PSYCHOLOGY

Themes and Variations / Second Edition

Study Guide

Richard B. Stalling

Bradley University

Ronald E. Wasden

Bradley University

Brooks/Cole Publishing Company
Pacific Grove, California

Brooks/Cole Publishing Company
A Division of Wadsworth, Inc.

Printed in the United States of America

10   9   8   7   6   5

ISBN 0-534-15331-3

Sponsoring Editor: Claire Verduin
Production: Del Mar Associates
Cover Art and Design: Martin Donald
Cover Photograph: Lee Hocker

CONTENTS

TO THE STUDENT

The two of us have written about eight study guides across the last couple of decades, and we've used a number of them written by others as well. Our goal in writing this study guide was to make it the best that we have ever written or used. We're pleased with the organization, the clear way in which each component parallels each part of the text, the fact that the practice material is in close proximity to the learning objectives, and the variety of the examples. We hope you find it as helpful a resource as we have tried to make it.

The first and major section of each chapter in the study guide is the Review of Key Ideas, consisting of approximately 20 learning objectives and several questions or exercises relating to each objective. The learning objectives tell you what you are expected to know, while the exercises quiz you, sometimes tutor you, and occasionally try to make a joke. Answers are provided at the end of each set of exercises.

The second section is the Review of Key Terms, which asks you to match 20 to 60 terms from the chapter with their definitions. The third section is the Review of Key Names, a matching exercise confined to the major researchers and theorists presented in each chapter. Finally, the Self-Quiz for each chapter gives you some idea of whether or not your studying has been on target.

What's the best way to work with this book? We suggest that you try this: (1) read each learning objective; (2) read the text subsection that relates to that learning objective; (3) answer the questions. After you complete the objectives, do the matching exercises and take the self-quiz. Of course, you may find a different procedure that works for you. Whatever method you use, the learning objectives will serve as an excellent review. At the end of your study of a particular chapter you can quiz yourself by reading over the learning objectives, reciting answers aloud, and checking your answers. This procedure roughly parallels the SQ3R study technique introduced in the Application section of Chapter 1.

On page 593 of your text Wayne Weiten, the author, illustrates a topic in social psychology by saying that "Years ago, one of my teachers told me that I had an 'attitude problem.'" Well, years ago—about 20, to be specific—we were Wayne's teachers in college, and although we don't recall reprimanding him, if we did, we apologize. Because now the tables are turned; now we are being instructed by and taking correction from Wayne.

We wish to acknowledge the help of a few people. First, we wish to thank Wayne Weiten, our former student. It has been a pleasure to work with him; he is an excellent teacher and superb writer, which makes our task much easier. If this guide achieves what we hope it does, Wayne deserves much of the credit. There are two other people who were of immense help to us. Thanks to Judy from Rick and to Kat from Ron.

Richard Stalling and Ron Wasden

1 THE EVOLUTION OF PSYCHOLOGY

REVIEW OF KEY IDEAS

FROM SPECULATION TO SCIENCE: HOW PSYCHOLOGY DEVELOPED

1. **Describe the methods used by philosophers and physiologists and discuss the contributions of these fields to the birth of psychology.**

   1-1.   In the field of philosophy, one starts with certain assumptions and eventually arrives at a set of conclusions. What is the major process or method that philosophers use to proceed from assumptions to conclusions? *reasoning*

   1-2.   In contrast, physiologists use the ___*scientific*___ method, which relies more heavily on ___*observation*___ than on pure logic.

   1-3.   In the first half of the 19th century, physiologists made several important discoveries relating to the nerve impulse, sensory processes, and perception. For the developing field of psychology, the importance of these discoveries was that they demonstrated that ___*mental*___ processes could be explored through ___*science*___.

   1-4.   Logic stimulated interest in areas relating to mental processes. It was the scientific method, however, as employed in the field of ___*physiology*___, that demonstrated that more stable information about psychological events could be obtained.

   Answers: 1-1. reasoning (or logic, or rational thought)   1-2. scientific, observation   1-3. mental (psychological), science (or the scientific method, etc.)   1-4. physiology.

2. **Summarize Wundt's accomplishments and contributions to the evolution of psychology.**

   2-1.   The name Wilhelm Wundt is hardly a household word, but Wundt is associated with several important firsts in psychology: (a) He established the first experimental psychology ___*lab*___ in Leipzig in 1879. (b) He established the first ___*journal*___ devoted to publishing psychological research.

2-2. If you ask most college graduate to name the founder of psychology they might well give you a name (maybe Sigmund Freud), but they would almost certainly <u>not</u> say Wilhelm Wundt. Among psychologists, however, Wundt is widely regarded as the "__founder__" of our field.

2-3. When did psychology, as an independent field of study, begin? If Wundt is its founder, then psychology's date of birth would be in __1879__, with the establishment of the first laboratory in __Leipzig__, Germany.

2-4. What was the subject matter of Wundt's psychology?

consciousness

2-5. One can summarize Wundt's contributions to the evolution of psychology as follows: (a) He is the founder of psychology as an independent academic __discipline__; (b) he insisted that psychology can and should use the __scientific__ method.

Answers: 2-1. (a) laboratory (b) journal 2-2. founder 2-3. 1879, Leipzig 2-4. consciousness 2-5. (a) discipline (field), (b) scientific (experimental).

3. Compare structuralism and functionalism and discuss their impact on the subsequent development of psychology.

3-1. Which "school" is characterized by each of the following descriptions? Place an "S" for structuralism or "F" for functionalism in the appropriate blanks.

__F__ Concerned with the purpose (or function) of consciousness.

__S__ Trained human beings to introspect about consciousness.

__S__ Assumed that consciousness could be broken down into basic elements (in the same way that physical matter is comprised of atoms).

__F__ Interested in the flow of consciousness.

__F__ Focused on the adaptive (evolutionary) value of consciousness.

__S__ Emphasized sensation and perception in vision, hearing, and touch.

__F__ Founded by William James.

3-2. While neither structuralism nor functionalism survived as viable theories of psychology, functionalism had a more lasting impact. What was that impact?
applied Psychology because of its emphasis on the practical it lead to behaviorism and

Answers: 3-1. F, S, S, F, F, S, F 3-2. The emphasis of functionalism on the practical (or the adaptive or purposeful) led to the development of two areas of modern psychology: behaviorism and applied psychology.

4. **Summarize Watson's view on the appropriate subject matter of psychology, nature versus nurture, and animal research.**

4-1. Recall that from a literal translation of its root words, psychology is the study of the ___mind___.
And, for both Wundt and James, the appropriate subject matter of psychology included human ___consciousness___. For Watson, however, the subject matter of psychology was ___behavior___.

4-2. Watson believed that psychology could not be a science unless it, like the other sciences, concentrated on ___observable___ rather than unobservable events.

4-3. Which of the following are observable behaviors? Place an "O" in the blank if the event is observable and a "N" if it is not.
___O___ writing a letter
___N___ feeling angry
___O___ saying "Please pass the salt"
___O___ passing the salt
___N___ perceiving a round object
___N___ experiencing hunger
___O___ walking rapidly

4-4. Watson largely discounted the importance of genetic inheritance. For Watson, behavior was governed by the ___environment___.

4-5. Watson also made a shift away from human introspection toward using ___animals___ as the subjects for research. Why the change in orientation? First, animal behavior is observable; human consciousness is not. Second, the environment of laboratory animals is subject to much more ___control___ than is that of human subjects.

Answers: 4-1. soul (or mind), consciousness, behavior 4-2. observable 4-3. O, N (you can't see or hear your own or another person's feelings of anger; you may see the results of anger), O, O, N (you can't see or hear perception), N (you can't see or hear hunger), O 4-4. environment 4-5. animals, control.

5. Explain how Gestalt psychologists challenged the views of structuralism and behaviorism.

5-1. Before taking up Gestalt psychology, let's briefly review structuralism and behaviorism.

(a) As defined by the structuralists, what was the subject matter of psychology?
analyze consciousness

(b) For behaviorists, what was the subject matter of psychology?
behavior - animal or human

(c) While structuralists and behaviorists differed in their views of the subject matter, their approach to the new field was similar in one major respect. In what way were the two systems similar?
both systems believed that the basic task of psychology was to find the smaller elements which made up the phenomena they were studying.

5-2. With the example of the *phi phenomenon* the gestalt theorists demonstrated one of their basic tenets involving parts and wholes.

(a) What is the phi phenomenon and what Gestalt principle does it illustrate?

the illusion of movement created by presenting non-moving stimuli in rapid succession.

(b) What, then, was Gestalt psychology's major objection both to structuralism and to behaviorism?

structuralism broke consciousness down to small parts, same w/behaviorism

Answers: 5-1. (a) conscience experience (consciousness) (b) animal or human behavior (c) Both systems believed that the basic task of psychology was to find the smaller elements which made up the phenomena they were studying. For the structuralists the smaller elements were the sensations or images which made up consciousness; for the behaviorists the elements were the stimulus-response bonds thought to make up behavior. 5-2. (a) The phi phenomenon is the illusion of movement created by presenting non-moving stimuli in rapid succession (as occurs in "motion" pictures). The illusion demonstrates that the whole (i.e., the illusion of movement) does not derive from the sum of its parts (the separate, non-moving stimuli), (b) Gestalt psychology asserted that by trying to study the parts of consciousness or behavior one would miss aspects of the whole phenomenon.

6. Summarize Freud's principal ideas and why they inspired controversy.

6-1. Recall that for Wundt, the subject matter of psychology was human consciousness. For Freud, the major subject matter was what he termed the __unconscious__. With this concept Freud asserted that human beings are (aware/<u>unaware</u>) of most of the factors that influence their thoughts and behavior.

6-2. There is a word beginning with *s* that means the same thing as feces. This word, however, may be more likely to cause laughter, embarrassment, or anger than the word feces. Why is it the case that two words that mean the same thing produce such differing emotional reactions? Freud would suggest that this irrational differentiation is caused by the __unconscious__.

6-3. How is the unconscious revealed? In several ways, according to Freud, including mistakes, like "__slip__ of the tongue," and symbolism in nighttime __dreams__.

6-4. Freud's ideas were (and still are) considered quite controversial. The general public tended to find Freud's ideas unacceptable because of his emphasis on __sexuality__. And scientific psychologists, increasingly emphasizing observable behavior, tended to reject Freud's notion that we are largely controlled by __unconscious__ forces. Nonetheless, Freud's theory gradually gained prominence and survives today as an influential theoretical perspective.

Answers: 6-1. unconscious, unaware 6-2. unconscious 6-3. slips, dreams 6-4. sexuality (sexual instincts), unconscious.

7. **Summarize Skinner's work, views, and influence.**

    7-1.   Summarize Skinner's viewpoint with regard to the following topics.

        (a) Internal drives, such as hunger or thirst:

        Skinner viewed speculation about unobservable, internal factors as unscientific and not helpful in building a science of behavior

        (b) The environment or external stimuli:

        Our behavior is controlled by the environment

        (c) The fundamental principle of operant conditioning:

        organisms will tend to repeat responses followed by positive outcomes

        (d) The factors that control human (and lower animal) behavior:

        external stimuli

        (e) Free will: *an illusion*

Answers: 7-1. (a) Skinner viewed speculation about unobservable, internal factors as unscientific and not at all helpful in building a science of behavior. (b) Our behavior is controlled by the environment; one need not resort to explanations in terms of internal states (needs and wants) to account fully for behavior. (c) Organisms will tend to repeat responses followed by positive outcomes. (d) external stimuli (or environmental events; consequences, outcomes) (e) Free will is an illusion (because, he asserts, behavior is under the lawful control of the environment).

8. **Summarize Rogers's and Maslow's ideas and the contributions of humanistic psychology.**

    8-1.   Both Rogers and Maslow, like other ___humanistic___ psychologists, emphasized the (similarities/ differences) between human beings and the other animals.

    8-2.   While Freud and Skinner stressed the way in which behavior is *controlled* (by unconscious forces or by the environment), Rogers and Maslow emphasized human beings' ___freedom___ to determine their own actions.

    8-3.   Rogers and Maslow also asserted that human beings have a drive to express their inner potential, a drive toward personal ___growth___.

    8-4.   Perhaps the greatest contribution of the humanistic movement has been in producing (scientific findings/new approaches) in psychotherapy.

Answers: 8-1. humanistic, differences 8-2. freedom 8-3. growth (expression) 8-4. new approaches.

9. **Explain how historical events since World War I have contributed to the emergence of psychology as a profession.**

9-1. World War I ushered in the field of applied psychology, primarily the extensive use of

intelligence _____ testing. World War II created demand for yet another applied area, the field of

clinical _____ psychology.

9-2. World War II brought an increased need for screening recruits and treating emotional casualties. With

the increased demand, the Veterans Administration began funding many new training programs in

clinical _____ psychology. Thus, the two wars accelerated the development of psychology as a

profession _____ as opposed to psychology as strictly an academic or research endeavor.

Answers: 9-1. intelligence (or mental), clinical   9-2. clinical, profession (i.e., as an applied field).

10. **Describe two recent trends in research in psychology that reflect a return to psychology's intellectual roots.**

10-1. Two recent trends in research in psychology involve the reemergence of areas largely discarded or ignored by the behaviorists. What are these two areas?

physiological processes, consciousness

10-2. Think about sucking on a lemon. When you do, the amount of saliva in your mouth will increase

measurably. While it would certainly suffice to describe your observable response as a function of my

observable instruction, it is obvious that the "organism" is involved: My instruction changed your

mental _____ image, which was accompanied by a change in salivation.

10-3. The study of mental imagery, problem solving, and decision making involves *cognitive* _____

processes. Research on electrical stimulation of the brain, brain specialization, and biofeedback refers to

physiological _____ processes.

Answers: 10-1. cognition (consciousness or thinking) and physiological processes   10-2. mental   10-3. cognitive, physiological.

PSYCHOLOGY TODAY: VIGOROUS AND DIVERSIFIED

11. **List and describe seven major research areas in psychology.**

11-1. Read over the descriptions of the research areas in Table 1.6. Then check your understanding by matching the names of the areas with the following research topics. Place the appropriate letters in the blanks. (Note that the separation between these areas is not always perfectly clear. For example, a personality theorist might also be a psychometrician with an interest in genetics or child development. Nonetheless, the following topics have been chosen so that one answer is correct for each.)

A. Experimental   *g*   attitude change, group behavior

B. Physiological   *e*   personality and intelligence assessment, test design, new statistical procedures

C. Cognitive   *f*   personality assessment, personality description

D. Developmental   *a*   "core" topics (e.g., perception, conditioning, motivation)

E. Psychometrics   *b*   influence of the brain, bodily chemicals, genetics

F. Personality   *d*   child, adolescent, and adult development

G. Social   *c*   memory, decision making, thinking

11-2. In case you want to remember the list of seven research areas, here's a mnemonic device: *Peter Piper Picked Some Exquisite California Dills*. List the seven research areas by matching them with the first letter of each word. *Personality, Experimental, Developmental, Psychometrics, Cognitive, Personality, Social*

Answers: 11-1. G, E, F, A, B, D, C 11-2. physiological, psychometrics, personality, social, experimental, cognitive, developmental.

12. List and describe the four professional specialties in psychology.

12-1. Match the following specialties with the descriptions by placing the appropriate letters in the blanks.

A. Clinical   _b_   Treatment of less severe problems and problems involving family, marital, and career difficulties.

B. Counseling   _a_   Treatment of psychological disorders, behavioral and emotional problems

C. Educational and school   _c_   Involves work on curriculum design and achievement testing in school settings.

D. Industrial and organizational   _d_   Psychology applied to business settings; deals with personnel, job satisfaction, etc.

Answers: 12-1. B, A, C, D.

13. Explain the difference between psychology and psychiatry.

13-1. The major difference between psychiatry and clinical psychology is a matter of degree (pun intended). Psychiatrists have ___medical M.D.___ degrees. Clinical psychologists generally have ___Ph.D.___ degrees, although some clinical psychologists have Ed. D. or Psy. D. degrees.

13-2. The major portion of psychiatrists' training occurs in ___medical___ schools and in the residency programs in psychiatry which follow medical school. Clinical psychologists' training occurs in ___graduate___ schools.

13-3. As physicians, ___psychiatrists___ are licensed to prescribe drugs and engage in other medical treatment. While clinical psychologists and psychiatrists frequently use the same psychotherapeutic treatment procedures, clinical psychologists do not administer drugs or in any other way engage in the practice of ___medicine___.

Answers: 13-1. medical (M.D.), Ph.D. 13-2. medical, graduate 13-3. psychiatrists, medicine.

PUTTING IT IN PERSPECTIVE: SIX KEY THEMES

14. Discuss the text's three organizing themes relating to psychology as a field of study.

14-1.   When my (R. S.'s) older daughter Samantha was about three years old, she pulled a sugar bowl off a shelf and broke it while I was not present. When I saw the mess later I said, "I see you've broken something." She said, "How do yer know, did yer see me do it?" I was amused, because while it was obvious who had broken it, her comment reflected psychology's foundation in direct observation. Theme 1 is that psychology is _empirical_. Empiricism is the point of view that knowledge should be acquired through _direct observation_.

14-2.   My daughter's comment caused me to think about one other aspect of empiricism: she expressed *doubt* (albeit somewhat self-serving in her case). One can describe belief systems along a continuum from *credulity*, which means ready to believe, to *skepticism*, which means disposed toward doubt. Psychology, and the empirical approach, is more disposed toward the _skepticism_ end of the continuum.

14-3.   We would ordinarily think that if one theory is correct, any other used to explain the same data must be wrong. While scientists do pit theories against each other, it is also the case that apparently contradictory theories may both be correct—as with the explanation of light in terms of both wave and particle theories. Thus, theme 2 indicates that psychology is _theoretically diverse_.

14-4.   Psychology tolerates different theories because:

there are many theories

14-5.   Why has research on the psychology of women increased dramatically in the last decade or so? This particular topic is undoubtedly influenced by, and in turn influences, the various feminist movements. It is clear that the topics, methods, and principles of any science, including psychology, do not evolve in a vacuum but are influenced by the vogues and trends within our _society_.

14-6.   The patterns of society change across the course of _history_; these changes are influenced by and in turn influence psychology. As stated in Theme 3, psychology evolves in a _sociohistorical_ context.

Answers: 14-1. empirical, observation   14-2. skepticism   14-3. theoretically diverse   14-4. more than one theory may be correct or because one theory may not adequately explain all of the observations   14-5. society 14-6. history, sociohistorical.

15. Discuss the text's three organizing themes relating to psychology's subject matter.

15-1.   When looking for an explanation of a particular behavior, someone might ask: "Well, why did he do it? Was it greed or ignorance?" The question implies that if one cause were present another could not be, and it illustrates the very human tendency to reason in terms of (one cause/multiple causes).

15-2.   What influences the course of a ball rolled down an inclined plane? Gravity. And also friction. And the presence of other objects, and a number of other factors. That is the point of Theme 4: even more than is the case for physical events, behavior is determined by _multiple_ _causes_.

15-3. Theme 5 relates to the influence of heredity and environment. What is the current consensus about the effect of heredity and environment on behavior?

behavior is affected by both heredity and environment

15-4. The scientific method relies on observation, but observation by itself isn't sufficient. Why isn't it?

people's experience of the world is highly subjective

15-5. What does it mean to say that our experience is subjective?

our experiences and perceptions are different

Answers: 15-1. one cause   15-2. multiple causes   15-3. Theme 5 states that behavior is affected by both heredity and environment operating jointly. While the relative influence of each is still debated, theorists no longer assert that behavior is entirely a function of one or the other.   15-4. because (Theme 6) people's experience of the world is highly subjective   15-5. Different people experience different things; even if we observe the same event at the same time, we do not "see" the same things.

APPLICATION: IMPROVING ACADEMIC PERFORMANCE

16. **Discuss three important considerations in designing a program to promote adequate studying.**

16-1. Three features of successful studying are listed below. Elaborate on them by providing some of the details asked for.
(a) A schedule: When should you plan your study schedule? Should you write it down?

(b) A place: What are the major characteristics of a good study place?

(c) A reward: When should you reward yourself? What kinds of rewards are suggested?

Answers: 16-1. (a) It's probably useful to set up a general schedule for a particular quarter or semester and then, at the beginning of each week, plan the specific assignments you intend to work on during each study session. Put your plans in writing. (b) Find a place to study with minimal distractions: little noise, few interruptions. (c) Reward yourself shortly after you finish a particular amount of studying; snacking, watching TV, or calling a friend are suggested.

Suggestion: You are studying now. Is this a good time for you? If it is, why not WRITE OUT YOUR WEEKLY SCHEDULE NOW. Include schedule preparation as part of your study time.

17. **Describe the SQ3R method and explain what makes it effective.**

17-1. Below are descriptions of an individual applying the five steps of the SQ3R method to Chapter 1 of your text. The steps are not in the correct order. Label each of the steps and place a number in the parentheses which indicates the correct order.

( ) _____ Vanessa is R. S.'s other daughter. Let's assume that all goes well and she is taking an introductory psychology course using this book in 1993. She looks at the title of the first sub-section of the chapter. After wondering briefly what it means for psychology to have "parents," she formulates this question: How was the field of psychology influenced by philosophy and physiology?

( ) _____ Vanessa turns to the back of Chapter 1 and notes that there is a chapter review. She turns back to the first page of the chapter, sees that the outline on that page matches the review at the end, and browses through some of other parts of the chapter. She has a rough idea that the chapter is going to define the field and discuss its history.

( ) _____ Keeping in mind the question she has posed, Vanessa reads the section about the meeting of psychology's "parents" and formulates a tentative answer to her question. She also asks some additional questions: "Who was Descartes?" and "What method did philosophers use?"

( ) _____ Vanessa answers her first question as follows: "One parent, philosophy, posed questions about the mind that made the study of human actions acceptable; the other parent, physiology, contributed the scientific method." She decides to note down her answer for later review.

( ) _____ When she has finished steps 2 through 4 for all sections, Vanessa looks over all the entire chapter, section by section. She repeats the questions for each section and attempts to answer each one.

17-2. What makes the SQ3R technique so effective?

Answers: 17-1. (2) Question (1) Survey (3) Read (4) Recite (5) Review   17-2. It breaks the reading assignment into manageable segments; it requires understanding before you move on.

18. **Summarize advice provided on how to get more out of lectures.**

18-1. Using a few words for each point, summarize the four points on getting more out of lectures.

Answers: 18-1. Listen actively, read ahead, organize in terms of importance, ask questions.

19. **Summarize advice provided on improving test-taking strategies.**

19-1. Is it better to change answers on multiple-choice tests or to go with one's first hunch?

19-2. Following are situations you might encounter while taking a test. Reread the section on general test-taking tips and then indicate what you would do in each situation.

(a) You run into a particularly difficult item:

(b) The answer seems to be simple, but you think you may be missing something.

(c) The test is a timed test:

(d) While taking the test you have a question but hesitate to ask:

(e) You have some time left at the end of the test:

19-3. Following are samples of the situations mentioned under the discussion of tips for multiple-choice and essay exam questions. Based on the suggestions, what would you do?

(a) In a multiple-choice test, item *c* seems to be correct, but you have not yet read items *d* and *e*:

(b) You know that items *a* and *b* are correct, are unsure of items *c* and *d*, and item *e* is an "all of the above" option:

(c) You have no idea which multiple-choice alternative is correct. You note that option *a* has the word "always" in it, items *b* and *c* use the word "never," and item *d* says "frequently."

(d) You have read the stem of a multiple-choice item but you have not yet looked at the options:

Answers: 19-1. In general, changing answers seems to be better. Available research indicates that people are more than twice as likely to go from a wrong answer to a right one as from a right answer to a wrong one. 19-2. (a) Skip it and come back to it if time permits. (b) Maybe the answer is simple! Don't make the question more complex than it was intended to be. (c) Budget your time, checking the proportion of the test completed against the time available. (d) Don't hesitate to ask (unless questions are forbidden). (e) Review, reconsider, check over your answers. 19-3. (a) Read all options. (b) Answer *e*. (c) Answer *d*. (Still good advice and generally the best procedure to follow. But note that some professors, aware of the strategy, may throw in an item in which "always" is part of a correct answer! It's sort of like radar detectors: someone builds a better detector and someone else builds radar which can't be detected. The best defense is probably going the speed limit or, in the case of tests, studying.) (d) Try to anticipate the correct answer *before* reading the options.

REVIEW OF KEY TERMS

Applied psychology
Behavior
Behaviorism
Clinical psychology
Cognition
Dualism
Empiricism

Functionalism
Gestalt psychology
Humanism
Introspection
Phi Phenomenon
Psychiatry
Psychoanalytic theory

Psychology
SQ3R
Stimulus
Structuralism
Testwiseness
Theory
Unconscious

stimulus   **1.** Any detectable input from the environment.

applied psychology   **2.** The branch of psychology concerned with practical problems.

structuralism   **3.** School of thought based on notion that the task of psychology is to analyze consciousness into its basic elements.

introspection   **4.** Observation of one's own conscious experience.

functionalism   **5.** School of thought asserting that psychology's major purpose was to investigate the function or purpose of consciousness.

behaviorism   **6.** The theoretical orientation asserting that scientific psychology should study only observable behavior.

behavior   **7.** An observable activity or response by an organism.

dualism   **8.** The idea that mind and body are separate entities.

Gestalt psychology   **9.** School of psychology which asserted that the whole is greater than the sum of it's parts.

phi phenomenon   **10.** The illusion of movement created by presenting visual stimuli in rapid succession.

psychoanalytic theory   **11.** Freudian theory that explains personality and abnormal behavior in terms of unconscious processes.

unconscious   **12.** According to psychoanalytic theory, that portion of the mind containing thoughts, memories, and wishes not in awareness but nonetheless exerting a strong effect on human behavior.

humanism   **13.** The psychological theory asserting that human beings are unique and fundamentally different from other animals.

clinical psychology   **14.** The branch of psychology concerned with the diagnosis and treatment of psychological disorders.

cognition   **15.** Mental processes or thinking.

psychology   **16.** The science that studies behavior and the physiological and cognitive processes that underlie it and that applies this knowledge in solving various practical problems.

psychiatry   **17.** The branch of medicine concerned with the diagnosis and treatment of psychological problems and disorders.

empirical   **18.** The point of view that knowledge should be based on observation.

theory   **19.** A system of ideas used to link together or explain a set of observations.

_SQ3R_   **20.** A five-step procedure designed to improve study skills.

testwiseness   **21.** Ability to use the characteristics and formats of a test to maximize one's score.

Answers: 1. stimulus 2. applied 3. structuralism 4. introspection 5. functionalism 6. behaviorism 7. behavior 8. dualism 9. Gestalt psychology 10. the phi phenomenon 11. psychoanalytic theory 12. unconscious 13. humanism 14. clinical psychology 15. cognition 16. psychology 17. psychiatry 18. empiricism 19. theory 20. SQ3R 21. testwiseness.

REVIEW OF KEY PEOPLE

Sigmund Freud   William James   B. F. Skinner
G. Stanley Hall   Carl Rogers   John B. Watson
Wilhelm Wundt

Wundt _____ 1. Founded experimental psychology and the first experimental psychology laboratory.

Hall _____ 2. Established the first American research laboratory, launched America's first psychological journal, was first president of the APA.

James _____ 3. Chief architect of functionalism; described a "stream of consciousness."

Watson _____ 4. Founded behaviorism.

Freud _____ 5. Devised the theory and technique known as psychoanalysis.

Skinner _____ 6. Identified operant conditioning.

Rogers _____ 7. A major proponent of "humanistic" psychology.

Answers: 1. Wundt 2. Hall 3. James 4. Watson 5. Freud 6. Skinner 7. Rogers.

SELF-QUIZ

1. Structuralism is the historical school of psychology which asserted that the purpose of psychology was to:
    a. study behavior
    b. discover the smaller elements which comprise consciousness
    c. explore the unconscious
    d. examine the purposes of conscious processes

2. Of the two parents of psychology, physiology and philosophy, which provided the method? What is the method?
    a. philosophy; logic, reasoning
    b. philosophy; intuition, introspection
    c. physiology; observation, science
    d. physiology; anatomy, surgery

3. Who is Wilhelm Wundt?
    a. He founded the first experimental laboratory.
    b. He founded the American Psychological Association.
    c. He discovered the classically conditioned salivary reflex.
    d. He founded behaviorism.

4. For John B. Watson, the appropriate subject matter of psychology was:
   a. animal behavior
   b. the unconscious
   c. consciousness
   d. human physiology

5. Which of the following represents a major breakthrough in the development of applied psychology?
   a. the use of the method of introspection
   b. Binet's development of the intelligence test
   c. establishment of the first animal laboratory
   d. Wundt's founding of experimental psychology

6. Within the field of psychology, Freud's ideas encountered resistance primarily because he emphasized:
   a. human consciousness
   b. human behavior
   c. introspection
   d. the unconscious

7. Which of the following would be considered the major principle of operant conditioning?
   a. Human behavior derives in part from free will; animal behavior is determined by the environment.
   b. Humans and other animals tend to repeat responses followed by positive outcomes.
   c. The majority of human behavior is based on thoughts, feelings, and wishes of which we are unaware.
   d. Human beings are fundamentally different from other animals.

8. Which of the following theorists would tend to emphasize explanations in terms of freedom and potential for personal growth?
   a. Rogers and Maslow
   b. Sigmund Freud
   c. B. F. Skinner
   d. All of the above

9. Recent research trends in psychology involve two areas largely ignored by early behaviorists. These two areas are:
   a. observable and measurable responses
   b. cognition (thinking) and physiological processes
   c. classical and operant conditioning
   d. the effect of environmental events and the behavior of lower animals

10. Which core psychological research area is primarily devoted to the study of such topics as memory, problem solving, and thinking?
    a. physiological
    b. social
    c. cognitive
    d. personality

11. Which of the following schools of psychology objected both to attempts to break consciousness into constituent elements and attempts to analyze behavior into stimulus-response bonds?
    a. structuralism
    b. functionalism
    c. behaviorism
    d. Gestalt

12. The assertion that "psychology is empirical" means that psychology is based on:
    a. introspection
    b. logic
    c. observation
    d. mathematics

13. In looking for the causes of a particular behavior, psychologists assume:
    a. one cause or factor
    b. multifactorial causation
    c. free will
    d. infinite causation

14. Contemporary psychologists generally assume that human behavior is determined by:
    a. heredity
    b. environment
    c. heredity and environment acting jointly
    d. heredity, environment, and free will

15. What does SQ3R stand for?
    a. search, question, research, recommend, reconstitute
    b. silence, quietude, reading, writing, arithmetic
    c. summarize, quickly, read, research, reread
    d. survey, question, read, recite, review

    Answers: 1. b 2. c 3. a 4. a 5. b 6. d 7. b 8. a 9. b 10. c 11. d 12. c 13. b 14. c 15. d.

2 THE RESEARCH ENTERPRISE IN PSYCHOLOGY

REVIEW OF KEY IDEAS

LOOKING FOR LAWS: THE SCIENTIFIC APPROACH TO BEHAVIOR

1. **Explain science's main assumption and describe the goals of the scientific enterprise in psychology.**

   1-1. The sun came up this morning, as it has in our experience on previous occasions, and we expect that it will do so tomorrow as well. In other words, we assume that events occur in a(an) _sequential/consistent_ manner. A major assumption of science is also that events occur in an orderly or predictable manner.

   1-2. As absolutely correct as our gross prediction about the behavior of the sun seems to be, Einstein's theories suggest that the "laws" of orbiting bodies may no longer be considered the _absolute_ truth that they once seemed. Instead, scientists make predictions in terms of likelihood or _probability_.

   1-3. There are three interrelated goals of psychology and the other sciences: (a) measurement and description, (b) understanding and prediction, and (c) application and control. Match each of the following descriptions with the goal it represents by placing the appropriate letters in the blanks. (There is considerable overlap among these goals; pick the closest match.)

   _a_ A psychologist develops a test or procedure that measures anxiety.

   _b_ Researchers find that when individuals are exposed to an object they happen to fear (e.g., a cliff, rats, roaches, snakes, spiders, etc.), their concentration and memory deteriorate.

   _c_ Muscle relaxation techniques are used to reduce anxiety and improve concentration and memory.

   Answers: 1-1. consistent (or lawful, regular, predictable, orderly)   1-2. absolute (concrete), probability   1-3. a, b, c.

2. **Outline the steps in a scientific investigation.**

2-1. Following are the five steps generally used in performing a scientific investigation. Fill in the missing key words.

(a) Formulate a testable _hypothesis_ .

(b) Select the research _method_ and design the study.

(c) _collect_ the data.

(d) _analyze_ the data and draw _conclusions_ .

(e) _report_ the findings.

2-2. Following are descriptions of various phases in the project by Holmes and his coworkers (Wyler et al., 1968). Indicate which step of this study is being described by placing a letter from the previous question (a, b, c, d, or e) in the appropriate blank.

_e_ The authors prepared a report of their findings that was accepted for publication in a technical journal.

_d_ The patients' responses were converted into numbers and analyzed with statistics. The data indicated that high scores on the life change questionnaire were associated with high scores on physical illness.

_a_ Holmes and his coworkers thought that life change might be associated with increased illness. Before they began they made precise operational definitions of both life change and illness.

_b_ The researchers decided to use a survey procedure involving administration of questionnaires to a large number of people.

_c_ The researchers gathered questionnaire data from 232 patients.

Answers: 2-1. (a) hypothesis (b) method (c) collect (d) analyze, conclusions (e) report (publish, write up)
2-2. e, d, a, b, c.

3. **Discuss the advantages of the scientific approach.**

3-1. We all tend to agree with the idea that "haste makes waste." We are also likely to agree with a commonsense saying that has the opposite implication: "a stitch in time saves nine." What are the two major advantages of the scientific approach over the commonsense approach?

the scientific approach is measured for clarity and has an intolerance for error or contradictory conclusions.

Answers: 3-1. First, scientific descriptions generally have a clarity and precision lacking in commonsense proverbs. While we have a general idea about the meaning of haste, for example, we don't know precisely when or in what way or how much haste we should avoid. Second, science has an intolerance for error or for contradictory conclusions, while commonsense sayings may well be contradictory. (Note that the proverbs in our example have contradictory messages: one says to slow down, the other says to hurry up.)

LOOKING FOR CAUSES: EXPERIMENTAL RESEARCH

4. **Describe the experimental method of research, explaining independent and dependent variables, experimental and control groups, and extraneous variables.**

4-1. Schachter proposed that affiliation is caused (in part) by level of anxiety. What was his independent variable? _level of anxiety_ The dependent variable? _affiliation_

4-2. The variable that is manipulated or varied by the experimenter is termed the ___*independent*___ variable. The variable that is affected by, or is dependent on, the manipulation is termed the ___*dependent*___ variable.

4-3. What is the name of the variable that *results from* the manipulation? ___*dependent*___ What is the name of the variable that *produces* the effect? ___*independent*___

4-4. The group of subjects that receives the experimental treatment is known as the ___*experimental*___ group; the group that does not is known as the ___*control*___ group.

4-5. Control and experimental groups are quite similar in most respects. They differ in that the experimental group receives the experimental ___*treatment*___ and the control group does not. Thus, any differences found in the measure of the ___*dependent*___ variable are assumed to be due to differences in manipulation of the ___*independent*___ variable.

4-6. In Schachter's study, the experimental group was subjected to instructions that produced a high level of ___*anxiety*___. Results were that the experimental group was higher than the control group on the dependent measure, the tendency toward ___*affiliation*___ with others.

4-7. An extraneous variable is any variable other than the ___*independent*___ variable that seems likely to cause a difference between groups as measured by the ___*dependent*___ variable.

4-8. To review the parts of an experiment: Suppose a researcher is interested in the effect of a drug on the running speed of rats. The ___*experimental*___ group is injected with the drug and the ___*control*___ group is not. Whether or not the rats received the drug would be the ___*independent*___ variable, and running speed would be the ___*dependent*___ variable.

4-9. Suppose also that the average age of the experimental rats is two years while the average age of the control rats is 3 months. What is the extraneous variable in this experiment? ___*age*___ Why does this variable present a problem? ___*the age difference probability would affect running ability as much as the drug if not more*___

4-10. Researchers generally control for extraneous variables through random ___*assignment*___ of subjects to groups. Write a definition of this procedure: ___*all subjects have an equal chance of being assigned to any group or condition*___

Answers: 4-1. anxiety, affiliation 4-2. independent, dependent 4-3. dependent, independent 4-4. experimental, control 4-5. treatment, dependent, independent 4-6. anxiety, affiliation 4-7. independent, dependent
4-8. experimental, control, independent, dependent 4-9. age, any difference between groups could be due to age rather than the independent variable 4-10. assignment, all subjects have an equal chance of being assigned to any group or condition.

5. **Summarize the method, results, and implications of the Featured Study (Sanders & Simmons, 1983) on hypnosis and eyewitness memory.**

5-1.   (a) What did subjects observe as part of the procedure? *a pick pocket*

(b) What were the two independent variables? *hypnosis, whether or not the thief was in the lineup*

5-2.   Which group was more accurate, in terms of either correctly identifying the thief or indicating that he was not in the lineup? *control* Which group had somewhat more confidence in their judgments? *control* Which group recalled more details on the 10-item test? *control*

5-3.   What is the major implication to be drawn from this study? *hypnosis does not enhance recall of events*

Answers: 5-1. (a) a brief videotape of a thief stealing someone's wallet (b) whether or not the subject was hypnotized prior to recall and whether or not the thief was in the lineup   5-2. The control (nonhypnotized) group scored higher than the experimental group on all three dependent measures.   5-3. Rather than improving accuracy of eyewitness testimony, hypnosis in this study was found to make recall worse. The findings suggest that hypnosis should not be used in attempt to enhance accuracy of eyewitness testimony.

6. **Explain the major advantages and disadvantages of the experimental method.**

6-1.   What is the major advantage of the experimental method? *the experimental method allows researchers to make cause-effect conclusions*

6-2.   What are the two major disadvantages of the experimental method? *precise experimental control may make the situation so artificial that it does not apply to the real world. Ethical, practical considerations may prevent one from manipulating independent variables of interest*

6-3.   Suppose a researcher is interested in the effect of excessive coffee drinking on health (e.g., 15 cups per day over an extended period of time). What would be a major *disadvantage* of using the experimental method to examine this particular question? *an experimental groups health - it would probably be unethical. that much coffee could harm*

Answers: 6-1. The major advantage of the experimental method is that it permits researchers to make cause-effect conclusions.   6-2. The major disadvantages are that (a) precise experimental control may make the situation so artificial that it does not apply to the real world, and (b) ethical or practical considerations may prevent one from manipulating independent variables of interest.   6-3. To the extent that excessive coffee drinking is a suspected factor in health problems, it would be unethical and perhaps impossible to require an experimental group to drink that many cups daily.

LOOKING FOR LINKS: CORRELATIONAL RESEARCH

7. **Explain how experimental and descriptive research are different and discuss three descriptive research methods.**

   7-1. The major difference between the experimental method and descriptive research is that with descriptive research the experimenter cannot ___*control*___ variables. For this reason, the descriptive methods do not permit one to demonstrate ___*cause effect*___ relationships between variables.

   7-2. For example, suppose you have data indicating that the more coffee people drink, the more likely they are to have cardiovascular problems. Is this experimental or descriptive research?
   experimental

   7-3. List the three descriptive methods described. *survey, natural observation, case studies*

   7-4. What is naturalistic observation? *observing people/animals in their natural environment w/o directly intervening*

   7-5. Describe the case study method. *Indepth investigation of an individual subject derived from interviews, direct observation, examination of records & psychological testing.*

   7-6. The third descriptive procedure is the survey technique. *Surveys* use ___*questionnaires*___ to find out about specific aspects of human attitudes or opinions.

   Answers: 7-1. manipulate, cause-effect, (causal) 7-2. descriptive, because the variables are not manipulated by the experimenter 7-3. naturalistic observation, case studies, and surveys 7-4. observation of human beings or animals in their natural environments, conducted without directly intervening 7-5. an in-depth and generally highly subjective or impressionistic report on a single individual (derived from interviews, psychological testing, and so on) 7-6. questionnaires (interviews).

8. **Explain the major advantages and disadvantages of descriptive research methods.**

   8-1. Describe one major advantage and one major disadvantage of the descriptive approach.
   descriptive research broadens the scope of phenomena that psychologists are able to study
   investigators cannot control events to isolate cause and effect.

   Answers: 8-1. An advantage is that descriptive methods broaden the scope of phenomena studied. A disadvantage is that one generally cannot make cause-effect conclusions from descriptive data.

LOOKING FOR CONCLUSIONS: STATISTICS AND RESEARCH

9. **Describe three measures of central tendency and one measure of variability.**

9-1. To review the meaning of the three measures of central tendency, determine the mean, median, and mode of the following scores: 3, 5, 5, 5, 6, 6, 7, 9, 80.

Mean: _14_

Median: _6_

Mode: _5_

9-2. One can describe a group of data with a single number by using one of the measures of central tendency. In the blanks below indicate which measure of central tendency is being described.

mode The score that occurs most frequently.

mean The sum of all scores divided by the total number of scores.

median Half the scores fall above this measure and half below.

mean Very sensitive to extreme scores.

mean Usually the most useful because it may be used in further statistical manipulations.

median The middle score.

9-3. Refer to data sets A and B, below. What is the median of data set A? _50_ of set B? _50_ Which of these sets is more variable, A or B? _B_

A. 20, 30, 50, 50, 60   B. 10, 30, 50, 70, 90

9-4. What is the name of the statistic used as a measure of variability? _standard deviation_.

Answers: 9-1. 14, 6, 5   9-2. mode, mean, median, mean, mean, median   9-3. 50, 50, B   9-4. standard deviation.

10. **Distinguish between positive and negative correlations and explain how the size of a correlation coefficient relates to the strength of an association.**

10-1. Some examples will help illustrate the difference between positive and negative correlations. Which of the following relationships are positive (direct) and which negative (inverse)? (Indicate with a + or – sign.)

_+_ The better that students' grades are in high school, the better their grades tend to be in college.

_–_ The more alcohol one has drunk, the slower his or her reaction time.

_–_ The higher the anxiety, the poorer the test performance.

_+_ The greater the fear, the greater the need for affiliation.

10-2. Which of the following indicates the *strongest correlational relationship*?

a. 1.12   (b.) –.92   c. .58   d. .87

10-3. What is the relationship between the size of the correlation coefficient and prediction?

the stronger the correlation +1.00 or -1.00, the greater the predictive power

Answers: 10-1. +, –, –, +   10-2. b (not *a*, because correlations cannot exceed +1.00 or –1.00)   10-3. The stronger the correlation (the closer to –1.00 or +1.00), the greater the predictive power.

11. **Explain how correlations relate to prediction and causation.**

11-1. Suppose you have some data indicating that the more money people make (i.e., the higher their annual incomes), the greater happiness they report on an attitude survey. Is this data correlational data or experimental data? Why? *correlational data because neither of the variables in the relationship was manipulated.*

11-2. What kind of conclusion is justified on the basis of the previous relationship, a conclusion involving prediction or one involving a statement about causation? *prediction. generally one can't make causal conclusions from a correlation*

11-3. Consider the same relationship as in the previous question: You discover that the more money people make, the greater their happiness. Which of the following conclusions is justified? Explain why.
a. Money makes people happy.
b. Happiness causes people to earn more money.
c. Both happiness and money result from some unknown third factor.
d. None of the above.
the data is correlation therefore no causal conclusions are justified.

11-4. Again consider the relationship between money and happiness. Assume that money does not cause happiness and happiness does not cause money. What possible *third factor* can you think of that could cause both? (I'm asking you to make a wild speculation here just to get the idea of how third variables may operate.) *poor health might cause one to be both unhappy and poverty stricken and good health might have the opposite effect.*

11-5. We aren't justified in making causal conclusions from a correlation, but we can predict. Let's examine what prediction means in the case of our hypothetical example. What prediction would you make if you knew that a comparable group of people were rich, for example? What prediction would you make concerning a group that was unhappy? *group of rich people would be happy. the unhappy group would be poor.*

Answers: 11-1. correlational, because neither of the variables in the relationship was manipulated. 11-2. prediction. Generally one can't make causal conclusions from a correlation. 11-3. d. Any of the statements is a possible causal explanation of the relationship, but we don't know which may be correct because the data are correlational. Therefore, *no causal conclusions* are justified. 11-4. Poor health might cause one to be both unhappy and poverty stricken (while good health would cause one to be both happy and wealthy). Intelligence or aggressiveness or stubbornness or a number of other physiological or behavioral factors could be causally related both to income and to happiness without those two factors being causes of one another. 11-5. You would predict that a group that was rich would also be happy and that a group that was unhappy would be poor. No causation is implied in these statements.

12. **Explain the logic of hypothesis testing and the meaning of statistical significance.**

12-1. In the hypothetical experiment described in your text there are two groups, largely equivalent except that the _experimental_ group receives the computerized tutoring sessions and the _control_ group does not. What is the experimental hypothesis?

that the student who receive tutoring will have better reading scores.

12-2. Researchers statistically evaluate the hypothesis by comparing means and determining the likelihood or probability that a difference between means of the size obtained (or larger) would occur by _chance_. If the probability that such a difference would occur by chance is very low, say less than 5 times in 100, the researchers would conclude that the difference (is/is not) due to chance. They would declare the difference statistically _significant_ at the _.05_ level of significance.

12-3. Statistically significant does not mean important or significant in the usual sense of that word. What does statistically significant mean?

the probability that the observed findings are due to chance is very low.

Answers: 12-1. experimental, control. The hypothesis is that special tutoring would increase reading scores. 12-2. chance, is not, significant, .05   12-3. It means that the difference is rare on a chance basis, so it is assumed not to be due to chance; or, more simply, it means that the difference between means is due to treatment.

LOOKING FOR FLAWS: EVALUATING RESEARCH

13. **Describe four common flaws in research (sampling bias, placebo effects, distortions in self-report, and experimenter bias).**

13-1. Dr. Brutalbaum distributes a questionnaire in an attempt to find out how the students in a particular course react to his teaching. Unfortunately, the day he selects for the evaluation is the day before a scheduled vacation, and about half the students are absent. He knows, however, that he does not have to test the entire class, and the sample which remains is large enough. Is the sample representative? What is a representative sample?

probably not representative. a representative sample is one that is similar in composition to the population from which it is drawn.

13-2. Brutalbaum is now concerned about class attendance and decides to find out what proportion of students miss class regularly. He distributes a questionnaire asking students to indicate how many classes they have missed during the course of the semester. What problem is he likely to encounter?

the students will probability not be accurate in reporting their absences

13-3. Cosmo, a student in Brutalbaum's classes, orders some audio tapes that promise sleep learning for psychology students. Brutalbaum is dubious, because from his observations students sleep a lot in his classes but still don't seem to learn very much. Nonetheless, Cosmo decides to run an experiment. There are two sections of the course, *so Cosmo decides to use one class section as the control group and the other as the experimental group*. He then distributes tapes to his experimental group and not to his control group, and after the first test he analyzes the results. The mean of the experimental group is statistically significantly higher than that of the control group, so Cosmo concludes that the tapes have produced the superior learning.

(a) What is the independent variable? *listening / not listening to tapes*

(b) What is the major flaw, in terms of sampling, in his procedure? *he doesn't pick the groups - they're already determined*

(c) In a sentence, what is wrong with Cosmo's conclusions (i.e., what is a reasonable alternative explanation for his results)? *the one section might've been more intelligent*

13-4. The following semester Cosmo hands the work over to Osmo, another student of Brutalbaum's. He obtains an appropriate sample of students, distributes the tapes to a random half, carefully informs them of the anticipated sleep-learning benefits, and tells them to use the tapes each night for one month. He has no contact with the remaining random half, his "control" group. After the next test Osmo analyzes the results. The mean test score of the experimental group is statistically significantly higher than that of the control group. He concludes that the higher grades are due to the taped messages.

(a) What is the independent variable? *tape / no tape*

(b) What did Osmo unintentionally manipulate other than the independent variable? Answer this question by listing the names of two flaws (of the four listed in the text) in this study and by clearly explaining how the terms apply to this particular study. (Note that these two flaws overlap somewhat in meaning.)

experimenter bias effect
placebo effects

(c) What two procedures would you have used to correct Osmo's experiment?

placebo control
double blind procedure

Answers: **13-1.** Probably not representative. A representative sample is one that is similar in composition to the population from which it is drawn. In this case, it seems likely that students who attend are different from those who do not (e.g., perhaps more enthusiastic, harder working, etc.).   **13-2.** He is likely to encounter distortions in self-report (which may include the self-serving bias, misunderstanding of the questionnaire, memory errors, and tendencies to agree or disagree regardless of content).   **13-3.** (a) the tapes (versus no tapes) (b) The two classes are not samples from the same population; it may well be that a class that meets at 2 p.m., for example, is very different from one that meets at 9 a.m., both in terms of the presentation by the instructor and the characteristics of the students enrolled. (c) The difference between groups could have been due to the fact that the samples were not from the same population.   **13-4.** (a) the tapes versus no tapes (b) Through contact with the experimental group Osmo may have produced an experimenter bias effect, an unintended manipulation of subjects' behavior; this contact and the use of the tapes may also have created placebo effects. Thus, the procedural flaws in this study are *experimenter bias* and *placebo* effects. (c) A placebo control and double-blind procedure: Both groups would receive tapes, but the placebo control group would receive a fake "sleep-learning" tape; and, neither the experimenter nor subjects would know who is in the experimental group and who is in the control group.

LOOKING AT ETHICS: DO THE ENDS JUSTIFY THE MEANS?

14. **Discuss the pros and cons of deception in research with human subjects.**

    14-1. In the space below present one or two of the arguments in favor of using deception and one or two arguments against.

Answers: **14-1.** On the con side, deception is, after all, lying; it may undermine people's trust in others; it may cause distress. On the pro side, many research issues could not be investigated without deception; the "white lies" involved are generally harmless; research indicates that deception studies are not actually harmful to subjects; the advances in knowledge obtained may improve human welfare.

15. **Discuss the controversy about the use of animals as research subjects.**

    15-1. What is the major reason that some people object to using animal subjects in research? In view of this objection, what moral considerations are raised by those who favor using animals in research?

Answers: **15-1.** Some people believe that it is morally wrong to use animals in research, especially in painful or harmful treatments that would be unacceptable for human subjects. In defense of the practice, others cite the significant advances in treatment of a variety of mental and physical disorders as a result of animal research.

PUTTING IT IN PERSPECTIVE

16. **Explain how this chapter highlighted two of our unifying themes: (a) psychology is empirical and (b) our experience of the world is highly subjective.**

    16-1. Theme 1 is that psychology is empirical, which means that its conclusions are based on systematic _observation_ and that it tends to be _skeptical_ rather than credulous.

    16-2. In what way did the discussion of methodology suggest that psychology tends to be skeptical of its results? _the field pays attention only to results considered highly unlikely to have occurred by chance_

16-3. Which of the methodological problems discussed point up psychology's awareness of the subjective nature of our experience?

Subjective reactions due to experimental bias and placebo effects.

APPLICATION: FINDING AND READING JOURNAL ARTICLES

17. Describe the *Psychological Abstracts* and explain how its author and subject indexes can be used to locate information.

    17-1. *Psychological Abstracts* contains abstracts or concise _____ of articles published in psychological journals. To find information about a particular article, consult either the author index or the _____ index found at the back of each monthly issue of the *Abstracts*. Cumulative indexes appear after each _____ -month period.

    17-2. If you know the author's name you can easily find the article. Next to the author's name, each article he or she has published within the period is identified by a particular number, its _____ number.

    17-3. Once you know the index number you can find the abstract. As you can see in Figure 2.17 in your text, the abstract provides not only a summary but the exact reference for the article, including publication date, page numbers, and name of the _____ in which the article was published.

    17-4. The subject index works the same way as the author index, but it's a little more like looking through the yellow pages of a phone book (e.g., do you look under Doctors or under Physicians?). As with the author index, you can locate the abstract once you find the _____ _____ of a particular article, and a quick glance at the abstract will generally tell you whether the article is in the subject area you are looking for.

18. Describe the standard organization of journal articles reporting on psychological research.

    18-1. In the blanks below list the six parts of the standard journal article in the order in which they occur.

        (a) _____   (d) _____

        (b) _____   (e) _____

        (c) _____   (f) _____

18-2. In the blanks below write the letters (from your list above) that correctly designate the sections of the standard journal article.

_____ States the hypothesis and reviews the literature relevant to the hypothesis.

_____ Lists of all the sources referred to in the paper.

_____ A summary.

_____ Presents the data; may include statistical analyses, graphs, and tables.

_____ Describes what the researchers did in the study, includes subjects, procedures, and data collection techniques.

_____ Interprets or evaluates the data and presents conclusions.

Answers: **18-1.** (a) abstract (b) introduction (c) method (d) results (e) discussion (f) references **18-2.** b, f, a, d, c, e.

REVIEW OF KEY TERMS

Case study
Confounding of variables
Control group
Correlation
Correlation coefficient
Data collection techniques
Dependent variable
Descriptive statistics
Double-blind procedure
Experiment
Experimental group
Experimenter bias
Extraneous variables

Hypothesis
Independent variable
Inferential statistics
Journal
Mean
Median
Mode
Naturalistic observation
Operational definition
Placebo effects
Population
Random assignment
Replication

Research method
Sample
Sampling bias
Social desirability bias
Standard deviation
Statistical significance
Statistics
Subjects
Survey
Variability
Variables

_____ 1. Any of the factors in an experiment that are controlled or observed by an experimenter or that in some other way affect the outcome.

_____ 2. A tentative statement about the expected relationship between two or more variables.

_____ 3. Precisely defines each variable in a study in terms of the operations needed to produce or measure that variable.

_____ 4. Persons or animals whose behavior is being studied.

_____ 5. Differing ways of conducting research, which include experiments, case studies, surveys, and naturalistic observation.

_____ 6. A research method in which independent variables are manipulated and which permits causal interpretations.

_____ 7. A condition or event that an experimenter varies in order to observe its impact.

_____ 8. The variable that results from the manipulation in an experiment.

_____ 9. The group in an experiment that receives a treatment as part of the independent variable manipulation.

_____ 10. The group in an experiment that does not receive the treatment.

_____ 11. Any variables other than the independent variables that seem likely to influence the dependent measure in an experiment.

_____ 12. Distribution of subjects in an experiment in which each subject has an equal chance of being assigned to any group or condition.

_____ 13. A link or association between variables such that one can be predicted from the other.

_____ 14. The statistic that indicates the degree of relationship between variables.

_____ 15. A research method in which the researcher observes behavior in the natural environment without directly intervening.

_____ 16. An in-depth, generally subjective, investigation of an individual subject.

_____ 17. A questionnaire or interview used to gather information about specific aspects of subjects' behavior.

_____ 18. Procedures for making empirical observations, including questionnaires, interviews, psychological tests, and physiological recordings.

_____ 19. Mathematical techniques that help in organizing, summarizing, and interpreting numerical data.

_____ 20. Mathematical techniques helpful in organizing and summarizing (but not interpreting) data.

_____ 21. The measure of central tendency that falls in the exact center of a distribution of data.

_____ 22. The arithmetic average.

_____ 23. The score that occurs most frequently.

_____ 24. The spread or dispersion of data, including the extent to which scores vary from the mean.

_____ 25. A measure of variability in data.

_____ 26. Statistical procedures used to help interpret data and draw conclusions.

_____ 27. A judgment inferred from statistics that the probability of the observed findings occurring by chance is very low.

_____ 28. A repetition of a study to determine whether the previously obtained results can be duplicated.

_____ 29. A group of subjects taken from a larger population.

_____ 30. A larger group from which a sample is drawn and to which the researcher wishes to generalize.

_____ 31. Exists when a sample is not representative of the population from which it was drawn.

_____ 32. Occurs when a researcher's expectations influence the results of the study.

_____ 33. Effects that occur when subjects experience a change due to their expectations (or to a "fake" treatment).

_____ 34. Occurs when an extraneous variable makes it difficult to sort out the effects of the independent variable.

_____ 35. The tendency to answer questions about oneself in a socially approved manner.

_____ 36. A research strategy in which neither the subjects nor experimenters know which condition or treatment the subjects are in.

_____ 37. A periodical that publishes technical and scholarly material within a discipline.

REVIEW OF KEY PEOPLE

Thomas Holmes   Robert Rosenthal
Neal Miller   Stanley Schachter

_____   1.   Examined the relationship between stress and physical illness.

_____   2.   Studied the effect of anxiety on affiliation.

_____   3.   Studied experimenter bias, a researcher's unintended influence on the
                                      behavior of subjects.

_____   4.   Asserted that the benefits of animal research (e.g., the resulting
                                      treatments for mental and physical disorders) far outweigh the harm
                                      done.

Answers: 1. Holmes 2. Schachter 3. Rosenthal 4. Miller.

SELF-QUIZ

1.   Which of the following is a major assumption of science?
     a. Events occur in a relatively orderly or predictable manner.
     b. Cause and effect is indicated by correlational relationships.
     c. In contrast to the behavior of lower animals, human behavior is in part a function of free will.
     d. Events are largely randomly determined.

2.   An experimenter tests the hypothesis that physical exercise helps people's mood (makes them happier).
     Subjects in the experimental group participate on Monday and Tuesday and those in the control group
     on Wednesday and Thursday. What is the *independent* variable?
     a. the hypothesis
     b. day of the week
     c. the exercise
     d. the mood (degree of happiness)

3.   An experimenter tests the hypothesis that physical exercise helps people's mood (makes them happier).
     Subjects in the experimental group participate on Monday and Tuesday and those in the control group
     on Wednesday and Thursday. What is the *dependent* variable?
     a. the hypothesis
     b. day of the week
     c. the exercise
     d. the mood (degree of happiness)

4. An experimenter tests the hypothesis that physical exercise helps people's mood (makes them happier). Subjects in the experimental group participate on Monday and Tuesday and those in the control group on Wednesday and Thursday. What is the *extraneous* (confounding) variable?
   a. the hypothesis
   b. day of the week
   c. the exercise
   d. the mood (degree of happiness)

5. The major advantage of the experimental method over the correlational approach is that the experimental method:
   a. permits one to make causal conclusions
   b. allows for prediction
   c. is generally less artificial than correlational procedures
   d. permits the study of people in groups

6. In looking through some medical records you find that there is a strong relationship between depression and chronic pain: the stronger the physical pain that people report, the higher their scores on an inventory that measures depression. Which of the following conclusions are justified?
   a. Depression tends to produce chronic pain.
   b. Chronic pain tends to produce depression.
   c. Both chronic pain and depression result from some unknown third factor.
   d. None of the above.

7. What is the mode of the following data? 2, 3, 3, 3, 5, 5, 7, 12
   a. 3
   b. 4
   c. 5
   d. 6

8. What is the median of the following data? 1, 3, 4, 4, 5, 6, 9,
   a. 3
   b. 4
   c. 4.57
   d. 6

9. Researchers tend to find an inverse relationship between alcohol consumption and speed of response. Which of the following fictitious statistics could possibly represent that relationship?
   a. −4.57
   b. −.87
   c. .91
   d. .05

10. The term *statistical significance* refers to:
    a. how important the data are for future research on the topic
    b. the conclusion that there are no reasonable alternative explanations
    c. the inference that the observed effects are unlikely to be due to chance
    d. the representativeness of the sample

11. An instructor wishes to find out whether a new teaching method is superior to his usual procedures, so he conducts an experiment. Everyone in his classes is quite excited about the prospect of learning under the new procedure, but of course he cannot administer the new teaching method to everyone. A random half of the students receive the new method and the remaining half receive the old. What is the most obvious flaw in this experiment?
    a. Subjects should have been systematically assigned to groups.
    b. The sample is not representative of the population.
    c. Placebo effects or experimenter bias will affect results.
    d. Distortions in self-report will affect results.

12. What procedure helps correct for experimenter bias?
    a. extraneous or confounding variables
    b. sleep learning or hypnosis
    c. a higher standard for statistical significance
    d. use of the double-blind procedure

13. With regard to the topic of deception in research with human subjects, which of the following is true?
    a. Researchers are careful to avoid deceiving subjects.
    b. Some topics could not be investigated unless deception were used.
    c. It has been empirically demonstrated that deception causes severe distress.
    d. All psychological research must involve some deception.

14. Which of the following is among the six standard parts of a psychological journal article?
    a. conclusions
    b. bibliography
    c. data summary
    d. results

15. The Author Index in the *Psychological Abstracts* provides:
    a. names of current APA members
    b. registration and biographical information about frequent authors
    c. index numbers that locate article summaries
    d. names of authors who specialize in abstractions

Answers: 1. a 2. c 3. d 4. b 5. a 6. d 7. a 8. b 9. b 10. c 11. c 12. d 13. b 14. d 15. c.

3 THE BIOLOGICAL BASES OF BEHAVIOR

REVIEW OF KEY IDEAS

COMMUNICATION IN THE NERVOUS SYSTEM

1. **Describe the main functions of the two types of nervous tissue.**

   1-1.   One of the major types of nervous tissue provides very important services to the other type, such as structural support, insulation, and supplying nutrients and removing waste. Individual members of this kind of nervous tissue are called _glia cells_.

   1-2.   The other type of nervous tissue receives, integrates, and transmits information. Individual members of this type of tissue are called _neurons_.

   1-3.   While most neurons just receive and transmit information from one neuron to another, two kinds of neurons are specialized for additional tasks. Name the two types and describe their specialization below.

   ① sensory neurons receive information from the outside environment
   ② motor neurons activate the muscles.

   Answers: 1-1. glia cells   1-2. neurons   1-3. Sensory neurons receive information from the outside environment, while motor neurons activate the muscles.

2. **Describe the various parts of the neuron.**

   2-1.   The neuron has three basic parts, the *dendrites*, the *cell body* or *soma*, and the *axon*. The major mission of the average neuron is to receive information from one neuron and pass it on to the next neuron. The receiving part is the job of the branch-like parts called _dendrites_. They then pass the message along to the nucleus of the cell, called the *cell body*, or _soma_. From there the message is sent down the _axon_ to be passed along to other neurons.

2-2. Many axons are wrapped in a fatty jacket called the _myelin_ , which permits for faster transmission of information and prevents messages from getting on to the wrong track. Like the covering on an electrical cord, myelin acts as an _insulating_ material.

2-3. When the neural message reaches the end of the axon it excites projections called *terminal* _buttons_ , which then release a chemical substance into the junction that separates them from other neurons. This junction between neurons is called the _synapse_ .

2-4. Identify the major parts of a neuron in the figure below. Note that the arrow indicates the direction of the flow of information.

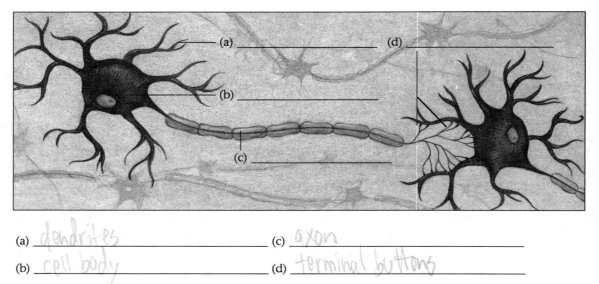

(a) _____   (d) _____

(b) _____

(c) _____

(a) _dendrites_   (c) _axon_

(b) _cell body_   (d) _terminal buttons_

Answers: 2-1. dendrites, soma, axon 2-2. myelin sheath, insulating 2-3. buttons, synapse 2-4. (a) dendrites, (b) cell body or soma, (c) axon, (d) terminal buttons.

3. Describe the neural impulse.

3-1. When it is at rest, the neuron is like a tiny battery in that it contains a weak (<u>negative</u>/positive) charge. When the neuron is stimulated, the cell membrane becomes more permeable. This allows positively charged _sodium_ ions to flow into the cell, thus lessening the cell's negative charge.

3-2. The change in the charge of the cell caused by the inflow of positively charged sodium ions is called an _action_ _potential_ , which travels down the _axon_ of the neuron. After the firing of an action potential there is a brief period in which no further action potentials can be generated. This brief period is called the *absolute* _refractory_ *period*.

3-3. The text likens the neuron to a gun in that it either fires or it does not fire. This property of the neuron is called the _all or none_ law. Neurons transmit information about the strength of a stimulus by variations in the number of action potentials generated. For example, in comparison to a weak stimulus, a strong stimulus will generate a (<u>higher</u>/lower) rate of action potentials.

Answers: 3-1. negative, sodium 3-2. action potential, axon, refractory 3-3. all-or-none, higher.

4. **Describe how neurons communicate at chemical synapses and discuss how researchers track neurotransmitter activity.**

4-1. A neuron passes its message on to another neuron by releasing a chemical messenger into the gap or
synaptic _cleft_ that separates it from other neurons. The sending neuron,
called the _presynaptic_ neuron , releases a chemical messenger into the synaptic cleft, which
then excites the _postsynaptic_ neuron.

4-2. The chemical messenger that provides this transmitting service is called a _neurotransmitter_. The
chemical binds with specifically tuned receptor sites on the postsynaptic neurons. In other words, the
receptor sites accept some neurotransmitters and reject _others_. The notion that a specific
neurotransmitter can bind with only a specific type of receptor site is called the _lock and key_
model.

4-3. When the neurotransmitter combines with a molecule at the receptor site it causes a voltage change at
the receptor site called a _postsynaptic_ potential (PSP). One type of PSP is excitatory and thus
increases the probability of producing an action potential in the receiving neuron. The
other type is inhibitory and thus _decreases_ the probability of producing an action potential.

4-4. Whether or not a neuron fires depends on the number of excitatory PSPs it is receiving and the number
of _inhibitory_ PSPs it is receiving.

4-5. Answer the following questions about how researchers track neurotransmitter activity.
(a) Since it is very difficult to directly measure neurotransmitter activity in an intact human brain, how do
researchers assess this activity in live human subjects? _blood, urine, cerebrospinal fluid._

(b) What other source do researchers have for obtaining and studying neurotransmitters?
dead animals from slaughter houses

Answers: 4-1. synaptic cleft, presynaptic, postsynaptic   4-2. neurotransmitter, others, lock and key   4-3. postsynaptic, increases, decreases   4-4. inhibitory   4-5. (a) They measure metabolic byproducts from blood, urine, and cerebrospinal fluid. (b) Dead animals obtained from slaughterhouses.

5. **Discuss how acetycholine, the bioamines, GABA, and endorphins are related to behavior.**

5-1. Our moods, thoughts and actions all depend on the action of neurotransmitters. For example, the
movement of all muscles depends on _acetycholine_ (ACh). An inadequate supply of
acetycholine has also been implicated in the memory losses seen in _Altzheimers_ disease.

5-2. Three neurotransmitters, dopamine, norepinephrine, and serotonin, are collectively known as
bioamines. Both Parkinsonism and schizophrenia have been linked with alterations in
dopamine activity, while the mood changes found in bipolar mood disorder have been
linked to receptor sites for _norepinephrine._

5-3. Still another group of neurotransmitters, including GABA, are unlike other neurotransmitters in that they only have (excitatory/<u>inhibitory</u>) effects at receptor sites. Most other neurotransmitters can have either inhibitory or excitatory effects. Lowered levels of GABA in the brain may allow for heightened neural activity which translates into feelings of ___*anxiety*___. Tranquilizers appear to work by increasing inhibitory activity at GABA synapses, a task that would normally be accomplished by ___*GABA*___ itself.

5-4. Endorphins are neuropeptides produced by the body that have effects similar to those produced by the drug ___*opium*___ and its derivatives. That is, they are able to reduce pain and also induce ___*pleasure*___. Endorphins work in two different ways. Some bind to specific receptor sites and thus serve as ___*neurotransmitters*___. Most endorphins, however, work by *modulating* the activity of specific neurotransmitters. In this role they are said to serve as ___*neuromodulators*___.

Answers: 5-1. acetycholine, Alzheimer's 5-2. bioamines, dopamine, norepinephrine 5-3. inhibitory, anxiety, GABA 5-4. opium, pleasure, neurotransmitters, neuromodulators.

ORGANIZATION OF THE NERVOUS SYSTEM

6. Provide an overview of the organization of the nervous system.

With approximately 100 to 180 billion individual neurons to control, it is important that the central nervous system have some kind of organizational structure. This organizational structure is depicted in Figure 3.6 of the text, and it will prove helpful if you have this figure in front of you while answering the following questions.

6-1. Answer the following questions regarding the organization of the nervous system.
(a) What are the two major divisions of the nervous system?
central nervous system and peripheral nervous system

(b) What two subdivisions make up the peripheral nervous system?
somatic nervous system and autonomic nervous system

(c) What two subdivisions make up the autonomic nervous system?
sympathetic and parasympathetic

(d) What are the two major divisions of the central nervous system?
the brain and the spinal cord

6-2. Describe the opposing roles of the sympathetic and parasympathetic nervous systems.
"fight or flight"
conserves resources

6-3. What is the role of the meninges covering and the cerebrospinal fluid?
serve as protective features for the brain & spinal cord

Answers: 6-1. (a) the central nervous system and the peripheral nervous system (b) the somatic nervous system and the autonomic nervous system (c) the sympathetic nervous system and the parasympathetic nervous system (d) the brain and the spinal cord 6-2. The sympathetic system prepares the body for fight or flight and the parasympathetic system conserves the body's resources. 6-3. They serve as protective features for the brain and spinal cord.

LOOKING INSIDE THE BRAIN: RESEARCH METHODS

7. **Describe how the EEG, lesioning, and ESB are used to investigate brain function.**

   7-1.   The electroencephalograph, or _____EEG_____, is a device that can measure the brain's
           _____electrical_____ activity. Electrodes are placed on the scalp and the brain's electrical activity is
           then monitored by the EEG machine and transformed into line tracings called _____brain_____ waves.

   7-2.   Answer the following questions regarding the use of lesioning and ESB to investigate brain function.
           (a) What technique involves the actual destruction of brain tissue so as to examine the resulting effect on
           behavior?   *lesioning*

           (b) What technique would most likely be employed by a neurosurgeon to map the brain of a patient?
           electrical stimulation of the brain

           (c) What technique employs the use of electrodes and electrical currents?
           lesioning & ESB

           (d) In what fundamental way does lesioning differ from ESB?
           lesioning destroys tissue - ESB is used to elicit behavior

Answers: 7-1. EEG, electrical, brain 7-2. (a) lesioning (b) ESB (c) lesioning and ESB (d) Lesioning is used to actually destroy tissue whereas ESB is used to merely elicit behavior.

8. **Describe the new brain imaging methods (CT, PET, MRI scans) that are used to study brain structure and function.**

   8-1.   There are three new kinds of brain imaging procedures that have come into recent use. One of these
           procedures consists of a computer enhanced X-ray machine that compiles multiple X rays of the brain
           into a single vivid picture. The resulting images are called _____CT_____ scans. An even newer
           device that produces clearer three dimensional images of the brain goes by the name of magnetic
           resonance imaging scanner, and the images it produces are known as _____MRI_____ scans.

   8-2.   Unlike CT and MRI scans, which can only show the structure of the brain, the positron emission
           tomography scanner can portray the brain's actual _____activity_____ across time. The images
           produced by this procedure are called _____PET_____ scans.

Answers: 8-1. CT, MRI 8-2. activity, PET.

9. **Summarize the methods and implications of the Featured Study (Suddath et al., 1990) linking brain structure to schizophrenia.**

9-1. Answer the following questions regarding the Featured Study.
(a) Who comprised the 15 experimental and 15 control subjects?

(b) What was the major difference in these subjects?

(c) What did the MRI scans show?

(d) What led to the clearer results in this study as compared to previous studies?

Answers: 9-1. (a) fifteen sets of identical twins (b) One twin in each set had schizophrenia. (c) Twelve of the schizophrenic twins showed enlarged ventricles in their brains (as compared to their identical twin). (d) Improved methods of observation; namely MRI scans.

10. **Summarize the key structures and functions of the hindbrain and midbrain.**

10-1. The brain can be subdivided into three major structures. Moving up from the top of the spinal cord, one first encounters the hindmost part of the brain, or _hind brain_. Next comes the middle part or _mid brain_. At the top we encounter the _fore brain_.

10-2. Three separate structures make up the hindbrain: the cerebellum, the pons, and the medulla. The structure that attaches to the top of the spinal cord and controls many essential functions such as breathing and circulation is called the _medulla_. The section that forms a bridge of fibers between the brainstem and the cerebellum is called the _pons_. The structure that is essential for executing and coordinating physical movement is called the _cerebellum_.

10-3. Helping to control sensory processes and voluntary movements is one of the major roles of the _midbrain_. It also shares a structure with the hindbrain that is essential for the regulation of sleep and wakefulness. This structure is called the _reticular_ formation.

Answers: 10-1. hindbrain, midbrain, forebrain 10-2. medulla, pons, cerebellum 10-3. midbrain, reticular.

11. **Summarize the key functions of the thalamus, hypothalamus, and limbic system.**

11-1. The structure which serves as a way station for all sensory information (except for smell) headed for the brain is called the _thalamus_. The thalamus also appears to play an active role in _integrating_ the sensory information.

11-2. The hypothalamus is a small but important structure that plays a major role in the regulation of basic biological drives. What two routes does the hypothalamus use to carry out this function?
connections w/ autonomic nervous system and endocrine system

11-3. An interconnected network of structures that are involved in the control of emotion, motivation, and memory are collectively known as the ___limbic___ system. Damage to one of these structures, the hippocampus, is found in Alzheimer's disease patients; thus it must play a key role in the formation of ___memories___. However, the limbic system is best known for its role as the seat of ___emotion___. Electrical stimulation of particular areas of the limbic system in rats and monkeys appears to produce intense pleasure. Similar research with human subjects has shown the pleasure to be (more/___less___) intense than is apparently the case in rats and monkeys.

Answers: 11-1. thalamus, integrating   11-2. It has connections with the autonomic nervous system and the endocrine system.   11-3. limbic, memories, emotion, less.

12. Describe the structure of the cerebrum and the key function of the four lobes in the cerebral cortex.

12-1. The cerebrum is the brain structure that is responsible for our most complex ___mental___ activities. Its folded outer surface is called the ___cerebral___ cortex. The cerebrum is divided into two halves, known as the ___left___ and ___right___ cerebral hemispheres. The two hemispheres communicate with each other by means of a wide band of fibers called the ___corpus callosum___.

12-2. Each cerebral hemisphere is divided into four parts called lobes. Match these four lobes (occipital, parietal, temporal, and frontal) with their key function:
(a) Contains the primary motor cortex that controls the movement of muscles.
___frontal___

(b) Contains the primary visual cortex that initiates the processing of visual information.
___occipital___

(c) Contains the primary auditory cortex that initiates the processing of auditory information.
___temporal___

'(d) Contains the somatosensory cortex that registers the sense of touch.
___parietal___

Answers: 12-1. mental, cerebral, right, left, corpus callosum   12-2. (a) frontal (b) occipital (c) temporal (d) parietal.

RIGHT BRAIN/LEFT BRAIN: CEREBRAL SPECIALIZATION

13. Summarize evidence that led scientists to view the left hemisphere as the dominant hemisphere and describe how research on cerebral specialization changed this view.

13-1. Until recent years it was believed that the left hemisphere was the dominant hemisphere, with the right hemisphere playing a much less important role. Evidence for this belief came from several sources that all seemed to indicate that the left hemisphere played the dominant role with respect to ___language___. For example, damage to an area in the frontal lobe known as ___Broca's___ area was associated with speech deficits. Also, damage to another area located in the temporal lobe was found to be associated with difficulty in speech comprehension. This area is called ___Wernicke's___ area. Both of these areas are located in the ___left___ cerebral hemisphere.

13-2. Answer the following questions regarding split-brain research.
(a) What was the result of severing the corpus callosum in these patients?

separate communication of the two cerebral hemispheres

(b) Which hemisphere was found to be primarily responsible for verbal and language tasks in general?

left

(c) Which hemisphere was found to be primarily responsible for visual and spatial tasks?

right

13-3. What can be concluded with respect to hemispheric domination from both split-brain and intact brain studies? *neither hemisphere dominates - each has its own specialized tasks.*

Answers: 13-1. language, Broca's, Wernicke's, left   13-2. (a) The two cerebral hemispheres could no longer communicate with each other. (b) the left cerebral hemisphere (c) the right cerebral hemisphere   13-3. Neither hemisphere dominates, rather each has its own specialized tasks.

THE ENDOCRINE SYSTEM: ANOTHER WAY TO COMMUNICATE

14. Describe the workings of the endocrine system.

14-1. Answer the following questions regarding the workings of the endocrine system.
(a) What is the role played by the hormones in the endocrine system?

chemical messengers

(b) While many glands comprise the endocrine system, which one functions as a master gland to control the others? *pituitary gland*

(c) What structure is the real power behind the throne here? *hypthalmus*

14-2. Fill in the boxes in the diagram below showing the role of the pituitary gland in the "fight or flight" response to stress.

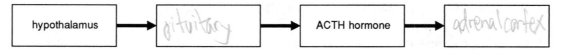

hypothalamus → *pituitary* → ACTH hormone → *adrenal cortex*

14-3. Fill in the boxes in the diagram below showing the role of the pituitary gland in controling sexual development.

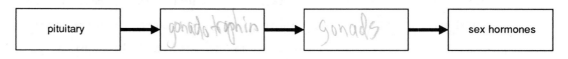

pituitary → *gonadotrophin* → *gonads* → sex hormones

14-4. What is the role of sexual hormones:
(a) Prior to birth? *direct formation of external sex organs*

(b) At puberty? *emerge of secondary sexual characteristics*

Answers: 14-1. (a) They serve as chemical messengers. (b) the pituitary gland (c) the hypothalamus 14-2. pituitary, adrenal cortex 14-3. gonadotrophin, gonads (or sex glands) 14-4. (a) They direct the formation of the external sexual organs. (b) They are responsible for the emergence of the secondary sexual characteristics.

HEREDITY AND BEHAVIOR: IS IT ALL IN THE GENES?

15. **Describe the structures and processes involved in genetic transmission.**

15-1. When a human sperm and egg unite at conception they form a one-celled organism called a ___*zygote*___. This cell contains 46 chromosomes, half of which are contributed by each ___*parent*___, thus making 23 pairs. Each member of a pair operates in conjunction with its ___*opposite*___ member. The zygote then evolves to form all of the cells in the body, all of which, except for the sex cells, have ___*23*___ pairs of chromosomes.

15-2. Each chromosome is actually a threadlike strand of a ___*DNA*___ molecule, and along this threadlike structure are found the individual units of information, called ___*genes*___, that determine our biological makeup. Like chromosomes, genes operate in ___*pair*___. For example, eye color is determined by a pair of genes. If both parents contribute a gene for the same color, the child will inherit this eye color and the two genes are said to be ___*homozygous*___. If the parents contribute two different genes for eye color, the genes are said to be ___*heterozygous*___ and the child will inherit the eye color carried by the dominant gene. When heterozygous genes are paired, the dominant gene masks the ___*recessive*___ gene.

Answers: 15-1. zygote, parent, opposite, 23 15-2. DNA, genes, pairs, homozygous, heterozygous, recessive.

16. **Explain the difference between genotype and phenotype and the meaning of polygenic inheritance.**

16-1. Answer the following questions about the difference between genotype and phenotype.
(a) What are the two genes that make up your eye color said to be?
genotype

(b) What is the resulting eye color you now have said to be?
phenotype

(c) Can your genotype and phenotype change over time?
phenotype can

16-2. What is meant when it is said that most human traits are polygenic?
determined by (2) or more pairs of genes

Answers: 16-1. (a) Your genotype. (b) Your phenotype. (c) Only your phenotype can change. 16-2. They are determined by two or more pairs of genes.

17. **Explain the special methods used to investigate the influence of heredity on behavior.**

17-1. If a trait is due to heredity, then more closely related members of a family should show a (lesser/greater) resemblance on this trait than less closely related family members. Studies using this method are called _____ studies. Data gathered from family studies (can/cannot) furnish conclusive proof as to the heritability of a specific trait. Even when it is demonstrated that a particular trait is highly related to the degree of family relationship, the cause for this relationship could be either heredity or _____.

17-2. A second method in this line of investigation is to compare specific traits across identical twins and fraternal twins. This method, called _____ studies, assumes that inherited traits are much more likely to be found among _____ twins than among fraternal twins. These studies do in fact show that for many characteristics, such as mental ability, the resemblance is closest for _____ twins. Again, the data are only correlational and (do/do not) provide conclusive proof that these traits are due completely to heredity.

17-3. A third method in this line of investigation is to study children who have been separated from their biological parents at a very early age and raised by adoptive parents. The idea behind these _____ studies is that if the adoptive children more closely resemble their biological parents with respect to a specific trait then it can be assumed that _____ plays a major role. On the other hand, if the adoptive children more closely resemble their adoptive parents with respect to a specific trait, it would indicate that _____ plays a major role. Studies using this method to study the inheritability of intelligence have found that adoptive children more closely resemble their _____ parents on this particular trait, but not by much. This would indicate that a trait such as intelligence is influenced by both heredity and _____.

Answers: 17-1. greater, family, cannot, environment 17-2. twin, identical, identical, do not 17-3. adoption, heredity, environment, biological, environment.

18. **Explain how heredity may influence behavior and how its influence may be moderated by environment.**

18-1. The answer now appears to be quite clear with respect to the question, "Is it all in the genes?" The answer is no. However, neither is it all in the environment. What does this mean with respect to most behavioral traits?

18-2. How can the interaction between heredity and environment be used to explain the development of schizophrenic disorders?

Answers: 18-1. They result from an interaction between heredity and environment. 18-2. One can inherit a vulnerability to schizophrenia, but the actual expression of this disorder will depend on environmental factors.

PUTING IT IN PERSPECTIVE

19. **Explain how this chapter highlighted three of the texts unifying themes.**

    19-1.   Indicate which of the three unifying themes (the interaction of heredity and environment, multiple causation of behavior, and the empirical nature of psychology) is particularly illustrated by each of the following situations.

        (a) The development of schizophrenic disorders.

        (b) The discovery of cerebral specialization.

        (c) The evidence showing that identical twins are more alike than fraternal twins.

        (d) The difference between your genotype and your phenotype.

    Answers: 19-1. (a) the interaction of heredity and environment and multiple causation of behavior (b) the empirical nature of psychology (c) the empirical nature of psychology (d) the interaction of heredity and environment.

APPLICATION: RIGHT BRAIN/LEFT BRAIN: TWO MODES OF THOUGHT

20. **Outline five popular ideas linking cerebral specialization to cognitive processes and evaluate each of these in light of currently available evidence.**

    20-1.   Your text lists five popular ideas that have found support among some neuroscientists and psychologists. These ideas are:

        (a) Our right and left brains actually give us _____ minds in a single brain.

        (b) Each half of the brain (does/does not) have its own mode of thinking.

        (c) Some people are left-brained while others are _____ - brained.

        (d) The creative half of the brain is located in the _____ hemisphere.

        (e) Our schools should devote more effort to teaching the overlooked _____ side of the

brain.

20-2. We will now proceed through each of these five assumptions to show how each has to be qualified in light of currently available evidence.

(a) The evidence that each hemisphere has its own mind, or stream of consciousness, is actually very weak, except for persons who have undergone _____-_____ surgery. The resulting "two minds" in these patients appears to be a byproduct of the surgery.

(b) The idea that the left and right brains are specialized to handle different kinds of information (is/is not) supported by research. However, there is evidence that this specialization hardly occurs in some persons, while in other persons the specialization is reversed, particularly among _____-handed persons. Moreover, most tasks require the ongoing cooperation of _____ hemispheres.

(c) The assertion that some people are left-brained, while others are right brained (is/is not) conclusive at the present time. Even if more evidence were found to support this assertion, it would only mean that some people consistently display a greater amount of activity in one _____ compared to the other.

(d) Present evidence (does/does not) support the supposition that creative ability is related to right-brainedness.

(e) The notion that most schooling overlooks the education of the right brain (does/does not) really make sense. Since both hemispheres are almost always sharing in accomplishing an ongoing task, it would be _____ to teach only one hemisphere at a time.

Answers: 20-1. (a) two (b) does (c) right- (d) right (e) right   20-2. (a) split-brain (b) is, left, both (c) is not, hemisphere (d) does not (e) does not, impossible.

REVIEW OF KEY TERMS

Absolute refractory period
Action potential
Adoption studies
Afferent nerve fibers
Agonist
Antagonist
Autonomic nervous system (ANS)
Axon
Blood-brain barrier
Central nervous system (CNS)
Cerebral cortex
Cerebral hemispheres
Cerebrospinal fluid (CSF)
Chromosomes
Corpus callosum
Dendrites
Dominant gene
Efferent fibers
Electrical stimulation of the brain (ESB)
Electroencephalograph (EEG)
Endocrine system

Endorphins
Excitatory PSP
Family studies
Forebrain
Genes
Genotype
Glia
Hindbrain
Hormones
Hypothalamus
Inhibitory PSP
Lesioning
Limbic system
Midbrain
Motor neurons
Myelin sheath
Nerves
Neuromodulators
Neurons
Neurotransmitters

Parasympathetic division
Peripheral nervous system
Phenotype
Pituitary gland
Polygenic traits
Postsynaptic potential (PSP)
Recessive gene
Resting potential
Sensory neurons
Soma
Somatic nervous system
Split-brain surgery
Sterotaxic instrument
Sympathetic division
Synapse
Synaptic cleft
Terminal buttons
Thalamus
Twin studies
Zygote

_____ 1. Neurons that receive information from outside the nervous system.

_____ 2. Neurons that transmit information to the muscles that actually move the body.

_____ 3. Cells found throughout the nervous system that provide structural support and insulation for neurons.

_____ 4. Individual cells in the nervous system that receive, integrate, and transmit information.

_____ 5. Neuron part that contains the cell nucleus and much of the chemical machinery common to most cells.

_____ 6. Branchlike parts of a neuron that are specialized to receive information.

_____ 7. A long, thin fiber that transmits signals away from the soma to other neurons, or to muscles or glands.

_____ 8. An insulating jacket, derived from glia cells, that encases some axons.

_____ 9. Small knobs at the end of the axon that secrete chemicals called neurotransmitters.

_____ 10. A junction where information is transmitted between neurons.

_____ 11. The stable, negative charge of an inactive neuron.

_____ 12. A brief change in a neuron's electrical charge.

_____ 13. The minimum length of time after an action potential during which another action potential cannot begin.

_____ 14. A microscopic gap between the terminal buttons of the sending neuron and the cell membrane of another neuron.

_____ 15. Chemicals that transmit information from one neuron to another.

_____ 16. A voltage change at the receptor site of a neuron.

_____ 17. An electric potential that increases the likelihood that a postsynaptic neuron will fire action potentials.

_____ 18. An electric potential that decreases the likelihood that a postsynaptic neuron will fire action potentials.

_____ 19. A technique for assessing hereditary influence by examining blood relatives to see how much they resemble each other on a specific trait.

_____ 20. A chemical that mimics the action of a neurotransmitter.

_____ 21. A chemical that opposes the action of a neurotransmitter.

_____ 22. An entire family of internally produced chemicals that resemble opiates in structure and effects.

_____ 23. Chemicals that increase or decrease (modulate) the activity of specific neurotransmitters.

_____ 24. System that includes all those nerves that lie outside the brain and spinal cord.

_____ 25. Bundles of neuron fibers (axons) that travel together in the peripheral nervous system.

_____ 26. System made up of the nerves that connect to voluntary skeletel muscles and sensory receptors.

_____ 27. Axons that carry information inward to the central nervous system from the periphery of the body.

_____ 28. Axons that carry information outward from the central nervous system to the periphery of the body.

_____ 29. System made up of the nerves that connect to the heart, blood vessels, smooth muscles and glands.

_____ 30. The branch of the autonomic nervous system that mobilizes the body's resources for emergencies.

_____ 31. The branch of the autonomic nervous system that generally conserves bodily resources.

_____ 32. System that consists of the brain and spinal cord.

_____ 33. A solution that fills the hollow cavities (ventricles) of the brain and circulates around the brain and spinal cord.

_____ 34. A semipermeable membranelike mechanism that stops some chemicals from passing between the bloodstream and brain cells.

_____ 35. A device that monitors the electrical activity of the brain over time by means of recording electrodes attached to the surface of the scalp.

_____ 36. Assessing hereditary influence by comparing the resemblance of identical twins and fraternal twins on a trait.

_____ 37. Method that involves destroying a piece of the brain by means of a strong electric current delivered through an electrode.

_____ 38. A device used to implant electrodes at precise locations in the brain.

_____ 39. Method that involves sending a weak electric current into a brain structure to stimulate (activate) it.

_____ 40. Part of the brain that includes the cerebellum and two structures found in the lower part of the brainstem —the medulla and the pons.

_____ 41. The segment of the brainstem that lies between the hindbrain and the forebrain.

_____ 42. Part of the brain encompassing the thalamus, hypothalamus, limbic system, and cerebrum.

_____ 43. A structure in the forebrain through which all sensory information (except smell) must pass to get to the cerebral cortex.

_____ 44. A structure found near the base of the forebrain that is involved in the regulation of basic biological needs.

_____ 45. A densely connected network of structures located beneath the cerebral cortex, involved in the control of emotion, motivation and memory.

_____ 46. The convulated outer layer of the cerebrum.

_____ 47. The right and left halves of the cerebrum.

_____ 48. The structure that connects the two cerebral hemispheres.

_____ 49. Assessing hereditary influence by examining the resemblance between adopted children and both their adoptive and biological parents.

_____ 50. Surgery in which the the corpus callosum is severed to reduce the severity of epileptic seizures.

_____ 51. System of glands that secrete chemicals into the bloodstream that help control bodily functioning.

_____ 52. The chemical substances released by the endocrine glands.

_____ 53. The "master gland" of the endocrine system.

_____ 54. Threadlike strands of DNA molecules that carry genetic information.

_____ 55. A one-celled organism formed by the union of a sperm and an egg.

_____ 56. DNA segments that serve as the key functional units in hereditary transmission.

_____ 57. A gene that is expressed when the paired genes are different (heterozygous).

_____ 58. A gene that is masked when paired genes are heterozygous.

_____ 59. A person's genetic makeup.

_____ 60. The ways in which a person's genotype is manifested in observable characteristics.

_____ 61. Characteristics that are influenced by more than one pair of genes.

Answers: 1. sensory neurons 2. motor neurons 3. glia 4. neurons 5. soma 6. dendrites 7. axon 8. myelin sheath 9. terminal buttons 10. synapse 11. resting potential 12. action potential 13. absolute refractory period 14. synaptic cleft 15. neurotransmitters 16. postsynaptic potential (PSP) 17. excitatory PSP 18. inhibitory PSP 19. family studies 20. agonist 21. antagonist 22. endorphins 23. neuromodulators 24. peripheral nervous system 25. nerves 26. somatic nervous system 27. afferent nerve fibers 28. efferent fibers 29. autonomic nervous system (ANS) 30. sympathetic division 31. parasympathetic division 32. central nervous system (CNS) 33. cerebrospinal fluid (CSF) 34. blood-brain barrier 35. electroencephalograph (EEG) 36. twin studies 37. lesioning 38. sterotaxic instrument 39. electrical stimulation of the brain (ESB) 40. hindbrain 41. midbrain 42. forebrain 43. thalamus 44. hypothalamus 45. limbic system 46. cerebral cortex 47. cerebral hemispheres 48. corpus callosum 49. adoption studies 50. split-brain surgery 51. endocrine system 52. hormones 53. pituitary gland 54. chromosomes 55. zygote 56. genes 57. dominant gene 58. recessive gene 59. genotype 60. phenotype 61. polygenic traits.

REVIEW OF KEY PEOPLE

Alan Hodgkin & Andrew Huxley   Candice Pert & Solomon Snyder
James Olds & Peter Milner   Roger Sperry & Michael Gazzaniga

_____ 1. Unlocked the mystery of the neural impulse.

_____ 2. Known for their work with the split-brain.

_____ 3. Showed that morphine works by binding to specific receptors.

_____ 4. Discovered "pleasure-centers" in the limbic system.

Answers: 1. Hodgkin & Huxley 2. Sperry & Gazzaniga 3. Pert & Snyder 4. Olds & Milner.

SELF-QUIZ

1. Most neurons are involved in transmitting information:
   a. from one neuron to another
   b. from the outside world to the brain
   c. from the brain to the muscles
   d. none of the above

2. Neurons that are specialized to communicate directly with the muscles of the body are called:
   a. sensory neurons
   b. motor neurons
   c. actuator neurons
   d. muscle neurons

3. Which part of the neuron has the responsibility for receiving information from other neurons?
   a. the cell body
   b. the soma
   c. the axon
   d. the dendrites

4. The myelin sheath serves to:
   a. permit faster transmission of the neural impulse
   b. keep neural impulses on the right track
   c. both of the above
   c. none of the above

5. The change in the polarity of a neuron that results from the inflow of positively charged ions and the outflow of negatively charged ions is called the:
   a. presynaptic potential
   b. postsynaptic potential
   c. synaptic potential
   d. none of the above

6. The task of passing a message from one neuron to another is actually carried out by:
   a. the myelin sheath
   b. the glia cells
   c. the action potential
   d. neurotransmitters

7. Which of the following neurotransmitters can only have an inhibitory effect at receptor sites?
   a. GABA
   b. dopamine
   c. norepinephrine
   d. serotonin

8. Which of the following techniques is often used by neurosurgeons to map the brain when performing brain surgery?
   a. EEG recordings
   b. ESB
   c. lesioning
   d. all of the above

9. The seat of emotion is to be found in the:
   a. reticular formation
   b. hindbrain
   c. limbic system
   d. forebrain

10. Persons having difficulty with language and speech following an accident that resulted in injury to the brain are most likely to have sustained damage in the:
    a. right cerebral hemisphere
    b. left cerebral hemisphere
    c. right cerebral hemisphere if they are a male and left cerebral hemisphere if they are a female
    d. I have no idea what you are talking about

11. In the Featured Study linking brain structure to schizophrenia it was found that when compared to the nonschizophrenic twin, the schizophrenic twin was more likely to have:
    a. a different genotype
    b. enlarged ventricles in the brain
    c. a less placid autonomic nervous system
    d. a more stressful environment

12. In carrying out the "fight or flight" response, the role of supervisor is assigned to the:
    a. adrenal gland
    b. pituitary gland
    c. hypothalamus
    d. parasympathetic nervous system

13. A person's current weight and height could be said to exemplify his or her:
    a. genotype
    b. phenotype
    c. both of the above
    d. none of the above

14. Which of the following kinds of studies can truly demonstrate that specific traits are indeed inherited?
    a. family studies
    b. twin studies
    c. adoption studies
    d. none of the above

15. Current evidence indicates that schizophrenia results from:
    a. genetic factors
    b. environmental factors
    c. multiple causes that involve both genetic and environmental factors
    d. completely unknown factors

16. Psychology as a science can be said to be:
    a. empirical
    b. rational
    c. analytic
    d. both b and c

17. Which of the following statements is/are correct?
    a. the right side of the brain is the creative side
    b. the right and left brains are specialized to handle different kinds of information
    c. language tasks are always handled by the left brain
    d. all of the above

Answers: 1.a 2.b 3.d 4.c 5.d 6.d 7.a 8.b 9.c 10.b 11.b 12.c 13.b 14.d 15.c 16.a
17. b.

4 SENSATION AND PERCEPTION

REVIEW OF KEY IDEAS

PSYCHOPHYSICS: BASIC CONCEPTS AND ISSUES

1. **Explain how thresholds are determined and how stimulus intensity is related to absolute thresholds.**

   1-1.   You are sitting on a secluded beach at sundown with a good friend. You make a bet as to who can detect the first evening star. Since you have just recently covered this chapter in your text, you explain to your friend doing so involves the detection of a stimulus ___threshold___. In this case, the first star that provides the minimal amount of stimulation to be detected can be said to have crossed the ___absolute___ threshold. All of our senses have absolute thresholds, but research clearly shows that the minimal amount of stimulation necessary to be detected by any one of our senses (is/is not) always the same. Therefore, the absolute threshold is defined as the stimulus intensity that can be detected _50_ percent of the time.

   1-2.   How short does a line have to be before you can no longer see it? Your text described two different methods that Fechner devised for measuring absolute thresholds; he called them the method of limits and the method of constant stimuli. Each of these methods is illustrated below to locate the shortest line that you can see. Which is which?

   (a) This is the method of ___constant stimuli___.

   (b) This is the method of ___limits___.

   Answers: 1-1. threshold, absolute, is not, 50   1-2. (a) constant stimuli (b) limits.

2. **Explain Weber's law and what Fechner and Stevens found when they related stimulus intensity to perceived magnitude.**

   2-1.   Weber's law states that the size of a just noticeable difference (JND) is a constant proportion of the intensity (size) of the initial stimulus. This means that it would be more difficult to detect a slight increase in the length of a (1-inch/20-inch) line and it would be more difficult to detect a JND in a (quiet/loud) tone.

   2-2.   Fechner's law states that larger and larger increases in stimulus intensity are required to produce perceptible increments, or _____JNDs_____, in the magnitude of sensation. What this means is that as the intensity of a stimulus increases, the size of the JND we are able to detect (decreases/increases).

   2-3.   Stevens, using a different approach, found that the shape of his curves relating stimulus intensity of perceived magnitude for some dimensions (did/did not) vary dramatically from Fechner's curves. However, both approaches found that our subjective measurements of sensory experience (can/cannot) be measured on an absolute scale. Rather, our sensory experience is always ___relative___.

   Answers: 2-1. 20-inch, loud   2-2. JNDs, increases   2-3. did, cannot, relative.

3. **Summarize the basic thrust of signal detection theory.**

   3-1.   The major idea behind signal detection theory is that our ability to detect signals depends not only on the initial intensity of a stimulus, but also on other sensory and decision processes. What two factors are particularly important here? *background noise & criterion*

   3-2.   Thus, according to signal detection theory, the concepts of absolute thresholds and JNDs need to be replaced by the notion that the probability of detecting any given stimulus will depend on all of the above factors; this is called the concept of ___detectability___.

   Answers: 3-1. background noise and subjective factors within the perceiver   3-2. detectability.

4. **Discuss the meaning and significance of sensory adaptation.**

   4-1.   Which of the following examples best illustrates what is meant by sensory adaptation?
   (a) You are unable to clearly hear the conversation at the next table even though it sounds intriguing and you are straining to listen.
   (b) The strawberries you eat at grandma's farm at the age of 20 seem not to taste as good as when you ate them at the age of 6.
   (c) The wonderful smell you encounter upon first entering the bakery seems to have declined considerably by the time you make your purchase and leave. *c.*

   4-2.   If you answered c to the above question, you are right on track and understand that sensory adaptation involves a gradual ___decrease___ in the sensitivity to prolonged stimulation. This automatic process means that we are not as likely to be as sensitive to the constants in our sensory environments as we are to the ___changes___.

   Answers: 4-1. c   4-2. decrease, changes.

OUR SENSE OF SIGHT: THE VISUAL SYSTEM

5. **List the three properties of light and the aspects of visual perception that they influence.**

   5-1. Before we can see anything, _lightwaves_ must be present. There are three characteristics of lightwaves that directly effect how we perceive visual objects; match each of these characteristics with its psychological effect.

   _1_ (a) wavelength   1. color

   _3_ (b) amplitude   2. saturation

   _2_ (c) purity   3. brightness

   Answers: 5-1. lightwaves or light, (a) 1 (b) 3 (c) 2.

6. **Describe the role of the lens and pupil in the functioning of the eye.**

   6-1. Getting light rays entering the eye to properly focus on the retina is the job of the _lens_. It accomplishes this task by either thickening or flattening its curvature, a process called _accomodation_. Controlling the amount of light entering the eye is the job of the _iris_. It accomplishes this task by opening or closing the opening in the center of the eye called the _pupil_.

   Answers: 6-1. lens, accomodation, iris, pupil.

7. **Describe the role of the retina in light sensitivity and in visual information processing.**

   7-1. The structure that transduces the information contained in light rays into neural impulses that are then sent to the brain is called the _retina_. All of the axons carrying these neural impulses exit the eye at a single opening in the retina called the optic _disk_. Since the optic disk is actually a hole in the retina, this part of the retina cannot sense incoming visual information and for this reason it is called the _blind spot_.

   7-2. The specialized receptor cells that are primarily responsible for visual acuity and color vision are called the _cones_. The cones are mainly located in the center of the retina in a tiny spot called the _fovea_. The specialized receptor cells that lie outside of the fovea and towards the periphery of the retina are called the _rods_. The rods are primarily responsible for peripheral vision and for _night_ vision.

   7-3. Both dark and light adaptation are accomplished through _chemical_ reactions in the rods and cones. This chemical reaction occurs more quickly in the _cones_, so they are quicker to show both dark adaptation and light adaptation.

   7-4. Light rays striking the rods and cones initiate neural impulses that are then transmitted to _bipolar_ cells and then to _ganglion_ cells. From here the visual information is transmitted to the brain via the axons running from the retina to the brain, collectively known as the _optic_ nerve.

7-5. The processing of visual information begins within the receiving area of a retinal cell called the _receptive_ field. Stimulation of the receptive field of a cell causes signals to be sent inward towards the brain and sideways, or _laterally_, to nearby cells, thus allowing them to interact with one another. The most common of these interactive effects, the inhibition of one cell by another, is called lateral _antagonism_. Lateral antagonism allows the visual system to compute the (absolute/~~relative~~) amount of light; it occurs in both the retina and the brain.

Answers: 7-1. retina, disk, blind spot **7-2.** cones, fovea, rods, night **7-3.** chemical, cones **7-4.** bipolar, ganglion, optic **7-5.** receptive, laterally, antagonism, relative.

8. Describe the routing of signals from the eye to the brain and the brains role in visual information processing.

8-1. Visual information from the right side of the visual field exits from the retinas of both eyes via the optic nerves and meet at the _optic_ chiasma, where it is combined and sent to the _left_ side of the brain. Visual information from the left side of the visual field follow a similar pattern, meeting at the optic chiasma, and then on to the _right_ side of the brain.

8-2. After leaving the optic chiasma on their way to the visual cortex, the optic nerve fibers diverge along two pathways. Fill in the missing parts of these pathways in the figures below.

Major pathway

(a) Optic chiasma _thalamus_   _lateral geniculate nucleus_   Visual cortex

Secondary pathway

(a) Optic chiasma _midbrain (superior colliculus)_   _thalamus_   Visual cortex

8-3. What purpose is served by having these two separate pathways dumping their information into different areas of the visual cortex. _the two visual pathways are specialized. they engage in parallel processing (simultaneously extracting different information from the same input)._

8-4. Because the cells in the visual cortex respond very selectively to specific features of complex stimuli, they have been described as _feature_ detectors. There are three major types of cells in the visual cortex, simple cells, complex cells, amd hypercomplex cells: identify them from their descriptions given below.

(a) These cells are particular about the width and orientation of a line but respond to any position in their receptive field.
complex

(b) These cells are very particular about the width, orientation, and position of a line.
simple

(c) These cells are like complex cells, but they are particular about the length of the lines that will cause them to fire.
hypercomplex

8-5. Each of these groups of cells responds to particular features of incoming stimuli. This means that the cells in the visual cortex (do/do not) provide a photographic-like picture of the outside world. Rather they provide a coding system that can then be transformed into such a picture.

Answers: 8-1. optic, left, right 8-2. (a) thalamus, lateral geniculate nucleus (b) superior colliculus, thalamus 8-3. It allows for parallel processing (simultaneously extracting different information from the same input). 8-4. feature, (a) complex cells (b) simple cells (c) hypercomplex cells 8-5. do not.

9. Discuss the trichromatic and opponent process theories of color vision, and the modern reconciliation of these theories.

9-1. The trichromatic theory of color vision, as its name suggests, proposes three different kinds of receptors (channels) for the three primary colors red, ___green___, and ___blue___. The opponent process theory of color vision also proposes three channels for color vision, but these channels are red versus ___green___, yellow versus ___blue___, and black versus ___white___.

9-2. These two theories of color vision can be used to explain different phenomenon. Use T (trichromatic) or O (opponent process) to indicate which theory best explains the following phenomena.

  _O_ (a) The color of an afterimage is the complement of the original color.

  _T_ (b) The different kinds of color blindness suggest three different kinds of receptors.

  _T_ (c) Any three appropriately spaced colors can produce all other colors.

  _O_ (d) Cultures that describe colors require at least four different names.

9-3. The evidence is now clear that both theories are (incorrect/correct). Each is needed to explain all of the phenomena associated with color vision. Three different kinds of cones have been found in the retina which are sensitive to one of the three primary colors; this supports the ___trichromatic___ theory. It has also been found that visual cells in the retina and thalamus respond in opposite (antagonistic) ways to complementary colors, thus supporting the ___opponent___ ___process___ theory.

Answers: 9-1. green, blue, green, blue, white 9-2. (a) O (b) T (c) T (d) O 9-3. correct, trichromatic, opponent process.

10. Summarize the procedure, results, and implications of the Featured Study (Johnston & McClelland, 1974) on perceptions of letters in words.

10-1. Explaining the perception of form is not easy because the same sensory input (can/cannot) result in radically different perceptions. One view of form perception assumes that the perception of form comes from building up the elements into a whole. This is the idea of ___visual___ analysis. The text describes it as bottom-___down___ processing. The discovery of cells in the visual cortex highly specialized for feature detection supports this theory. However, it has also been found that we can perceive words more quickly than we can perceive their individual letters. This argues against bottom-up processing and for ___top___-___down___ processing.

10-2. Answer the following questions regarding the Featured Study.
  (a) What was the task given to both groups in this study?

  to identify the letter that appeared in a particular position

  (b) What was the dependent variable?

  their accuracy in identifying the specific letters

  (c) Half of the subjects were briefly exposed to displays containing four random letters. What were the other half of the subjects exposed to? *sets of letters that formed words*

  (d) On half of the trials the subjects in both groups were instructed to focus their attention in the middle of the stimulus array and pay attention to the stimulus as a whole. What were they instructed to do on the other half of the trials? *focus their attention on the position where the critical letter would appear*

  (e) The study found that the subjects exposed to random letters did best when instructed to pay attention to the critical position. What instruction was best for the subjects exposed to words?

  focus on the stimulus as a whole

  (f) What does this study suggests about our perception of words? *we perceive words before their individual letters - top down processing.*

Answers: 10-1. can, feature, up, top-down 10-2. (a) identify the letter that appeared in a particular position (b) their accuracy in identifying the specific letters (c) letters that formed words (d) focus their attention on a specific position (e) focus their attention on the array as a whole (f) we perceive words before their individual letters (top-down processing).

11. **Explain the basic premise of Gestalt psychology and describe Gestalt principles of visual perception.**

  11-1. The Gestalt view of form perception assumes that form perception is not constructed out of individual elements; rather the form, or whole, is said to be __greater__ than the sum of its individual elements. The illusion of movement, called the __phi__ phenomenon, is used to support the Gestalt view of form perception because the illusion of movement (is/~~is not~~) completely contained in the individual chunks of stimuli that give rise to it. In other words, the illusion, or whole, appears to be __greater__ than the sum of its parts.

11-2. Five Gestalt principles of visual perception are illustrated below. Match each illustration with its correct name.

Proximity

Similarity

Continuity

Closure

Simplicity

(a) _proximity_

(b) _closure_

(c) _similarity_

(d) _simplicity_

(e) _continuity_

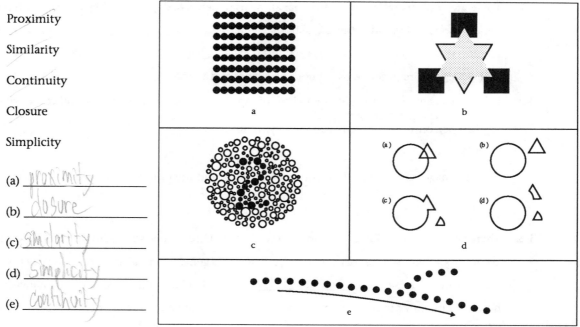

11-3. What Gestalt principle is illustrated by:
(a) The fact that the words printed on this page appear to stand out from the white paper they are printed on? _figure/ground_

(b) The fact that things that move in the same direction together get grouped together.
common fate

Answers: 11-1. greater (more), phi, is not, greater (more)   11-2. (a) proximity (b) closure (c) similarity (d) simplicity (e) continuity   11-3. (a) figure and ground (b) common fate.

12. Explain how form perception can be a matter of formulating perceptual hypotheses.

12-1. The objects that surround us in the world outside of our bodies are called _distal_ stimuli; the images the objects project on our retinas are called _proximal_ stimuli. When perceived from different angles or distances, the same distal stimulus projects (similar/**different**) proximal images on the retina. This forces us to make perceptual _hypotheses_ about the distal stimulus.

Answers: 12-1. distal, proximal, different, hypotheses or guesses

13. **Describe the monocular and binocular cues employed in depth perception.**

13-1. There are two general kinds of cues that allow us to perceive depth and they are easy to remember because one kind involves the use of both eyes and is called __binocular__ cues; the other kind requires the use of only one of the eyes and is called __monocular__ cues. Depth perception (does/~~does not~~) require the use of both binocular and monocular cues.

13-2. Below are examples of two different kinds of binocular cues, retinal disparity and convergence. Identify them from the examples given below.
(a) As a person walks towards you your eyes turn inward. *convergence*

(b) The images are slightly different on each retina and the differences change with distance.
retinal disparity

13-3. There are two general kinds of monocular cues. One kind involves the active use of the eye, such as the accommodation used for focusing the eye. The other general kind is used to indicate depth in flat pictures and thus is called __pictoral__ cues. No further discussion of pictoral cues is needed here because they are adequately reviewed in the Concept Check 4.2 of your text. If you have not already done so, review this Concept Check now.

Answers: 13-1. binocular, monocular, does not 13-2. (a) convergence (b) retinal disparity 13-3. pictoral.

14. **Describe perceptual constancies in vision and illusions in vision, and discuss their importance.**

14-1. The tendency to experience stable perceptions in spite of constantly changing sensory input is called perceptual __constancy__. The text lists several of these visual perceptual constancies; identify the ones being illustrated below.
(a) Even though the retinal image shrinks as a friend walks away, she continues to remain her usual height.
size constancy

(b) The retinal image warps as you track a basketball through the air but the ball always appears perfectly round. *shape constancy*

(c) Indoors or on the ski slope the light blue sweater always looks light blue.
color constancy

14-2. Being fooled by the discrepancy between the appearance of a visual stimulus and its physical reality is what is meant by an optical __illusion__. Both perceptual constancies and optical illusions illustrate the point we are continually formulating __hypotheses__ about what we perceive and also that these perceptions can be quite (subjective/~~objective~~).

Answers: 14-1. constancy, (a) size constancy (b) shape constancy (c) color constancy 14-2. illusion, hypotheses, subjective.

OUR SENSE OF HEARING: THE AUDITORY SYSTEM

15. **List the three properties of sound and the aspects of auditory perception that they are most closely associated with.**

15-1. Name the perceived qualities that are associated with the following properties of sound waves.

Physical property	Description	Perceived Quality
(a) purity	kind of mixture	timbre
(b) amplitude	wave height	loudness
(c) wavelength	wave frequency	pitch

Answers: 15-1. (a) timbre (b) loudness (c) pitch.

16. **Summarize the information on human hearing capacities and describe how sensory processing occurs in the ear.**

16-1. Below are questions concerning human hearing capacities. Match the questions with their correct answers.

Answers
1. 90 to 120 decibels (dB).
2. 1,000 to 5,000 Hz.
3. 20 to 20,000 Hz.

Questions

___3___ (a) What is the frequency range of human hearing?

___1___ (b) How loud do sounds have to be to cause damage to human hearing?

___2___ (c) To what frequency range is human hearing the most sensitive?

16-2. Below is a scrambled sequence of events that occurs when a sound wave strikes the ear. Put these events in their correct order using the numbers 1 through 4.

___3___ Fluid waves travel down the choclea causing the hair cells on the basilar membrane to vibrate.

___1___ The pinna directs air to the eardrum.

___4___ The hair cells convert fluid motion into neural impulses and send them to the brain.

___2___ The motion of the vibrating eardrum is converted to fluid motion by the ossicles.

Answers: 16-1. (a) 3 (b) 1 (c) 2   16-2. 3, 1, 4, 2.

17. **Describe the routing of auditory signals from the ear to the brain and auditory information processing in the brain.**

17-1. After leaving the ear, the auditory nerves ascend through the lower ___brainstem___ and then through the thalamus before ending in the ___auditory___ cortex.

17-2. Answer the following questions regarding this pathway.
(a) Which cerebral hemisphere receives most of the information from the left ear?

right cerebral hemisphere

(b) What three kinds of information are extracted during the ascension through the lower brain centers?

location in pitch, loudness & timbre

(c) What kind of information does the auditory cortex appear to process?

complex patterns such as speech

Answers: 17-1. brainstem, auditory   17-2. (a) the right cerebral hemisphere (b) location in space, pitch, and loudness (c) complex patterns of sound such as speech.

18. Compare and contrast the place and frequency theories of pitch perception and discuss the resolution of the debate.

18-1. One theory of pitch perception assumes that the hair cells respond differentially to pitch depending on their location along the basilar membrane. This is the main idea of the __*place*__ theory of pitch perception. A second theory assumes a one to one correspondence between the actual frequency of the sound wave and the frequency at which the entire basilar membrane vibrates. This is the main idea of the __*frequency*__ theory of pitch perception.

18-2. Below are several facts uncovered by research. Tell which theory of pitch is supported by each of these facts.
(a) The hair cells vibrate in unison and not independently.

Frequency theory

(b) Even when they fire in volleys, auditory nerves can only handle up to 5000 Hz.

Frequency theory

(c) A wave pattern caused by the vibrating basilar membrane peaks at a particular place along the membrane.

Place theory

18-3. The above facts mean that the perception of pitch depends on both __*place*__ and __*frequency*__ coding.

Answers: 18-1. place, frequency   18-2. (a) frequency theory (b) place theory (c) place theory   18-3. place, frequency.

19. Discuss the cues employed in auditory localization.

19-1. The sound shadow cast by the head is in a large part responsible for enhancing two important cues used for auditory localization. What are these two cues?

slight difference in intensity (loudness) and timing of sounds arriving at each ear

19-2. What behavior is commonly used in both vision and audition for localization?

scanning, or head & body movement

19-3. What do the eyes have to do with locating sound in space?

the eyes are used to locate sources of sound.

OUR CHEMICAL SENSES: TASTE AND SMELL

20. **Describe the stimulus and receptors for taste and discuss factors that may influence perceived flavor.**

   20-1.   The stimuli for taste perception are __chemicals__ absorbed in the saliva that stimulate taste cells

   located in the tongue's __taste__ __buds__. It is generally thought that there are four

   fundamental tastes; these are __sweet__, __sour__, __salty__, __bitter__.

   20-2.   Answer the following questions regarding the role of visual input and odors on perceived flavor.
   (a) Why is the same meal likely to taste better when served in a fine resturant than in a shabby diner?

   Appearance influences perceived flavor

   (b) Why do most persons prefer not to have their steak liquified in a food processor?

   _they don't have the chewing sensation - it changes the texture
   of the steak_

   (c) What additional effect is added to the flavor of wine by first swirling it in the glass?

   _helps to release the wine's odor - odor is a major determinant
   of flavor_

   Answers: 20-1. chemicals, taste buds, sweet, sour, salty, bitter.   20-2. (a) Appearance influences perceived flavor.
   (b) It changes the texture of the steak. (c) It helps to release the wine's odor and odor is a major determinant of flavor.

21. **Describe the stimulus and receptors for smell and discuss the sensitivity of human olfaction.**

   21-1.   The stimuli for the sense of smell are __chemical__ molecules floating in the air. The receptors

   for smell are hairlike structures located in the nasal passages called __olfactory__

   __cilia__. If there are any primary odors they must be (large/small) in number. Human

   sensitivity to smell (does/does not) compare favorably with that of many other animals, although some

   animals surpass us in this respect.

   Answers: 21-1. chemical, olfactory cilia, large, does.

22. **Describe processes involved in the perception of pressure, temperature, and pain.**

   22-1.   The statements below pertain to either the sense of pressure (P), the sense of temperature (T), or in some
   cases, both (B) senses. Indicate the correct answers below using the letters P, T, or B.

   __B__ (a) The primary receiving area in the brain is called the somatosensory cortex.

   __P__ (b) The sensitivity is particularly acute in the fingers, lips, and tongue.

   __T__ (c) The receptors are particularly sensitive to context and contrast.

   __T__ (d) Has receptors specific for either warmth or cold.

   __P__ (e) Cells in the somatosensory cortex show similarities to the feature detectors found in the visual
   cortex.

   __T__ (f) Shares the same nerve pathway to the brain with the sense of pain.

22-2. Pain signals travel to the brain by two slightly different pathways. One pathway sends signals directly and immediately to the cortex and is called the _fast_ pathway. The other first sends signals through the limbic system and then on to the cortex and is called the _slow_ pathway. Lingering, less localized pain is mediated by the _slow_ pathway.

22-3. Answer the following questions regarding the perception of pain.
(a) What phenomenon did the gate-control theory of pain perception attempt to explain?

why the perception of pain is so subjective

(b) What effect do endorphins have with respect to pain? _morphinelike painkillers_

(c) What appears to be the role of the periaqueductal gray (PAG) area in the midbrain with respect to the perception of pain? _periaqueductal gray (PAG) sends signals down the spinal cord that block incoming pain signals._

Answers: 22-1. (a) B (b) P (c) T (d) T (e) P (f) T   22-2. fast, slow, slow   22-3. (a) why the perception of pain is so subjective (b) an analgesic effect (c) It sends signals down the spinal cord that block incoming pain signals.

23. Describe the perceptual experiences mediated by the kinesthetic and vestibular senses.

23-1. The system that monitors the positions of various parts of the body is called the _kinesthetic_ system. This systems sends information to the brain about body position and movement obtained from receptors located in the joints and _muscles_.

23-2. The system that monitors the body's location in space is called the _vestibular_ system. The receptors for the vestibular system are primarily hair cells contained within the _semicircular_ canals.

23-3. What point does the text make about the kinesthetic and vestibular systems, and indeed all sensory systems, in carrying out their tasks?

they integrate information from other senses.

Answers: 23-1. kinesthetic, muscles   23-2. vestibular, semicircular   23-3. They integrate information from other senses (in carrying out their tasks).

24. Explain how this chapter highlighted the text's themes about theoretical diversity and the subjectivity of experience.

24-1. The fact that competing theories of both color vision and pitch were eventually reconciled attests to the value of theoretical diversity. Why is this?

24-2. Why must our experience of the world always be highly subjective?

Answers: 24-1. Competing theories drive and guide the resolving research.   24-2. The perceptual processes themselves are inherently subjective.

25. **Discuss how the paintings shown in the Application illustrate various principles of visual perception.**

    25-1.   After reading the Application section in your text, answer the following questions by only looking at the paintings.

        ____ (a) Which painting particularly depends on the Gestalt principles of continuity and common fate for its effect?

        ____ (b) Which painting uses variations in context, shading, and texture gradients to make identical triangles appear very different?

        ____ (c) Which painting builds a total picture out of geometric forms (feature analaysis applied to canvas)?

        ____ (d) Which two paintings incorporate impossible figures to achieve their effect?

        ____ (e) Which painting makes particular use of monocular cues to enhance the illusion of depth?

        ____ (f) Which painting manipulates the figure and ground relationship to achieve its special effect?

        ____ (g) Which painting makes use of color mixing to illustrate how different spots of colors can be blended into a picture that is more than the sum of its parts?

        ____ (h) Which painting makes use of a reversible figure to enchance a feeling of fantasy?

    Answers: 25-1. (a) 4.49 (b) 4.54 (c) 4.48 (d) 4.52 & 4.53 (e) 4.46 (f) 4.51 (g) 4.47 (h) 4.50.

REVIEW OF KEY TERMS

Absolute threshold
Additive color mixing
Afterimage
Auditory localization
Basilar membrane
Binocular cues
Bottom-up processing
Cochlea
Color blindness
Complementary colors
Cones
Dark adaptation
Depth perception
Distal stimuli
Feature analysis
Feature detectors
Fechner's law
Fovea
Frequency theory

Gate-control theory
Gustatory system
Impossible figures
Just noticeable difference (JND)
Kinesthetic sense
Lateral antagonism
Lens
Light adaptation
Monocular cues
Olfactory system
Opponent process theory of
   color vision
Optical illusion
Perception
Perceptual constancy
Perceptual hypothesis
Perceptual set
Phi phenomenon

Place theory
Proximal stimuli
Psychophysics
Pupil
Receptive field of a visual cell
Retina
Reversible figure
Rods
Sensation
Sensory adaptation
Signal detection theory
Subtractive color mixing
Threshold
Top-down processing
Trichromatic theory of color vision
Vestibular system
Volley principle
Weber's law

    _____   1.   The stimulation of sense organs.

    _____   2.   The selection, organization, and interpretation of sensory input.

    _____   3.   The study of how physical stimuli are translated into psychological (sensory) experience.

    _____   4.   A dividing point between energy levels that do and do not have a detectable effect.

    _____   5.   The minimum amount of stimulation that can be detected by an organism for a specific type of sensory input.

_____ 6. The smallest amount of difference in the amount of stimulation that can be detected in a sense.

_____ 7. States that the size of a just noticeable difference is a constant proportion of the size of the initial stimulus.

_____ 8. Proposes that sensory sensitivity depends on a variety of factors besides the physical intensity of the stimulus.

_____ 9. Involves a gradual decline in sensitivity to prolonged stimulation.

_____ 10. States that larger and larger increases in stimulus intensity are required to produce perceptible increments in the magnitude of sensation.

_____ 11. The transparent eye structure that focuses the light rays falling on the retina.

_____ 12. The opening in the center of the iris that helps regulate the amount of light passing into the rear chamber of the eye.

_____ 13. The neural tissue lining the inside back surface of the eye that absorbs light, processes images, and sends visual information to the brain.

_____ 14. Specialized receptors that play a key role in daylight vision and color vision.

_____ 15. Specialized receptors that play a key role in night vision and peripheral vision.

_____ 16. A tiny spot in the center of the retina that contains only cones, where visual acuity is greatest.

_____ 17. The process in which the eyes become more sensitive to light in low illumination.

_____ 18. The process in which the eyes become less sensitive to light in high illumination.

_____ 19. A variety of deficiencies in the ability to distinguish among colors.

_____ 20. The retinal area that, when stimulated, affects the firing of a particular cell.

_____ 21. Occurs when neural activity in a cell opposes activity in surrounding cells.

_____ 22. Neurons that respond selectively to very specific features of more complex stimuli.

_____ 23. Works by removing some wavelengths of light, leaving less light than was originally there.

_____ 24. Works by superimposing lights, leaving more light in the mixture than in any one light by itself.

_____ 25. Proposes that the human eye has three types of receptors with differing sensitivities to different wavelengths.

_____ 26. Pairs of colors that can be added together to produce gray tones.

_____ 27. A visual image that persists after a stimulus is removed.

_____ 28. Proposes that color is perceived in three channels, where an either-or response is made to pairs of antagonistic colors.

_____ 29. A drawing compatible with two different interpretations that can shift back and forth.

_____ 30. A readiness to perceive a stimulus in a particular way.

_____ 31. A process in which we detect specific elements in visual input and assemble these elements into a more complex form.

_____ 32. A progression from individual elements to the whole.

_____ 33. A progression from the whole to the elements.

_____ 34. An apparently inexplicable discrepancy between the appearance of a visual stimulus and its physical reality..

_____ 35. The illusion of movement created by presenting visual stimuli in rapid succession.

_____ 36. Stimuli that lie in the distance (in the world outside us).

_____ 37. The stimulus energies that impinge directly on our sensory receptors.

_____ 38. An inference about what distal stimuli could be responsible for the proximal stimuli sensed.

_____ 39. Involves our interpretation of visual cues that tell us how near or far away objects are.

_____ 40. Clues about distance that are obtained by comparing the differing views of the two eyes.

_____ 41. Clues about distance that are obtained from the image in either eye alone.

_____ 42. A tendency to experience a stable perception in the face of constantly changing sensory input.

_____ 43. Locating the source of a sound in space.

_____ 44. A fluid-filled, coiled tunnel that makes up the largest part of the inner ear.

_____ 45. A membrane running the length of the cochlea that holds the actual auditory receptors, called hair cells.

_____ 46. Holds that our perception of pitch corresponds to the vibration of different portions, or places, along the basilar membrane.

_____ 47. Holds that our perception of pitch corresponds to the rate, or frequency, at which the entire basilar membrane vibrates.

_____ 48. Holds that groups of auditory nerve fibers fire neural impulses in rapid succession, creating volleys of impulses.

_____ 49. Our sense of taste.

_____ 50. Our sense of smell.

_____ 51. Objects that can be represented in two-dimensional figures but cannot exist in three-dimensional space.

_____ 52. Holds that incoming pain sensations pass through a "gate" in the spinal cord that can be opened or closed.

_____ 53. The sense that monitors the positions of the various parts of the body.

_____ 54. The system that provides the sense of balance.

Answers: 1. sensation 2. perception 3. psychophysics 4. threshold 5. absolute threshold 6. just noticeable difference (JND) 7. Weber's law 8. signal detection theory 9. sensory adaptation 10. Fechner's law 11. lens 12. pupil 13. retina 14. cones 15. rods 16. fovea 17. dark adaptation 18. light adaptation 19. color blindness 20. receptive field of a visual cell 21. lateral antagonism 22. feature detectors 23. subtractive color mixing 24. additive color mixing 25. trichromatic theory of color vision 26. complementary colors 27. afterimage 28. opponent process theory of color vision 29. reversible figure 30. perceptual set 31. feature analysis 32. bottom-up processing 33. top-down processing 34. optical illusion 35. phi phenomenon 36. distal stimuli 37. proximal stimuli 38. perceptual hypothesis 39. depth perception 40. binocular cues 41. monocular cues 42. perceptual constancy 43. auditory localization 44. cochlea 45. basilar membrane 46. place theory 47. frequency theory 48. volley principle 49. gustatory system 50. olfactory system 51. impossible figures 52. gate-control theory 53. kinesthetic sense 54. vestibular system.

REVIEW OF KEY PEOPLE

Gustav Fechner   David Hubel & Torston Weisel   Anna Treisman
Herman von Helmholtz   Ernst Weber   Max Wertheimer

_____ 1. Pioneered the early work in the detection of thresholds.

_____ 2. His law states that the size of a just noticeable difference is a constant
                             proportion of the size of the initial stimulus.

_____ 3. These two men won the Nobel Prize for their discovery of feature
                             detector cells in the retina.

_____ 4. One of the originators of the trichromatic theory of color vision.

_____ 5. Made use of the phi phenomenon to illustrate some of the basic
                             principles of gestalt psychology.

_____ 6. Has proposed that the perception of objects involves two stages
                             characterized by different types of processing.

Answers: 1. Fechner 2. Weber 3. Huber & Weisel 4. Helmholtz 5. Wertheimer 6. Treisman.

SELF-QUIZ

1. Stimuli cannot be perceived when they are presented below the absolute threshold. This statement is:
    a. true
    b. false

2. According to Weber's law, which of the following changes would be the most difficult to detect?
    a. a 36-inch line lengthened by 1 inch
    b. a 60-inch line lengthened by 2 inches
    c. a 90-inch line lengthened by 3 inches
    d. all of the above would be equally difficult to detect

3. Which law or theory of detecting stimuli places a major emphasis on subjective factors?
    a. Weber's law
    b. Fechner's law
    c. Steven's power factor
    d. signal detection theory

4. The receiving area of a retinal cell is called the:
    a. cone
    b. fovial field
    c. rod
    d. receptive field

5. The fact that we are generally much more aware of the changes in our sensory environments rather than
    the constants is the general idea behind:
    a. signal detection theory
    b. sensory adaptation
    c. the method of constant stimuli
    d. sensory equalization

6. The major difference between a green light and a blue light is the:
    a. wave frequency
    b. wave purity
    c. wavelength
    d. wave saturation

7. If the eye is compared to a camera, the role of the retina would most closely resemble the role of the:
    a. lens
    b. film
    c. shutter
    d. flash cube

8. Which theory of color vision best explains why the color of an afterimage is the complement of the original color?
    a. the trichromatic theory
    b. the opponent process theory
    c. both theories explain this phenomenon equally well
    d. neither theory adequately explains this phenomenon

9. When watching a wild car chase scene in a movie we can be thankful for:
    a. chunking
    b. lateral processing
    c. bottom-up processing
    d. the phi phenomenon

10. Which of the following is one of the binocular distance cues?
    a. convergence
    b. linear perspective
    c. relative height
    d. texture gradients

11. Which of the following is an example of what is meant by perceptual constancy?
    a. moths are always attracted to light
    b. a round pie tin always appears to us as round
    c. proximal and distal stimuli are always identical
    d. none of the above

12. Middle C sounded on a piano sounds different than middle C on a violin because of the difference in:
    a. wavelengths
    b. purity
    c. amplitude
    d. all of the above

13. Research has shown that the perception of pitch depends on:
    a. the area stimulated on the basilar membrane
    b. the frequency at which the basilar membrane vibrates
    c. both of the above
    d. none of the above

14. Which of the following is *not* considered to be one of the four fundamental tastes?
    a. sour
    b. sweet
    c. burnt
    d. bitter

15. Our sense of balance depends upon:
    a. the semicircular canals
    b. the kinesthetic senses
    c. visual cues
    d. all of the above

16. Which of the following terms perhaps best describes human perception?
    a. accurate
    b. objective
    c. subjective
    d. unknowable

Answers: 1. b   2. a   3. d   4. d   5. b   6. c   7. b   8. b   9. d   10. a   11. b   12. b   13. c   14. c   15. d   16. c.

5 VARIATIONS IN CONSCIOUSNESS

REVIEW OF KEY TERMS

ON THE NATURE OF CONSCIOUSNESS

1. **Discuss the nature of consciousness (its transitions, its levels, and its relation to brain activity).**

    1-1. The personal awareness of internal and external events is how psychologists define
    _____consciousness_____. Consciousness is like a moving stream in that it is constantly _____changing_____.

    1-2. Not only is consciousness constantly changing, but it also exists at different levels. Freud believed that at
    its deepest level we would find the _____unconscious_____. Most psychologists today feel that there are at
    least three major levels of consciousness. Match each of these three levels with its appropriate activity.

_2_ (a) Controlled processes	1. Some processing.	
_3_ (b) Automatic processes	2. High concentration.	
_1_ (c) Deepest layers	3. Daydreaming and well-practiced skills.	

    1-3. EEG recordings reveal that there (is/is not) some relationship between brain waves and levels of consciousness. There are four principal bands of brain wave activity, based on the frequency of the wave patterns, these are alpha, beta, delta, and theta. Identify these wave patterns from their descriptions given below.

    (a) alert (13-24 cps) _____beta_____   (c) deep sleep (4-7 cps) _____theta_____
    (b) drowsy (8-12 cps) _____alpha_____   (d) deepest sleep (1-4 cps) _____delta_____

Answers: 1-1. consciousness, changing.   1-2. unconscious, (a) 2 (b) 3 (c) 1   1-3. is (a) beta (b) alpha (c) theta
(d) delta.

THE SLEEP AND WAKING CYCLE

2. Describe how sleep research is conducted.

2-1.   Sleep research is conducted by electronically monitoring various bodily activities, such as brain waves, heart contractions, eye movements, etc., while persons actually ___sleep___ in a specially prepared laboratory setting. Through the use of a television camera or a window, researchers also ___observe___ the subjects during sleep. Data collection usually begins (before/after) allowing the subject to adjust to the novel sleeping environment.

Answers: 2-1. sleep, observe (or watch), after.

3. Summarize what is known about our biological clocks and the relationship of circadian rhythms to sleep.

3-1.   The daily, or 24-hour rhythm is called the ___circadian___ rhythm and is responsible for the regulation of sleep and wakefulness. This is accomplished through the regulation of several bodily processes, including body temperature. Describe below what happens to body temperature when we:
(a) begin to fall asleep. ___decreases___

(b) continue into deeper sleep. ___continues to decrease___

(c) begin to awaken. ___begins to increase___

3-2.   There is evidence that exposure to ___sunlight___ is responsible for regulating the 24-hour circadian clock. Sunlight affects the suprachiasmatic nucleus in the hypothalamus which in turn signals the ___pineal___ gland. The pineal gland then secretes the hormone melatonin. which is a major player in adjusting biological clocks. There is also evidence that most persons tend to drift from a 24-hour cycle to a ___25___ hour cycle.

3-3.   Getting out of time with the circadian rhythms can greatly affect the quality of ___sleep___. This is commonly found among persons suffering from jet lag. Research on jet lag has shown that there are two kinds of alterations in circadian rhythms. One kind called *phase-delay shift* occurs when the day is ___lengthened___. Another kind, called *phase-advance shift*, occurs when the day is ___shortened___. Since there already seems to be a natural tendency to shift to a 25-hour circadian cycle, most people find it is easier to make a phase ___delay___ shift. This explains why air travel is likely to be less disturbing when flying in a ___westerly___ direction.

Answers: 3-1. circadian (a) Temperature decreases. (b) Temperature continues to decrease. (c) Temperature begins to increase.   3-2. sunlight, pineal, 25   3-3. sleep, lengthened, shortened, delay, westerly.

4. **Summarize the Featured Study (Czeisler et al., 1982) on how to make shift rotation more compatible with circadian rhythms.**

4-1. The Featured Study looked at two different factors that may help to make shift rotation more compatible with circadian rhythms. One factor was to change from phase-advance shift rotations to phase-___delay___ shift rotations. The investigators also looked at what differences may occur between weekly shift rotations and rotations that occurred every ___three___ weeks. All of the workers in the experimental group were switched to phase delay shift rotations and were compared to similar workers not subjected to shift rotations. In addition, some of the workers in the experimental group experienced shift rotations every 3 weeks, while others were rotated on a ___weekly___ basis. Measures of worker satisfaction, health, and productivity served as the ___dependent___ variables.

4-2. What did the results of this study show regarding worker satisfaction for the workers changed to phase-delay shift rotations? Worker satisfaction improved.

4-3. What group showed the greatest improvement in worker satisfaction? Workers rotated @ 3-week intervals.

Answers: 4-1. delay, 3, weekly, dependent   4-2. Worker satisfaction improved.   4-3. Workers rotated at 3-week intervals.

5. **Compare and contrast REM sleep and NREM sleep.**

5-1. The four stages of sleep that do not involve rapid eye movement (REM) are collectively called ___NREM___ sleep. During NREM sleep one first descends into stage ___1___ sleep and then continues to descend into stages 2, 3 and 4. Each descent is accompanied by (slower/faster) brain wave activity, along with declines in body temperature, heart rate, respiration rate, and muscle tension.

5-2. What particularly differentiates NREM sleep from rapid eye movement sleep, or ___REM___ sleep, is that during REM sleep the brain wave pattern resembles that of a person who is wide ___awake___. However, REM sleep is actually a deep stage of sleep. This has led some researchers to refer to REM sleep as ___paradoxical___ sleep. It is also during REM sleep that ___dreaming___ is most likely to occur.

Answers: 5-1. NREM, 1, slower   5-2. REM, awake, paradoxical, dreaming.

6. **Describe how the sleep cycle evolves through the night and how the sleep cycle is related to age.**

6-1. The sleep cycle is representative of one of the ___90___ minute biological rhythms and is repeated approximately four times during an average night of sleep. NREM sleep dominates the early part of the sleep period, but ___REM___ sleep and dreaming dominate the later stages of sleep. As one progresses though the night the depth of NREM sleep tends to progressively (increase/decrease).

6-2. Not only do newborns sleep more frequently and for more total hours during a day than do adults, but they also spend a greater proportion of time in ___REM___ sleep. As they grow older, the children move toward longer but (more/**less**) frequent sleep periods and the total proportion of REM sleep declines from about 50 percent to the adult level of about __20__ percent. During adulthood there is a gradual shift towards the (**lighter**/deeper) stages of sleep.

Answers: 6-1. 90, REM, decrease   6-2. REM, less, 20, lighter.

7. Discuss the neural basis of sleep.

7-1. Sleep and wakefulness is apparently under the control of several neural structures, but one appears to stand out from the rest. The neural structure that is essential for both sleep and wakefulness is the reticular ___formation___. When a part of this system, called the ascending ___reticular___ ___activating___ system (ARAS) is severed in cats, the cats remain in continuous ___sleep___. When the ARAS is stimulated in normal cats, they act ___alert/awake___.

7-2. There are also at least four neurotransmitters that appear to influence the sleep-wakefulness cycle, but the neurotransmitter ___serotonin___ appears to be the most important one. Even so, it should be remembered that sleep depends on ___several___ brain structures and ___several___ neurotransmitters.

Answers: 7-1. formation, reticular activating, sleep, alert or awake   7-2. serotonin, several (or many), several (or many).

8. Summarize evidence on the effects of complete, partial, and selective sleep deprivation.

8-1. Answer the following questions regarding the effects of different kinds of sleep deprivation.
(a) What is the major effect of both complete and partial sleep deprivation?
Sleepiness!

(b) How would you describe the recovery period with respect to time from both complete and partial sleep deprivation? _next 24 hrs? very rapid_

8-2. Studies in which subjects were selectively deprived of REM sleep, leaving NREM sleep undisturbed, found (substantial/**little**) negative effects from REM deprivation. One curious effect that has been noted from selective REM deprivation is that subjects tend to increase their amount of (NREM/**REM**) sleep when given the first opportunity to do so. This same rebound effect has also been found with stage 4 or ___slow___ ___wave___ sleep.

Answers: 8-1. (a) weariness or sleepiness (b) It is very rapid.   8-2. little, REM, slow-wave.

9. Explain restorative and circadian theories of sleep and describe Borbely's integration of these views.

9-1. Some theories as to why we sleep believe the purpose is to recharge the body. These are known as ___restorative___ theories. Other theories propose that sleep has survival value since it conserves energy and protects from danger. These theories are known as ___circadian___ theories.

9-2. After reading the text you should be able to answer the following questions regarding Borbely's theory of sleep.
(a) Borbely's theory assumes that:
   (1) Restorative theories are correct.
   (2) Circadian theories are correct.
   (3) Both theories are correct.
(b) According to Borbely's theory, the need for sleep will be highest when (see Fig. 5.11):
   (1) Process C (circadian rhythm) is high.
   (2) Process S (hours awake) is high.
   (3) Both process C and Process S are high.
(c) Research evidence shows that:
   (1) Time spent in slow wave sleep depends on _hours spent awake_.
   (2) Time spent in REM sleep depends on _circadian rhythm_.

(d) If the theory and the research evidence are correct then a person suffering from jet lag will most likely experience a need for (REM/slow-wave) sleep.

Answers: 9-1. restorative, circadian. 9-2. (a) 3, (b) 3, (c) 1. hours spent awake 2. the circadian rhythm (d) REM.

10. Discuss the prevalence, causes, and treatments of insomnia.

10-1. While practically everybody will suffer from occasional bouts of insomnia, it is estimated that chronic problems with insomnia occur in about _30_ percent of all adults. There are three basic types of insomnia, which are easily remembered because one type occurs at the beginning of sleep, one type during sleep, and the third type at the end of sleep. Thus, one type involves difficulty in _falling_ asleep; one type involves difficulty in _staying_ asleep; and one type involves persistent _early_ awakening.

10-2. There are a number of different causes of insomnia, but perhaps the most common one results from stressful problems that generate excessive _stress/anxiety_. Another frequent cause results from physical problems, such as ulcers and back ailments, that cause _pain_, and asthma, that interferes with proper _breathing_. Certain drugs are also implicated in insomnia.

10-3. Since there are many different causes of insomnia, it seems reasonable that there (is/is not) a single form of treatment. However, researchers agree that the most commonly used form of treatment, using sedatives, or _sleeping_ pills, is not the treatment of choice. Evidence shows that while sleeping pills do promote sleep, they also interfere with the (REM/NREM) part of the sleep cycle.

Answers: 10-1. 30, falling, remaining, early 10-2. anxiety (or worry), pain, breathing 10-3. is not, sleeping, REM.

11. **Describe the symptoms of narcolepsy, sleep apnea, night terrors, nightmares, and somnambulism.**

11-1. Described below are six different case histories of persons suffering from six different sleep disorders. Make the appropriate diagnosis for each one.

(a) Throckmorton is a young child who frequently wakes up during the night with a loud piercing cry, but cannot describe what happened to him; he usually returns quickly to sleep. A night spent at the sleep clinic discloses that the episodes generally occur during NREM sleep. Throckmorton is most likely suffering from ___night___ ___terrors___.

(b) Galzelda reports that occasionally, even when typing a term paper or driving a car, she will quickly drop into a deep sleep. The sleep is often accompanied by dreams, which indicates REM sleep. Gazelda is most likely suffering from ___narcolepsy___.

(c) Ajax is a young child who frequently wakes up terrified and relates vivid dreams to his parents who rush to comfort him. The family physician tells the parents there is probably nothing to worry about, unless these episodes persist, and that the child will most likely outgrow this problem. The diagnosis here is probably ___nightmares___.

(d) Mr. Whistletoe will occasionally get up late at night and walk around the house. Unfortunately, Mr. Whistletoe is completely unaware of this behavior and usually returns to bed without awakening. Upon awakening the next morning he is surprised by a new bruise on his leg and he wonders how the chair in the living room got tipped over. Mr. Whistletoe would be diagnosed as suffering from ___somnambulism___, or sleep walking.

(e) Hendrieta complains that during a night's sleep she frequently wakes up gasping for breath. A visit to the sleep clinic discloses that indeed she does stop breathing for brief periods all through the night. Hendrieta undoubtedly suffers from ___sleep___ ___apnea___.

Answers: 11-1. (a) night terrors (b) narcolepsy (c) nightmares (d) somnambulism (e) sleep apnea.

THE WORLD OF DREAMS

12. **Summarize Hall's findings on dream content and discuss how dreams are affected by real world events.**

12-1. Calvin Hall, who analyzed the contents of more than 10,000 dreams, concluded that the content of most dreams is (exotic/mundane). Moreover, he found that dreams seldom involve events that are not centered around ___ourselves___. Hall also found that dreams tend to be like soap operas in that they revolve around such common themes as misfortune, ___sex___, and ___aggression___.

12-2. What did Freud mean when he stated that our dreams reflect *day residue*?
dream content is influenced by what happen to us in our daily lives.

12-3. What other factor has an inconsistent effect on our dreams?

Stimulus experienced while dreaming

Answers: 12-1. mundane, ourselves, sex, aggression   12-2. Dream content is influenced by what happens to us in our daily lives.   12-3. external stimuli (dripping water, ringing phones, etc.).

13. Describe the three theories of dreaming covered in the chapter.

13-1. The text mentions three theories as to why we need to dream. Identify these theories (what purpose do they serve) from the hints given below.
(a) This was Sigmund Freud's theory about the need to dream.

wish fulfillment

(b) This theory proposed by Rosalind Cartwright is cognizant of the fact that dreams are not restricted by logic or reality. *problem-solving view*

(c) This theory proposed by J. Allan Hobson does not believe dreams are of any cognitive significance.
activation-synthesis model - dreams are simply byproducts of physiological processes

Answers: 13-1. (a) Dreams serve the purpose of wish fulfillment. (b) Dreams allow for creative problem-solving. (c) Dreams are simply byproducts of physiological processes (in which the brain is being aroused to a waking state).

HYPNOSIS: ALTERED CONSCIOUSNESS OR ROLE PLAYING?

14. Discuss hypnotic susceptibility, list some prominent effects of hypnosis, and explain the role-playing and altered-state theories of hypnosis.

14-1. While there are many different hypnotic induction techniques, the common and essential feature in all of these techniques is the hypnotist's _____*verbal*_____ behavior. The hypnotist encourages the subject to give full attention to specific bodily sensations and this narrowing of attention under the constant suggestion of the hypnotist gradually leads to a _____*hypnotic*_____ state. Research shows that individuals (do/do not) vary in their susceptibility to hypnotic induction. In fact, approximately _____*10*_____ percent of the population does not respond at all and approximately _____*10*_____ percent are highly susceptible to hypnotic induction. People who are highly susceptible tend to have (vivid/poor) imaginations.

14-2. The text lists several of the more prominent effects that can be produced by hypnosis. Identify these effects from their descriptions given below.
(a) Reducing awareness of pain. _____*anesthesia*_____
(b) Engaging in acts one would not ordinarily do. _____*disinhibition*_____
(c) Perceiving things that do not exist or failing to perceive things that do exist. _____*hallucinations*_____
(d) Claiming that sour foods taste sweet. _____*sensory*_____ _____*distortion*_____
(e) Carrying out suggestions following the hypnotic induction session. _____*posthypnotic*_____ _____*suggestions*_____
(f) Claiming to forget what occurred during the induction session. _____*amnesia*_____

14-3. A theory of hypnosis proposed by Barber and Orne is that hypnosis is really a form of acting or *role playing* in which the subjects are simply playing as if they are hypnotized. What two lines of evidence support this theory?

① non-hypnotized subjects can duplicate the feats of hypnotized subjects

② it's been shown that hypnotized subjects are merely carrying out their expectations of how hypnotized subjects should act.

14-4. Another theory of hypnosis, proposed by Hilgard, is that hypnosis does in fact result in an altered state

of _consciousness_. This theory holds that hypnosis results in a split or _divided_

consciousness in which one half of the consciousness communicates with the hypnotist while the other

half remains _hidden_, even from the hypnotized subject. In this case, pain perceived by

the "hidden" part of the consciousness (is/is not) reported to the "aware" part of consciousness. The

divided state of consciousness proposed by Hilgard (is/is not) a common experience in everyday life.

One such example of this commonly experienced state is appropriately called "highway

hypnosis."

Answers: 14-1. verbal, hypnotized, do, 10, 10, vivid 14-2. (a) anesthetic (b) disinhibition (c) hallucinations (d) sensory distortions (e) posthypnotic suggestions (f) amnesia 14-3. Nonhypnotized subjects can duplicate the feats of hypnotized subjects and it has been shown that hypnotized subjects are merely carrying out their expectations of how hypnotized subjects should act. 14-4. consciousness, divided, hidden, is not, is, hypnosis.

MEDITATION: PURE CONSCIOUSNESS OR RELAXATION?

15. Summarize the evidence on the short-term and long-term effects of meditation.

15-1. Certain short-term physiological changes may occur during meditation. One of the most prominent of

these changes is that EEG brain waves change from the rapid beta waves to the slower

alpha and theta waves. This change to slower waves is accompanied by (an increase/a

decrease) in metabolic activity, such as heart rate, oxygen consumption, etc. All of these physiological

changes are characteristic of a normal state of _relaxation_. This state of relaxation (is/is not)

unique to meditation.

15-2. The claims made for the long-term effects of meditation may have some merit in that studies have shown that subjects have shown improved mood and lessened anxiety and fatigue, as well as better physical health and increased longevity. These changes can (also/not) be induced by other commonly used methods for inducing relaxation. Moreover, the claim that meditation can produce a unique state of pure consciousness (has/has not) been supported by scientific research.

Answers: 15-1. alpha, a decrease, relaxation, is not 15-2. also, has not.

ALTERING CONSCIOUSNESS WITH DRUGS

16. List and describe the major types of abused drugs and their effects.

16-1. The text lists six different categories of psychoactive drugs; identify these drugs from the descriptions given below.

(a) This drug is the most widely used of all psychoactive drugs and there are approximately 10 million Americans who suffer from chronic abuse of _alcohol_.

(b) This class of drugs is derived from opium and while this class of drugs is effective at relieving pain, it can also produce a state of euphoria, which is the principal reason that opiates, or _narcotics_, are attractive to recreational users.

(c) The drugs in this class, such as LSD, mescaline and psilocybin, are known for their ability to distort sensory and perceptual experiences, which is why they are given the collective name of _hallucinogens_.

(d) The drugs in this class include marijuana, hashish and THC. Although they vary in potency each of them can produce a mild and an easy going state of euphoria along with enhanced sensory awareness and a distorted sense of time. This class of drugs gets its name from the hemp plant _cannabis_ from which they are all derived.

(e) This class of drugs is known for its sleep-inducing (sedation) and behavioral depression effects, resulting in tension reduction and a relaxed state of intoxication. While there are several different drugs in this class, the barbiturates are the most widely abused. Commonly known as "downers," they are more properly called _sedatives_.

(f) This class of drugs produces arousal in the central nervous system and ranges from mildly arousing drugs like caffeine and nicotine, to strongly arousing drugs like cocaine and the amphetamines. Known for their ability to produce an energetic euphoria, the drugs in this class go by the name of _stimulants_.

Answers: 16-1. (a) alcohol (b) narcotics (c) hallucinogens (d) cannabis (e) sedatives (f) stimulants.

17. Explain why drug effects vary and how psychoactive drugs exert their effects on the brain.

17-1. Taking a specific drug (will/will not) always have the same effect on the same person. This is because drug effects have _multifactorial_ *causation*; individual, environmental, and drug factors can combine in many ways to produce the final effect. For example, one's expectations can strongly affect reactions to a drug. This is known as the _placebo_ effect. Moreover, as one continues to take a specific drug, it requires a greater amount of the drug to achieve the same effect. This phenomenon is called drug _tolerance_.

17-2. Psychoactive drugs affect the CNS by altering neurotransmitter activity at the juncture between neurons called the ___synapse___. Like neurotransmitters, psychoactive drugs are attracted to selective ___sites___ in the synapses. Some psychoactive drugs mimic the effects of naturally occuring neurotransmitters, while others act by increasing or decreasing the availability of selective ___neurotransmitters___. For example, barbiturates can mimic the effects of the neurotransmitter GABA, while alcohol produces a similar effect by amplifying the effect of naturally released GABA. When these two drugs are taken together, their combined depressive effect on the CNS may be greater than the sum of their individual effects. Drugs having this effect are said to be ___synergistic___.

Answers: 17-1. will not, multifactorial, placebo, tolerance   17-2. synapse, sites, neurotransmitters, synergistic.

18. Summarize which drugs carry the greatest risk of tolerance, physical dependence, and psychological dependence.

18-1. When a person must continue taking a drug to avoid withdrawal illness, addiction, or ___physical___ *dependence* is said to occur. When a person must continue taking a drug to satisfy intense emotional craving for the drug, then ___physiological___ *dependence* is said to occur. As can be seen in Table 5.4 in the text, the three riskiest drugs in terms of tolerance and physical and psychological dependence are the ___narcotics___, ___sedatives___, and ___stimulants___.

Answers: 18-1. physical, psychological, narcotics/opiates, sedatives, stimulants.

19. Summarize evidence on the major physical health risks associated with drug abuse.

19-1. What two physical effects were found in the study in which rats were allowed unlimited access to heroin or cocaine and which drug was the most deadly?
___loss of body weight & death — cocaine___

19-2. There are three major ways in which drugs may affect physical health. The most dramatic way is when a person takes too much of a drug, or drugs, and dies of an ___overdose___. Another way is when drug usage directly damages bodily tissue; this is referred to as a ___direct___ *effect*. The third way is when drug usage results in accidents, improper eating and sleeping habits, infections, etc. These effects are collectively called ___indirect___ effects.

Answers: 19-1. loss of body weight and death, cocaine   19-2. overdose, direct, indirect.

20. Discuss how drug abuse is related to psychological health.

20-1. There is good evidence of a linkage between excessive drug abuse and mental disorders. For many drugs, such as the narcotics, which leads to which is (known/unknown) at this time. However, some drugs are known to cause specific mental disorders. Korsakoff's syndrome, along with several other mental disorders, are known to follow the excessive use of ___alcohol___. The onset of a psychotic-like state that includes hallucinations, paranoia, and hyperactivity have been shown to follow excessive use of two of the stimulant drugs, amphetamine and ___cocaine___.

Answers: 20-1. unknown, alcohol, cocaine.

PUTTING IT IN PERSPECTIVE

21. **Explain how the chapter highlighted three of our unifying themes: psychology evolves in a sociohistorical context, experience is subjective, and psychology is theoretically diverse.**

> 21-1. Identify which of the underlying themes is illustrated by the following statements.
>
> (a) Psychologists have followed many different approaches and developed many different theories in their attempt to understand consciousness.
>
> (b) The study of consciousness by psychologists followed rather than preceded renewed public interest in this topic.
>
> (c) There are striking individual differences in the way people respond to hypnosis, meditation, and drugs.
>
> Answers: 21-1. (a) Psychology is theoretically diverse. (b) Psychology evolves in a sociohistorical context. (c) Experience is subjective.

APPLICATION: ADDRESSING PRACTICAL QUESTIONS ABOUT SLEEP AND DREAMS

22. **Summarize evidence on common questions about sleep and dreams, as discussed in the Application.**

> 22-1. Answer the following questions about sleep and napping.
>
> (a) How much sleep do we require?
>
> (b) How much napping do we require?
>
> (c) Why might napping be inefficient?
>
> (d) How might we determine which sleep and napping habits are best for us?
>
> 22-2. Drugs which depress the central nervous system, such as alcohol and the sedatives, promote going to sleep but they actually interfere with the normal sleep cycle because they suppress (NREM/REM) sleep. On the other hand, any kind of sleep may prove difficult when __Stimulant__ drugs, such as cocaine, amphetamines, and caffeine, are taken.
>
> 22-3. Evidence is quite clear that attempting to learn complex material, such as a foreign language, during deep sleep is likely to prove (beneficial/futile). While little if any learning occurs at the deeper levels of sleep, simple learning, such as the conditioning of a reflex, can occur at the lighter levels of (REM/NREM) sleep.

22-4. List four habits one should follow in order to avoid problems with sleep.

22-5. Temporary problems in going to sleep (do/do not) indicate that one is becoming an insomniac. These temporary problems often correct themselves. There are numerous methods for facilitating going to sleep, but a common feature in all of them is that they generate a feeling of _relaxation_. Some methods generate a feeling of boredom, which is akin to relaxation. The important point here is that one (does/does not) concentrate on the heavy events in life when attempting to go to sleep.

Answers: 22-1. (a) It varies across individuals. (b) It varies across individuals. (c) The deeper stages are generally too short. (d) Experiment with different schedules and times. 22-2. REM, stimulant 22-3. futile, NREM 22-4. (In any order) Do not nap during the day. Avoid drinks containing caffeine. Eat moderately during the evening hours. Establish a regular bedtime that coincides with the downswing in the circadian rhythm. 22-5. do not, relaxation or calmness, does not.

22-6. While there are some persons who claim they never dream, what is really happening is that they cannot _remember_ their dreams. The dreams that we are able to recall are those that occur just prior to waking from _REM_ sleep. Determination and practice (can/cannot) improve one's ability to recall dreams. A dream whose action takes place over a 20-minute period will actually last for approximately _20_ minutes. Most of us (do/do not) dream in color, although a minority of persons claim they never do.

22-7. Freud believed that dreams do require interpretation in order to get at their true meaning because their true meaning, which he called the _latent_ content, is symbolically encoded in the obvious plot of the dream, which he called the _manifest_ content. Freud's theory that dreams carry hidden symbolic meaning would mean that dream interpretation (is/is not) a very complicated affair. More recent researchers now believe that dreams are (more/less) complicated than Freud would have us believe. For example, Calvin Hall makes the point that dreams require some interpretation simply because they are mostly (visual/verbal). However, because of their very subjective nature, any interpretation of dreams is probably best done by the _person_ experiencing the dream.

22-8. Folklore has it that dreaming of one's own death can prove fatal. So far there are (a few/no) cases of persons reporting their own deaths as the result of a fatal dream. Moreover, a good many people will experience vivid dreams of their own deaths and _live_ to tell about it.

22-9. Which one of the three statements below is correct regarding the question as to whether people can influence their own dreams.
(a) Evidence shows that it is extremely difficult, if not impossible to exert any control over one's dreams.
(b) Evidence shows that some control over one's dreams may be possible, but it is not easy and results are not always consistent.
(c) Evidence shows that it is actually quite easy to learn to control one's own dreams and consistent results are possible.

Answers: 22-6. remember (or recall), REM or dream, can, 20, do 22-7. latent, manifest, is, less, visual, person 22-8. no, live 22-9. (b).

REVIEW OF KEY TERMS

Alcohol
Ascending reticular activating
    system (ARAS)
Automatic processes
Biological rhythms
Cannabis
Circadian rhythms
Consciousness
Controlled processes
Designer drugs
Dissociation
Dream
Electrocardiograph (EKG)

Electroencephalograph (EEG)
Electromyograph (EMG)
Electro-oculograph (EOG)
Hallucinogens
Hypnosis
Insomnia
Latent content
Manifest content
Meditation
Narcolepsy
Narcotics or opiates
Night terrors

Nightmares
Non-REM sleep
Physical dependence
Psychoactive drugs
Psychological dependence
REM sleep
Sedatives
Sleep apnea
Slow-wave sleep (SWS)
Somnambulism
Stimulants
Tolerance

_____   1.   Our awareness of internal and external stimuli.

_____   2.   Processes that require alert awareness, absorb our limited attention,
                                 and interfere with other ongoing activities.

_____   3.   Processes that occur with little awareness, require minimal attention,
                                 and do not interfere with other activities.

_____   4.   A device that monitors the electrical activity of the brain.

_____   5.   A device that records muscle activity and tension.

_____   6.   A device that records the contractions of the heart.

_____   7.   A device that records eye movements.

_____   8.   Periodic fluctuations in physiological functioning.

_____   9.   The 24-hour biological cycles found in humans and many other
                                 species.

_____   10.   Sleep involving rapid eye movements.

_____   11.   Sleep stages 1 through 4, which are marked by an absence of rapid eye
                                 movements.

_____   12.   Consists of the afferent fibers running through the reticular formation
                                 that influence physiological arousal.

_____   13.   Drugs that are derived from opium that are capable of relieving pain.

_____   14.   Involves chronic problems in getting adequate sleep.

_____   15.   A disease marked by sudden and irresistible onsets of sleep during
                                 normal waking hours.

_____   16.   Reflexive grasping for air that awakens a person and disrupts sleep.

_____   17.   Abrupt awakenings from NREM sleep accompanied by intense
                                 autonomic arousal and feelings of panic.

_____   18.   Anxiety arousing dreams that lead to awakening, usually from REM
                                 sleep.

_____   19.   Occurs when a sleeping person arises and wanders about in deep
                                 NREM sleep.

_____   20.   Illicitly manufactured variations on known recreational drugs.

_____   21.   A mental experience during sleep that includes vivid visual images.

_____   22.   A systematic procedure that typically produces a heightened state of
                                 suggestibility.

_____ 23. Involves a splitting off of mental processes into two separate, simultaneous streams of awareness.

_____ 24. A family of medical exercises in which a conscious attempt is made to focus attention in a nonanalytical way.

_____ 25. Chemical substances that modify mental, emotional or behavioral functioning.

_____ 26. Sleep stages 3 and 4 in which low-frequency delta waves become prominent in EEG recordings.

_____ 27. Drugs that have sleep-inducing and behavioral depression effects.

_____ 28. Drugs that tend to increase central nervous system activation and behavioral activity.

_____ 29. A diverse group of drugs that have powerful effects on mental and emotional functioning, marked most prominently by distortions in sensory and perceptual experience.

_____ 30. The hemp plant from which marijuana, hashish, and THC are derived.

_____ 31. A variety of beverages containing ethyl alcohol.

_____ 32. A progressive decrease in a person's responsiveness to a drug.

_____ 33. A condition that exists when a person must continue to take a drug to avoid withdrawal illness.

_____ 34. A condition that exists when a person must continue to take a drug to satisfy mental and emotional craving for the drug.

_____ 35. Freud's term that refers to the plot of a dream at the surface level.

_____ 36. Freud's term that refers to the hidden or disguised meaning of events in a dream.

Answers: 1. consciousness 2. controlled processes 3. automatic processes 4. electroencephalograph (EEG) 5. electromyograph (EMG) 6. electrocardiograph (EKG) 7. electro-oculograph (EOG) 8. biological rhythms 9. circadian rhythms 10. REM sleep 11. non-REM sleep 12. ascending reticular activating system (ARAS) 13. narcotics or opiates 14. insomnia 15. narcolepsy 16. sleep apnea 17. night terrors 18. nightmares 19. somnambulism 20. designer drugs 21. dream 22. hypnosis 23. dissociation 24. meditation 25. psychoactive drugs 26. slow-wave sleep (SWS) 27. sedatives 28. stimulants 29. hallucinogens 30. cannabis 31. alcohol 32. tolerance 33. physical dependence 34. psychological dependence 35. manifest content 36. latent content.

REVIEW OF KEY PEOPLE

Theodore Barber   Willian Dement   Ernest Hilgard
Alexander Borbely   Sigmund Freud   J. Alan Hobson
Rosalind Cartwright   Calvin Hall   William James

_____ 1. Originated the term, "the stream of consciousness."

_____ 2. Argued for the existence of the unconscious and the hidden meaning of dreams.

_____ 3. As one of the pioneers in early sleep research, he coined the term REM sleep.

_____ 4. His theory is an integration of restorative and circadian theories as to why we sleep.

_____ 5. After analyzing thousands of dreams, he concluded that their contents are generally quite mundane.

_____ 6. Proposes a problem-solving view as a reason for dreaming.

_____ 7. One of the authors of the role playing theory of hypnosis.

_____ 8. A proponent of the altered state (divided consciousness) theory of hypnosis.

_____ 9. His activation-synthesis model proposes that dreams are only side effects of neural activation.

Answers: 1. James 2. Freud 3. Dement 4. Borbely 5. Hall 6. Cartwright 7. Barber 8. Hilgard 9. Hobson.

SELF-QUIZ

1. While taking this exam you are probably operating at which level of consciousness?
   a. the deepest layers
   b. the controlled processes level
   c. the automatic processes level
   d. the shallowest layers

2. The circadian rhythm operates around a:
   a. 1-year cycle
   b. 28-day cycle
   c. 24-hour cycle
   d. 90-minute cycle

3. Most dreams occur during:
   a. REM sleep
   b. NREM sleep
   c. the early hours of sleep
   d. both b and c

4. Severing the ascending reticular activating system in cats caused them to:
   a. become very aggressive
   b. become very fearful
   c. remain in continuous wakefulness
   d. remain in continuous sleep

5. Which of the following is likely to be found among persons deprived of sleep for a long period of time?
   a. slower reaction times
   b. slurred speech
   c. both of the above
   d. none of the above

6. It has now been concluded that deprivation of REM sleep is more debilitating than deprivation of NREM sleep. This statement is:
   a. true
   b. false

7. According to Borbely's theory of sleep, the need for sleep is due to:
   a. the need to recharge the body
   b. circadian rhythms
   c. both a and b
   d. none of the above

8. The content of most dreams is usually:
   a. mundane
   b. exotic
   c. exciting
   d. both b and c

9. Which of the following sleep disorders is most life threatening?
   a. nightmares
   b. narcolepsy
   c. sleep apnea
   d. somnambulism

10. Persons can be made to act as if they are hypnotized even without the use of hypnotic induction. This statement is:
    a. true
    b. false

11. Which of the following physiological changes is unique to meditation?
    a. increased alpha rhythms
    b. increased heart rate
    c. increased oxygen consumption
    d. none of the above

12. Psychoactive drugs exert their effect on the brain by:
    a. decreasing blood supply to the brain
    b. altering neurotransmitter activity
    c. breaking down essential brain amino acids
    d. penetrating the nucleus of the neurons

13. The most widely abused drug in the United States is:
    a. alcohol
    b. cocaine
    c. heroin
    d. hallucinogens

14. Which of the following is likely to produce highly subjective events?
    a. hypnosis
    b. meditation
    c. psychoactive drugs
    d. all of the above

15. In order to maintain good psychological adjustment one should:
    a. sleep at least 8 hours per day
    b. take a short nap each afternoon
    c. both of the above
    d. none of the above are necessarily essential

16. Which of the following statements is correct?
    a. most people do not dream in color
    b. practice will not improve the ability to recall dreams
    c. dreams generally last only 1 or 2 minutes at most
    d. none of the above

Answers: 1. b 2. c 3. a 4. d 5. d 6. b 7. c 8. a 9. b 10. a 11. d 12. b 13. a 14. d 15. d 16. d.

CHAPTER FIVE

6 LEARNING THROUGH CONDITIONING

REVIEW OF KEY IDEAS

CLASSICAL CONDITIONING

1. **Describe Pavlov's demonstration of classical conditioning and the key elements in this form of learning.**

    1-1.   Classical conditioning is a type of learning that occurs when two stimuli are paired or associated closely in time. In Pavlov's initial demonstration, the two stimuli were a bell and _meat powder_.

    1-2.   The response to one of the two stimuli occurs naturally and does not have to be learned or acquired through conditioning. This "unlearned" stimulus, in this case the food, is technically known as the _unconditioned_ stimulus.

    1-3.   The other stimulus is said to be neutral in the sense that it does not initially produce a response. When a response to this neutral stimulus is *acquired* or *learned*, the technical name for it is the _conditioned_ stimulus. In Pavlov's initial study the conditioned stimulus was the sound of a _bell_.

    1-4.   The unconditioned stimulus in Pavlov's original study was the _meat powder_ and the conditioned stimulus was the _bell_. Salivation to the meat powder is known as the _unconditioned_ response; salivation to the bell is termed the _conditioned_ response.

    1-5.   Label the parts of the classical conditioning sequence. Place the commonly used abbreviations for these terms in the parentheses.
    (a) meat: _unconditioned stimulus_ (UCS)
    (b) salivation to meat: _unconditioned response_ (UCR)
    (c) bell: _conditioned stimulus_ (CS)
    (d) salivation to bell: _conditioned response_ (CR)

Answers: 1-1. meat powder (food)   1-2. unconditioned   1-3. conditioned, bell   1-4. meat powder, bell, unconditioned, conditioned   1-5. (a) unconditioned stimulus (UCS), (b) unconditioned response (UCR), (c) conditioned stimulus (CS), (d) conditioned response (CR).

2. Discuss how classical conditioning may shape phobias, other emotional responses, and physiological processes.

2-1.   The kids in the neighborhood where I (RS) grew up used to dig tunnels in a neighbor's backyard. One of the tunnels was exceptionally long, and one day Benny Schultz, who was a little bigger than the rest of us, got stuck halfway. He got out, but after that he didn't want to play in tunnels again. I ran into Benny a few years ago and discovered that he still has an intense fear not only of tunnels but of closed-in spaces in general. Label the parts of the classical conditioning process in Benny's phobia acquisition. (Hint: Even though "getting stuck" certainly involves a behavior or response, it also has stimulus components.)

(a) Getting stuck: _unconditioned stimulus (UCS)_

(b) Fear produced by getting stuck: _unconditioned response (UCR)_

(c) Tunnels and closed-in spaces: _conditioned stimulus (CS)_

(d) Fear of tunnels and closed-in spaces: _Conditioned response (CR)_

2-2.   Benny had developed an intense fear, or phobia, acquired quite likely through the process of

___classical___ conditioning. Other emotions can be conditioned as well. For example, the smell

of smoke and Beemans gum described in your text, the playing of "our song," and the sight of one's

home after a long absence could all produce a pleasant emotional response (or perhaps a slightly weepy,

sentimental feeling). Such smells, sounds, or sights would be considered ___conditioned___ stimuli.

2-3.   Similarly, certain physiological responses can be conditioned. Label the parts of the conditioning process in the study on immunosuppression in rats described in the text. (Use the abbreviations CS, CR, UCS, and UCR.)

UCS   Injection with the immunosuppressive drug.

_CS_   Unusual taste.

UCR   Decreased antibody production produced by the drug.

_CR_   Decreased antibody production produced by the taste.

Answers: 2-1. (a) unconditioned stimulus (UCS), (b) unconditioned response (UCR), (c) conditioned stimulus (CS), (d) conditioned response (CR)   2-2. classical, conditioned   2-3. UCS, CS, UCR, CR.

3. Describe the classical conditioning phenomena of acquisition, extinction, spontaneous recovery, and higher-order conditioning.

3-1.   The term *acquisition*, not surprisingly, refers to acquiring a conditioned response. Acquisition occurs when stimuli are contiguous, or paired. Not all pairings result in conditioning, however. What characteristics of the CS are more likely to produce acquisition of a conditioned response?

3-2. Timing is also important for acquisition. Label the following diagrams of CS-UCS arrangements as *trace, simultaneous,* or *short-delayed.*

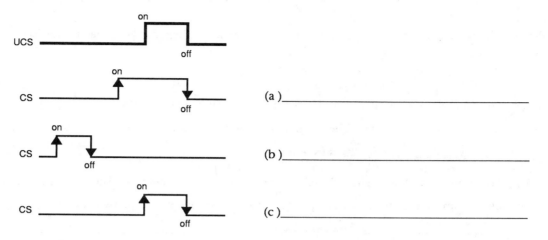

(a) _____

(b) _____

(c) _____

3-3. Which of the above arrangements is most likely to produce acquisition of the conditioned response?

3-4. Acquisition refers to the formation of a conditioned response. What is the term that refers to the weakening or disappearance of a CR? *Extinction*

3-5. What procedure results in extinction of a CR? *Removing the UCS*

3-6. CRs may be acquired, and they may extinguish. After they extinguish they may also reappear, even without further conditioning.
(a) What is the name of this "reappearance"? *spontaneous recovery*

(b) When, or under what circumstance, is this recovery likely to occur? *after extinction, following a period of non-exposure to the CS*

3-7. Suppose a bell and meat powder are paired, as in the original Pavlovian study, until a conditioned salivary response occurs to the bell alone. Suppose that the bell is then paired in a series of new trials with a clicking sound. Assuming that the stimuli are potent enough, that the timing is right, and so on:
(a) Will a CR now occur to the clicking sound? *yes*

(b) What is the name of this conditioning procedure? *higher order conditioning*

(c) Which stimulus acts as the UCS under this new arrangement? *the bell - the previous CS, nows acts as the UCS.*

Answers: 3-1. A novel or particularly intense CS is more likely to produce conditioning.   3-2. (a) short-delayed (b) trace (c) simultaneous   3-3. short-delayed   3-4. extinction   3-5. The CS is presented for a series of trials alone, without the UCS.   3-6. (a) spontaneous recovery (b) after extinction, following a period of nonexposure to the CS 3-7. (a) yes (b) higher-order conditioning (c) The bell, the previous CS, now acts as a UCS.

4. Describe the processes of stimulus generalization and discrimination and summarize the classic study of Little Albert.

4-1. With regard to the case of Little Albert:
(a) What was the CS? *White rat*

(b) The UCS? *loud noise*

4-2. Albert was also afraid of white dogs and white rabbits. What is the name of the process that resulted in his acquisition of these fear responses? *stimulus generalization*

4-3. Why would Albert be more likely to develop a fear of a white rabbit, say, than a white car or a dark horse? *Similarity to CS*

4-4. The more similar stimuli are to the CS, the more likely the organism will *generalize* from the CS to the other stimuli. The less similar stimuli are to the CS, the more likely the organism is to *discriminate* them from the CS.

4-5. You probably will not be astonished to hear that my cat salivates when she hears the sound of food being dumped into her bowl. The process by which this learned response occurs is *classical* *conditioning*. The food is a(an) *unconditioned* *stimulus*. The sound of the food is a(an) *conditioned* *stimulus*. Salivation to the sound is a(an) *conditioned* *response*.

4-6. Pets may also salivate when they hear other, similar sounds, like bags rustling in the kitchen or dishes being pulled from the cupboard. Salivation to these other sounds represents stimulus *generalization*.

4-7. With continued training, in which food is paired only with the sound of food entering the bowl and not with the other sounds, the animal will learn to salivate only to the rattling bowl. The process of learning to respond only to one particular stimulus and not to a range of similar stimuli is termed *discrimination*.

Answers: 4-1. (a) a white rat (b) a loud noise   4-2. stimulus generalization (or just generalization)   4-3. Because of similarity. The more similar the other stimuli to the CS, the more likely generalization is to occur.   4-4. generalize, discriminate   4-5. classical conditioning, unconditioned stimulus, conditioned stimulus, conditioned response 4-6. generalization   4-7. discrimination.

OPERANT CONDITIONING

5. Describe Thorndike's law of effect and Skinner's principle of reinforcement.

5-1. E. L. Thorndike's pioneering work on *instrumental* learning provided the foundation for Skinner's model of *operant* conditioning. According to Thorndike's law of *effect*, if a response leads to a satisfying effect in the presence of a stimulus, the association between the stimulus and response is strengthened. Thorndike's law of effect is similar to Skinner's principle of *reinforcement*.

5-2. A reinforcer is a stimulus or event that (1) is presented *after* a response and that (2) increases the tendency for the response to be repeated. Apply that definition to this example: Grundoon, a captive monkey, occasionally swings on a bar in his cage. Suppose that at some point Grundoon's trainers decide to give him a spoonful of applesauce whenever he swings. How would they know whether the applesauce is a reinforcer? *if his swinging increases, then the applesauce is a reinforcer*

5-3. The trainers switch to vinegar. Grundoon, an unusual primate, swings quite frequently when this behavior is followed by vinegar. Is vinegar a reinforcer here? How do you know? *yes*

5-4. The trainers try another approach. They present Grundoon with fresh fruit *just before* they think he is likely to jump. It so happens that Grundoon's rate of jumping does increase. Is the fruit a reinforcer? Why or why not? *the fruit is not a reinforcer. Reinforcing stimuli follow the response*

Answers: 5-1. instrumental, operant, effect, reinforcement 5-2. If the animal's rate of swinging increases when followed by applesauce, then applesauce is a reinforcer. 5-3. Yes. Because the vinegar is presented *after the response,* and because the *response rate increases.* (Note that this is an imaginary example to illustrate the point that reinforcement is defined in terms of consequences, not by our subjective judgment; I don't know of any monkeys that will respond for vinegar.) 5-4. No. Reinforcing stimuli, by definition, follow the response.

6. Describe the prototype experimental procedures and apparatus used in studies of operant conditioning.

6-1. The prototypic apparatus used in operant conditioning studies is the operant chamber, better know as the ___skinner box___. On one wall of the chamber is mounted a manipulandum, a device that makes for an easily discernible response. For rats, the manipulandum is usually a small ___lever/bar___; for pigeons, the device is a ___disk___ that the bird learns to peck.

6-2. A press of the lever or peck at the disk may produce a reinforcer, generally a small bit of food dispensed into the food cup mounted to one side or below the manipulandum. Each of these responses is recorded on a ___cumulative___ ___recorder___, a device that creates a graphic record of the number of responses per unit time.

6-3. The cumulative recorder records the *rate* of the behavior, that is, the number of ___responses___ made per unit ___time___.

6-4. Below is a highly stylized version of a cumulative record. About how many responses were made during the first 40 seconds? ___10___ Which section of the graph (a, b, c, d, or e) has the steepest slope? ___d___ Which section of the graph illustrates the fastest rate of responding? ___d___ About how many responses were made between the 40th and 70th seconds? ___20___

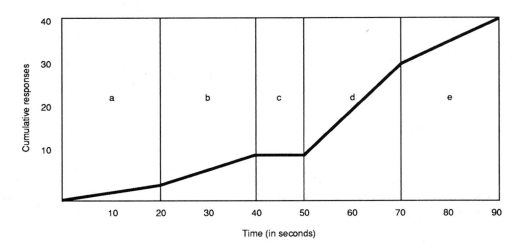

Time (in seconds)

Answers: 6-1. Skinner box, lever (or bar), disk   6-2. cumulative recorder   6-3. responses, time   6-4. 10, d, d, 20.

7. Describe the operant conditioning phenomena of acquisition, shaping, and extinction.

7-1. Acquisition refers to the formation of new responses. In classical conditioning, acquisition occurs through a simple pairing of the CS and UCS. In operant conditioning, acquisition involves the procedure known as ___shaping___.

7-2. What is shaping? When is it used?

Shaping - reinforcing closer & closer approximations to the desired behavior to form a new response.

7-3. Extinction in classical conditioning involves removing the UCS while still presenting the CS.
(a) What is the extinction procedure in operant conditioning?   *remove the reinforcer(s)*

(b) What is the effect of extinction on behavior (response rate)?   *decreases, stops*

Answers: 7-1. shaping   7-2. Shaping involves reinforcing closer and closer approximations to the desired behavior. It is used in the formation of a new response.   7-3. (a) removal or termination of the reinforcers (b) Response rate decreases; the behavior may eventually stop occurring altogether.

8. Explain how stimuli govern operant behavior and how generalization and discrimination occur in operant conditioning.

8-1. When a pig jumps through a hoop, the animal trainer may reward it with a bit of pig chow. With further training the pig may jump only when the trainer says "Jump!" The pig chow is a ___reinforcer___, and the word "Jump!" is a ___discriminative___ stimulus.

CHAPTER SIX

8-2. Reinforcers occur (after/before) the response occurs. Discriminative stimuli occur _____before_____ the response occurs.

8-3. To create a discriminative stimulus, one reinforces a response only in the presence of a particular stimulus and not in its absence. In time that stimulus will gain control of the response: Animals will tend to emit the response only if the discriminative stimulus is (present/absent) and not if it is _____absent_____ .

8-4. For example, rats can be trained to press a lever when a light comes on and not to press when the light is off. Lever presses that occur after the onset of the light are followed with a food pellet; those that occur in the dark are not. Label each component of this operant conditioning process by placing the appropriate letters in the blanks below.

_a_ light   a. discriminative stimulus

_b_ lever press   b. response

_c_ food   c. reinforcer

8-5. "Heel, Fido!" says the master. Fido runs to his master's side. Fido gets a pat on the head. Label the parts of the operant conditioning sequence by placing the appropriate letters in the blanks.

_a_ "Heel, Fido!"   a. discriminative stimulus

_c_ Fido gets a pat on the head.   b. response

_b_ Fido runs to his master's side. c. reinforcer

8-6. Phyllis will lend money to Ralph, but only after he promises to pay her back. Ralph is also careful to thank Phyllis for her help.

_c_ "Thank you very much, Phyllis." a. discriminative stimulus

_b_ Phyllis lends.   b. response

_a_ "I promise I'll pay you back." c. reinforcer

8-7. Generalization occurs in operant as well as in classical conditioning. For example, when I put the dishes in the sink, our cat *runs to her bowl* looking for food. In technical terms, our cat _____generalizes_____ between the sound of food being dropped in her bowl and similar sounds caused by the clatter of dishes: she has not learned to _____discriminate_____ between these sounds.

Answers: 8-1. reinforcer, discriminative **8-2.** after, before **8-3.** present, absent **8-4.** a, b, c **8-5.** a, c, b **8-6.** c, b, a **8-7.** generalizes, discriminate.

9. Discuss the role of delayed reinforcement and conditioned reinforcement in operant conditioning.

9-1. For those who smoke, the pleasure received is apparent. Giving up the habit, however, also has its rewards. Given the information about delay of reinforcement, why is it so hard to give up smoking?

9-2. Define the following:
  (a) Primary reinforcer: _food, water, sex, etc. reinforcer is unlearned and satisfies biological needs._

  (b) Secondary or conditioned reinforcer: _reinforcer that is learned -applause, praise, attention, awards, etc._

Answers: **9-1.** Because we, like the rest of the animal kingdom, are more affected by reinforcers that follow our behavior immediately than those which follow after a delay. Reinforcement for smoking is immediate; reinforcement for giving up smoking may occur only after a long delay.   **9-2.** (a) a reinforcer that is unlearned and that satisfies biological needs, such as food, water, sex, etc. (b) a reinforcer that is learned or acquired, such as applause, praise, attention, awards, etc.

10. Identify various types of schedules of reinforcement and conditioned reinforcement and discuss their typical effects on responding.

10-1. Schedules of reinforcement are either continuous or intermittent. If reinforcers follow each response, the schedule is referred to as a ___continuous___ reinforcement schedule. If reinforcers only follow some responses and not others (e.g., FR, VR), or occur as a function of the passage of time (e.g., FI, VI), the schedule is referred to as a/an ___intermittent___ schedule .

10-2. Identify the following schedules of reinforcement by placing the appropriate abbreviations in the blanks: continuous reinforcement (CRF), fixed ratio (FR), variable ratio (VR), fixed interval (FI), variable interval (VI).

  __FR__ A pigeon is reinforced whenever it has pecked a disk exactly 200 times.

  __VR__ A pigeon is reinforced for pecking a disk, on the average, 200 times.

  __FI__ A rat is always reinforced for the first response that follows a 2-minute interval.

  __VR__ ＊ A slot machine delivers a payoff, on the average, after every 10th pull of the lever.

  __CRF__ Every time the pigeon pecks a disk, it receives a pellet of food.

  __VI__ A rat is reinforced, on the average, for the first response following a two-minute interval.

  __VI__ A pig is reinforced for the first response after 30 seconds, then for the first response after 42 seconds, then for the first response after 5 seconds, etc.

  __FI__ Every two weeks Ralph picks up his payroll check at the office.

  __VR__ ＊ A rat is reinforced after the 73rd response, then after the 22nd response, then after the 51st response, etc.

10-3. What is the general effect of the intermittent schedules of reinforcement on resistance to extinction?
  greatest resistance to extinction with intermittent reinforcement

10-4. In terms of the effect on patterns of responding, what is the general difference between the *ratio* schedules (FR and VR) and the *interval* schedules (FI and VI)? _the ratio schedules tend to produce more rapid responding than the interval schedules._

10-5. In terms of the effect on patterns of responding, what is the general difference between *fixed* schedules and *variable* schedules? _Variable schedules tend to produce more regular, or steadier patterns of responding and more resistance to extinction than do the fixed schedules._

Answers: 10-1. continuous, intermittent (or partial)   10-2. FR, VR, FI, VR, CRF, VI, VI, FI, VR   10-3. The intermittent schedules increase resistance to extinction.   10-4. The ratio schedules tend to produce more rapid responding than the interval schedules.   10-5. The variable schedules tend to produce more regular, or steadier, patterns of responding and more resistance to extinction than do their fixed counterparts.

11. Explain the distinction between positive reinforcement and negative reinforcement.

11-1. Suppose that each time a rat presses a lever, the mild electric shock on the cage floor is turned off for a period of time. Will the lever-pressing behavior be *strengthened* or *weakened*?

Strengthened

11-2. By definition, what effect does reinforcement have on behavior? What is the effect of positive reinforcement on behavior? Negative reinforcement?

the frequency) of behavior. Both positive & negative reinforcement strengthen behavior. reinforcement strengthens/ increases

11-3. With positive reinforcement, a stimulus is *presented* after the response. What is the procedure with negative reinforcement?

after the response. the stimulus (aversive stimulus) is removed

Answers: 11-1. strengthened   11-2. Reinforcement strengthens (increases the frequency of) behavior. Both positive and negative reinforcement strengthen behavior.   11-3. The stimulus (an aversive stimulus) is *removed* after the response.

12. Describe and distinguish between escape learning and avoidance learning.

12-1. Label the following examples E for escape and A for avoidance.

___E___ The weather has changed, and Fahrquhart is getting extremely cold. He goes inside.

___E___ Little Sandy rapidly removes her hand from the hot stove.

___A___ Randolph has been told that he will be mugged if he goes outside, so he stays inside.

___E___ Sue has learned a new bit of verbal behavior. If she simply says, "No, I don't want that" shortly after a salesman starts his pitch, the salesman will stop bothering her.

___A___ Alice sees Ruppert in the distance. If Ruppert sees her he will ask for her course notes, which she doesn't want to lend him. She heads in the other direction.

___A___ A cue light comes on in the dog's shuttle box. It jumps the hurdle to the other side.

12-2. What is the major difference between escape learning and avoidance learning?

With escape learning there is no cue stimulus, so the animal must first experience the aversive stimulus —then escapes the aversive stimulus. In avoidance learning, a cue preceding the aversive stimulus permits the animal to avoid the aversive event altogether.

Answers: 12-1. E, E, A, E, A, A   12-2. The major difference is that with escape learning there is no cue stimulus, so the animal must first experience the aversive stimulus; it then escapes the aversive stimulus. In the case of avoidance learning, a cue preceding the aversive stimulus permits the animal to *avoid* the aversive event altogether.

13. Explain Mowrer's two-process theory and the role of negative reinforcement in avoidance behavior.

13-1. In successful avoidance learning, the organism never experiences the aversive stimulus. So why doesn't the response gradually extinguish? Why does the animal continue to avoid? Mowrer proposed the answer more than 40 years ago: The dog in the shuttle box isn't just avoiding the shock, it is avoiding (or escaping) something else as well. What else is it avoiding?

the cue light or conditioned fear of the cue light.

13-2. In Mowrer's explanation the cue stimulus becomes an aversive stimulus that elicits fear. Through what learning process does the cue stimulus acquire the capacity to produce a fear response?

classical conditioning

13-3. Why is Mowrer's theory called a two-process theory? *because it involves both classical and operant conditioning*

13-4. Some years ago Ajax was bitten by a dog on a couple of occasions. Even though he hasn't been bitten by a dog in years, the sight of a dog will send chills through his body, and he runs away. Use Mowrer's theory to explain why this phobic response hasn't extinguished. *the sight of a dog produces a classically conditioned response (fear). Ajax can avoid this aversive stimulus and the fear it produces (and internal stimulus) by running away.*

Answers: 13-1. the cue light, or conditioned fear of the cue light   13-2. classical conditioning   13-3. Because it integrates two processes, classical and operant conditioning.   13-4. The sight of the dog produces a classically conditioned fear response. Ajax can avoid this aversive stimulus and the fear it produces (an internal stimulus) by running away.

14. Describe punishment and its effects and list six guidelines for making punishment more effective.

14-1. To review the concepts of reinforcement and punishment, label each of the following descriptions with one of these terms: positive reinforcement, negative reinforcement, or punishment.
(a) A stimulus is presented after the response; response rate increases: *positive reinforcement*

(b) A stimulus is presented after the response; response rate decreases: *punishment*

(c) A stimulus is removed after the response; response rate increases: *negative reinforcement*

14-2. Response rate *increases*. Which of the following procedure or procedures may have been used?
a. positive reinforcement
b. negative reinforcement
c. punishment
d. either *a* or *b* above

14-3. Response rate *decreases*. Which of the following procedure or procedures may have been used?
a. positive reinforcement
b. negative reinforcement
c. punishment
d. either *b* or *c* above

14-4. When a rat presses a bar in an operant chamber, the electric shock stops. Bar pressing increases. What procedure has been used?
a. positive reinforcement
b. negative reinforcement
c. punishment
d. extinction

14-5. When the dog ran after the car, his master immediately threw a bucket of water on him. This sequence of events was repeated only twice, and the dog stopped running after the car. What has occurred?
a. positive reinforcement
b. negative reinforcement
c. punishment
d. extinction

14-6. When Randolph stepped out in his new outfit, everyone stared. If Randolph tends *not* to wear this outfit in the future, what has occurred?
a. positive reinforcement
b. negative reinforcement
c. punishment
d. extinction

14-7. Skinner has argued that punishment does not have a particularly potent effect on behavior. Recent research has found which of the following?
a. Punishment has as strong an influence on behavior as reinforcement.
b. The effects of punishment are weaker than those of reinforcement.
c. Punishment only temporarily suppresses behavior.
d. Punishment is even more effective than reinforcement.

14-8. In the space below list three negative side effects of punishment.

① can repress many responses besides the punished one

② can trigger strong emotional responses - fear, anxiety, anger, resentment

③ physical punishment often leads to an increase in aggressive behavior

14-9. Following are six hints that refer to the guidelines for making punishment more effective. Beneath each hint describe the appropriate guideline.

(a) When? immediately after the behavior

(b) How strong? just severe enough to be effective

(c) How consistently? every time the behavior occurs

(d) What explanations? if the reasons for the punishment are given to children, the punishment tends to be more effective

(e) Alternative responses? punishment tends to be more effective if alternative behaviors are reinforced at the same time.

(f) Spanking, or withdrawal of privileges? withdrawal of valued privileges can give children hours to contemplate the wisdom of changing their ways.

Answers: 14-1. (a) positive reinforcement (b) punishment (c) negative reinforcement   14-2. d, because if response rate increases, *either* positive *or* negative reinforcement may be involved.   14-3. c. Not d, because negative reinforcement *increases* response rate.   14-4. b   14-5. c   14-6. c   14-7. a   14-8. Punishment may (1) suppress responses in general rather than just the response punished, (2) produce unwanted emotional responses, including fear and anger, and (3) increase aggressive behavior.   14-9. (a) If possible, punishment should be delivered *immediately* after the behavior. (b) Since undesirable side effects increase with the intensity of punishment, it should be *only as strong as needed* to be effective. (c) To be effective punishment should be given *consistently*, after each instance of the behavior. (d) If the *reasons for the punishment* are given to children, the punishment tends to be more effective. (e) Punishment tends to be more effective if *alternative behaviors are reinforced* at the same time. (f) For the most part, *physical punishment should be avoided* because it tends to provide a model for, and hence to increase, aggressive behavior.

NEW DIRECTIONS IN THE STUDY OF CONDITIONING

15. **Discuss the implications of instinctive drift and conditioned taste aversion for traditional views of conditioning and learning.**

15-1. What is instinctive drift? *the tendency for instinctive or innate behavior to interfere with the process of conditioning*

15-2. Why was the occurrence of instinctive drift surprising to operant psychologists? Discuss this question in terms of the supposed generality of the laws of learning.

15-3. What is conditioned taste aversion? *if the distinctive taste of a particular food is followed some hours later by sickness, that taste will become aversive and hence will be avoided.*

15-4. Why is the occurrence of conditioned taste aversion surprising? Discuss this question with regard to classical conditioning and (1) CS-UCS delays and (2) the sense of taste compared with other senses. *1) classical conditioning generally does not occur if there are long CS-UCS delays and 2) taste is only one of several senses stimulated. We seem to have an innate tendency to associate taste (rather than sight, sound, etc.) with sickness that may occur much later.*

Answers: 15-1. It is the tendency for instinctive or innate behavior to interfere with the process of conditioning. 15-2. Operant psychologists of the 1960s assumed that one could operantly condition any response that animals are physically capable of emitting (and that behaviors are largely acquired rather than innate). Thus, it was surprising to find that conditioning was not as general a process as they had supposed and that some responses are, because of inherent characteristics of the animal, difficult or impossible to condition. 15-3. It is the fact that if the distinctive taste of a particular food is followed some hours later by sickness (nausea, vomiting, etc.), that taste will become aversive and hence will be avoided. 15-4. It is surprising because (1) classical conditioning generally does not occur if there are long CS-UCS delays, and (2) taste is only one of several senses stimulated. We seem to have an innate tendency to associate taste (rather than sight, sound, etc.) with sickness that may occur much later.

16. **Summarize the procedure, results, and implications of the Featured Study (Gustavson et al., 1976) on conditioned taste aversion and livestock predation.**

16-1. What was the purpose of the study? *to see whether conditioned taste aversion could be employed to make sheep unappetizing to coyotes - to reduce herd losses.*

16-2. How was conditioned taste aversion induced? *Sheep carcasses were treated with lithium - a chemical that causes nausea & illness, were fed (pilot study) to captive coyotes or made available for consumption by coyotes in the wild (field study)*

16-3. What were the results of the pilot study? The field study? *In the pilot study, coyotes and wolves in captivity actively avoided the sheep. In the field study, attacks on the sheep in the local ranch area seemed to decrease by between 30-60%.*

16-4. What were some of the problems encountered and what conclusions were drawn about the use of the conditioned taste aversion procedure in an applied setting?
because it was a field experiment, it was difficult to draw firm conclusions.

Answers: **16-1.** The purpose was to see whether conditioned taste aversion could be employed to make sheep unappetizing to coyotes, thereby reducing herd losses. **16-2.** Sheep carcasses treated with lithium, a chemical that causes nausea and illness, were fed to captive coyotes (in the pilot study) or made available for consumption by coyotes in the wild (in the field study). **16-3.** In the pilot study, coyotes (and wolves) in captivity actively avoided the sheep. In the field study attacks on the sheep in the local ranch area seemed to decrease by between 30% and 60%. **16-4.** The researchers did not have control of their subject population in the wild, so they did not know what proportion of the coyotes ate the tainted food nor what proportion remained in that geographical area. Thus, while the study suggests a potential practical use for the taste-aversion phenomenon, it was difficult to draw firm conclusions from the results of the field study. The study illustrates some of the problems encountered in interpreting field, as opposed to laboratory, studies.

17. **Describe research on blocking and on signal relations in classical conditioning and explain their theoretical importance.**

17-1. In phase one of the blocking study described, a tone was paired with shock in a classical conditioning arrangement.
(a) What was paired with shock in phase two? *a light*

(b) What happened when the tone and light were presented together (without the shock)? *elicited response (fear)*

(c) What happened when the light was presented alone? *no CR*

(d) In terms of traditional thinking about classical conditioning and the conditioned reflex, why is the blocking phenomenon surprising and of theoretical importance?

17-2.   In the example of a signal relations study described, the number of conditioning trials in which CS and UCS were paired was the same for two groups. The difference between the two treatment groups was that for one group the (CS/UCS) was presented alone for a series of trials.

17-3.   Theorists originally assumed that classical conditioning is an automatic, reflexive phenomenon which does not depend at all on higher mental processes. If this actually were the case, then what, supposedly, would have been the effect of presenting the UCS alone?
a. Extinction would occur.
b. The UCS trials would weaken conditioning.
c. The UCS trials would have no effect on conditioning.

17-4.   In fact, what did occur in the signal relations studies?
a. Extinction.
b. The UCS trials weakened conditioning.
c. The UCS trials had no effect on conditioning.

17-5.   Why are the signal relations results surprising and of theoretical importance?

As with blocking, the signal relations studies indicate that conditioning depends to a considerable degree on higher mental processes.

Answers: 17-1. (a) Both a tone and light were presented as conditioned stimuli. (b) A conditioned response was elicited. (c) There was no CR to the light alone. (d) The finding that the light did not become a CS, even though it was paired with shock, is surprising if one takes the traditional view that classical conditioning is an *automatic, mechanical* process. After all, a light alone paired with shock will produce classical conditioning, so why should the addition of the tone CS block conditioning? The blocking phenomenon suggests that some sort of *cognitive* processes are at work in classical conditioning in which the animal processes the fact that the light provides no new information.   17-2. UCS   17-3. c   17-4. b   17-5. As with blocking, the signal relations studies indicate that conditioning is not, as assumed earlier, an the automatic process; instead, conditioning depends to a considerable degree on higher mental processes.

18.   Explain how response-outcome relations (including noncontingent reinforcement) may influence operant behavior.

18-1.   "Response-outcome relations" refers to the connection between a response and its consequences. For example, for a rat in a Skinner box the relationship between the lever press (the response) and the food pellet (the outcome) is this: the rat gets the food only if it presses the lever. In other words, the reinforcer is ___contingent___ (contingent/not contingent) on the response.

18-2.   But suppose the rat is reinforced so that the food pellet is delivered on a timed basis, without regard to what the animal is doing. Whether the rat is jumping, sniffing, scratching, turning, or whatever, when the time comes it will receive a pellet of food. In this case the reinforcer is delivered ___noncontingently___ (contingently/noncontingently).

18-3.   As is the case with contingent reinforcement, when a reinforcer is delivered noncontingently the organism will tend to repeat what it was doing just before it was reinforced. Athletes, for example, may develop superstitious rituals (hat tugging, sock pulling, pants adjusting, etc.) that have been reinforced accidentally (by making a basket, hitting a home run, etc.). This accidental reinforcement is technically termed ___non-contingent___ reinforcement.

18-4. While noncontingent reinforcement does strengthen behavior, noncontingent reinforcement is (more/less) effective than reinforcement that is locally connected to the response. Even studies with animals have found that responses are more affected by reinforcers that appear to be _caused_ by the response than by reinforcers that do not.

18-5. Reinforcement, then, is not such an automatic process. Some response-outcome relations are more plausible than others, and the more plausible ones are (just as/more) likely to be strengthened than the less plausible ones.

18-6. Thus, research on blocking, signal relations, and response-outcome relations has forced the development of new theories which emphasize a much more _cognitive_ explanation of conditioning, an explanation in which organisms actively attempt to detect the relationship between their behaviors and environmental events.

Answers: 18-1. contingent   18-2. noncontingently   18-3. noncontingent   18-4. more, caused (produced)
18-5. more   18-6. cognitive (information processing, mental).

OBSERVATIONAL LEARNING

19. Discuss the nature and importance of observational learning.

19-1. In the space below list and define the four processes that Bandura has identified as crucial components of observational learning. The first letter of each concept is listed at the left.

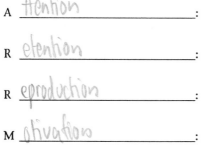

A _ttention_ :

R _etention_ :

R _eproduction_ :

M _otivation_ :

19-2. Why is the concept of observational learning so important? First, it extends classical and operant conditioning to include not only direct experience but indirect, or _vicarious_ , experience. We learn not only from experiencing classical and operant conditioning ourselves but by _observing_ conditioning that occurs in others.

19-3. Second, research on observational learning suggests a revision of the idea that learning does not occur unless one is reinforced. In Bandura's view, reinforcement is essential to (learning/performance) but not to _learning_ . We may learn, without being reinforced, simply by _observing_ the behavior of a model.

19-4. Third, Bandura's theory has helped explain some puzzling aspects of conditioning in human behavior. For example, while punishment by definition (increases/decreases) the behavior it follows, in the longer run it may ___increase___ aggressive behavior. The reason for these opposing effects is that while punishment weakens behavior it also provides a_n_ _example/model_ of aggression, so that tendencies toward aggression are acquired through _observational_ learning.

Answers: 19-1. Attention: Paying attention to a model's behavior and consequences. Retention: Retaining in memory a mental representation of what one has observed. Reproduction: Having the ability to reproduce what one sees, to convert the image to behavior. Motivation: Having the inclination, based on one's assessment of the likely payoff, to reproduce the observed behavior. 19-2. vicarious, observing 19-3. performance, learning (or acquisition), observing 19-4. decreases, increase (strengthen), model, observational (vicarious).

PUTTING IT IN PERSPECTIVE

20. **Explain how this chapter highlighted the joint influence of heredity and environment and psychology's impact on trends and values in society at large.**

   20-1.   Skinner has emphasized the importance of *environmental* events (reinforcers, punishers, discriminative stimuli, schedules of reinforcement) as the determinants of behavior. One of our unifying themes, however, is that heredity and environment interact. In support of this theme list the names of two phenomena that show that *biology* has a powerful effect on *conditioning*.

   instinctive drift and conditioned taste aversion

   20-2.   The second theme well illustrated in this chapter is that psychology evolves in a sociohistorical context. To illustrate this theme, list three areas in which operant psychology has influenced our everyday lives.

   ① parents' tendency to prefer reinforcement over punishment
   ② use of positive reinforcement in the business world
   ③ programmed learning & individualized instruction

   Answers: 20-1. instinctive drift, conditioned taste aversion 20-2. Operant psychology has probably influenced (1) parents' tendency to prefer reinforcement over punishment, (2) the use of positive reinforcement in the world of business, and (3) programmed learning and individualized instruction (including, by the way, the procedure of using learning objectives as used in your text and study guide).

APPLICATION: ACHIEVING SELF-CONTROL THROUGH BEHAVIOR MODIFICATION

21. **List and discuss the five steps in a self-modification program.**

   21-1.   In the space below list the five steps of a self-modification program in the order in which they are performed. The letters at the left are the first letters of the key words in each phase.

   T: Specify your ___target___ behavior.

   B: Gather ___baseline___ data.

   D: ___design___ your program.

   EE: ___execute___ and ___evaluate___ your program.

   E: ___end___ your program.

21-2. Match the letters from the previous question with the steps illustrated in the following story about a successful self-modification. Note that the sequence of events occurs in chronological order.

____ Thorson believes he has a nasty temper. He decides that what he needs to change is the number of violent outbursts he has.

____ He behaviorally defines a violent outburst as behavior involving a red face, loud voice, and pounding on a table or wall.

____ Thorson's goal is to have no violent outbursts. Expressions of irritation are o.k., but no violent outbursts.

____ Before trying to change anything, Thorson counts the number of his outbursts on a 3 × 5 card that he carries with him at all times.

____ Thorson also notes down the time of day and who he is with when an outburst occurs. He also tries to observe the consequences of his outbursts, especially the positive or negative reinforcers which may be maintaining them.

____ Thorson begins planning what he will do to change his behavior. He notes that the antecedents to the outbursts tend to involve contact with his children. He could avoid that antecedent, but he is actually very fond of his kids and finds this alternative undesirable. He decides on using reinforcement.

____ Thorson wishes he had a nice sports car with which to reinforce himself, but he doesn't. What he is able to enjoy, however, is reading in the evening. So, he decides that before he may read in the evening, he must check his card, and his card must indicate that he has had no outbursts that day.

____ To increase the chances of the success of his program, and so that he won't forget the contingencies, he writes down the agreement and signs it in the presence of his wife and children.

____ During the first day the program goes o.k., he has no outbursts, and he reads with pleasure in the evening. During the second day he counts one "little" outburst, which he thinks shouldn't count, but his wife remembers five.

____ They decide to make two changes: Mrs. Thorson and the older child will do the counting, and he will approach the target behavior more gradually. He is allowed two outbursts per day during the first week, one during the second, and none the third week.

____ During the second week two other modifications are introduced: Mr. Thorson will receive an additional reward for behaviors that compete with the outbursts. If he has five pleasant interactions with the children during a day (compliments them, plays a game with them, etc.) he avoids having to cook or do dishes. In addition, Mrs. Thorson takes control of the book he is currently reading.

____ The Thorsons judge that the program is successful, and they decide to terminate it. They also decide to institute a new program if the outbursts reoccur.

Answers: 21-1. target, baseline, design, execute and evaluate, end   21-2. T, T, T, B, B, D, D, D (or EE if added later), EE, EE, EE, E.

REVIEW OF KEY TERMS

Acquisition
Antecedents
Avoidance learning
Behavior modification
Behavioral contract
Blocking
Classical conditioning
Conditioned reinforcer
Conditioned response (CR)
Conditioned stimulus (CS)
Continuous reinforcement
Cumulative recorder
Discriminative stimuli
Elicit
Emit
Escape learning
Extinction
Fixed-interval (FI) schedule

Fixed-ratio (FR) schedule
Higher-order conditioning
Instinctive drift
Instrumental learning
Intermittent reinforcement
Law of effect
Learning
Negative reinforcement
Noncontingent reinforcement
Observational learning
Operant conditioning
Partial reinforcement
Pavlovian conditioning
Phobias
Positive reinforcement
Primary reinforcers
Programmed learning
Punishment

Reinforcement
Reinforcement contingencies
Resistance to extinction
Respondent conditioning
Schedule of reinforcement
Secondary reinforcers
Shaping
Skinner box
Spontaneous recovery
Stimulus contiguity
Stimulus discrimination
Stimulus generalization
Token economy
Trial
Unconditioned response (UCR)
Unconditioned stimulus (UCS)
Variable-interval (VI) schedule
Variable-ratio (VR) schedule

_____ 1. A relatively durable change in behavior or knowledge that is due to experience.

_____ 2. Irrational fears of specific objects or situations.

_____ 3. The most common name of a type of learning in which a neutral stimulus acquires the ability to evoke a response that was originally evoked by another stimulus.

_____ 4. Another name for classical conditioning derived from the name of the person who originally discovered the conditioning phenomenon.

_____ 5. A third name for classical conditioning that emphasizes the importance of the response.

_____ 6. A stimulus that evokes an unconditioned response.

_____ 7. The response to an unconditioned stimulus.

_____ 8. A previously neutral stimulus that has acquired the capacity to evoke a conditioned response.

_____ 9. A learned reaction to a conditioned stimulus that occurs because of previous conditioning.

_____ 10. To draw out or bring forth, as in classical conditioning.

_____ 11. Any presentation of a stimulus or pair of stimuli in classical conditioning.

_____ 12. The formation of a new response tendency.

_____ 13 Occurs when there is a temporal (time) association between two events.

_____ 14. The gradual weakening and disappearance of a conditioned response tendency.

_____ 15. The reappearance of an extinguished response after a period of nonexposure to the conditioned stimulus.

_____ 16. Occurs when an organism responds to new stimuli that are similar to the stimulus used in conditioning.

_____ 17. Occurs when an organism learns not respond to stimuli that are similar to the stimulus used in conditioning.

_____ 18. Occurs when a conditioned stimulus functions as if it were an unconditioned stimulus.

_____ 19. This term, introduced by Skinner, refers to learning in which voluntary responses come to be controlled by their consequences.

_____ 20. Another name for operant conditioning, this term was introduced earlier by Edward L. Thorndike.

_____ 21. Law stating that if a response in the presence of a stimulus leads to satisfying effects, the association between the stimulus and the response is strengthened.

_____ 22. Occurs when an event following a response strengthens the tendency to make that response.

_____ 23. A standard operant chamber in which an animal's responses are controlled and recorded.

_____ 24. Production of voluntary responses in responding in operant conditioning.

_____ 25. The circumstances or rules that determine whether responses lead to presentation of a reinforcer; or, the relationship between a response and positive consequences.

_____ 26. Device that creates a graphic record of operant responding as a function of time.

_____ 27. The reinforcement of closer and closer approximations of the desired response.

_____ 28. An approach to self-instruction in which information and questions are arranged in a sequence of small steps to permit active responding by the learner.

_____ 29. Occurs when an organism continues to make a response after the delivery of the reinforcer for it has been terminated.

_____ 30. Cues that precede operant behavior and that influence the behavior by indicating the probable consequences (reinforcement or no reinforcement) of a response.

_____ 31. Stimulus events that are inherently reinforcing because they satisfy biological needs.

_____ 32. Stimulus events that acquire reinforcing qualities by being associated with primary reinforcers.

_____ 33. A specific pattern of presentation of reinforcers over time.

_____ 34. Occurs when every instance of a designated response is reinforced.

_____ 35. The name for all schedules of reinforcement in which a designated response is reinforced only some of the time.

_____ 36. The schedule in which the reinforcer is given after a fixed number of nonreinforced responses.

_____ 37. The schedule in which the reinforcer is given after a variable number of nonreinforced responses.

_____ 38. The schedule in which the reinforcer is given for the first response that occurs after a fixed time interval has elapsed.

_____ 39. The schedule in which the reinforcer is given for the first response that occurs after a variable time interval has elapsed.

_____ 40. Occurs when a response is strengthened because it is followed by the arrival of a rewarding (presumably pleasant) stimulus.

_____ 41. Occurs when a response is strengthened because it is followed by the removal of an aversive ("unpleasant") stimulus.

_____ 42. Occurs when an organism engages in a response that brings aversive stimulation to an end.

_____ 43. Occurs when an organism engages in a response that prevents aversive stimulation from occurring.

_____ 44. Occurs when an event that follows a response weakens or suppresses the tendency to make that response.

_____ 45. Occurs when an animal's innate response tendencies interfere with conditioning processes.

_____ 46. Occurs when a stimulus paired with a UCS fails to become a CS because it is redundant with an established CS.

_____ 47. Occurs when a response is strengthened even though the delivery of the reinforcer is not a result of the response.

_____ 48. Occurs when an organism's responding is influenced by the observation of others, who are called models.

_____ 49. A systematic approach to changing behavior through the application of the principles of conditioning.

_____ 50. Events that typically precede your target behavior and may play a major role in governing your target response; also, another term for discriminative stimuli.

_____ 51. A system for distributing symbolic reinforcers that are exchanged later for a variety of genuine reinforcers.

_____ 52. A written agreement outlining a promise to adhere to the contingencies of a behavior modification program.

_____ 53. Another name for intermittent reinforcement, i.e, when a designated response is reinforced only some of the time.

_____ 54. Another name for secondary reinforcer.

Answers: 1. learning 2. phobias 3. classical conditioning 4. Pavlovian conditioning 5. respondent conditioning 6. unconditioned stimulus (UCS) 7. unconditioned response (UCR) 8. conditioned stimulus (CS) 9. conditioned response (CR) 10. elicit 11. trial 12. acquisition 13. stimulus contiguity 14. extinction 15. spontaneous recovery 16. stimulus generalization 17. stimulus discrimination 18. higher-order conditioning 19. operant conditioning 20. instrumental learning 21. law of effect 22. reinforcement 23. Skinner box 24. emit 25. reinforcement contingencies 26. cumulative recorder 27. shaping 28. programmed learning 29. resistance to extinction 30. discriminative stimuli 31. primary reinforcers 32. secondary reinforcers 33. schedule of reinforcement 34. continuous reinforcement 35. intermittent reinforcement 36. fixed-ratio (FR) schedule 37. variable-ratio (VR) schedule 38. fixed-interval (FI) schedule 39. variable-interval (VI) schedule 40. positive reinforcement 41. negative reinforcement 42. escape learning 43. avoidance learning 44. punishment 45. instinctive drift 46. blocking 47. noncontingent reinforcement 48. observational learning 49. behavior modification 50. antecedents 51. token economy 52. behavioral contract 53. partial reinforcement 54. conditioned reinforcer.

REVIEW OF KEY PEOPLE

Albert Bandura   Robert Rescorla   E. L. Thorndike
Ivan Pavlov   B. F. Skinner   John B. Watson

_____ 1. The first to describe the process of classical conditioning.

_____ 2. Founded behaviorism; examined the generalization of conditioned fear in a boy known as "Little Albert."

_____ 3. Developed a principle known as the law of effect; coined the term instrumental learning.

_____ 4. Elaborated the learning process known as operant conditioning; investigated schedules of reinforcement; developed programmed learning.

_____ 5. Asserted that environmental stimuli serve as signals and that some stimuli in classical conditioning are better signals than others.

_____ 6. Described and extensively investigated the process of observational learning.

Answers: 1. Pavlov 2. Watson 3. Thorndike 4. Skinner 5. Rescorla 6. Bandura.

SELF-QUIZ

1. In Pavlov's original demonstration of classical conditioning, salivation to the bell was the:
   a. conditioned stimulus
   b. conditioned response
   c. unconditioned stimulus
   d. unconditioned response

2. Sally developed a fear of balconies after almost falling from a balcony on a couple of occasions. What was the conditioned response?
   a. the balcony
   b. fear of the balcony
   c. almost falling
   d. fear resulting from almost falling

3. When the UCS is removed and the CS is presented alone for a period of time, what will occur?
   a. classical conditioning
   b. generalization
   c. acquisition
   d. extinction

4. Sally developed a fear of balconies from almost falling. Although she has had no dangerous experiences on bridges, cliffs, and the view from tall buildings, she now fears these stimuli as well. Which of the following is likely to have produced a fear of these other stimuli?
   a. instinctive drift
   b. spontaneous recovery
   c. generalization
   d. discrimination

5. A researcher reinforces closer and closer approximations to a target behavior. What is the name of the procedure she is using?
   a. shaping
   b. classical conditioning
   c. discrimination training
   d. extinction

6. John says, "Please pass the salt." Ralph passes the salt. "Thank you," says John. John's request precedes a behavior (salt passing) which is reinforced ("Thank you"); thus, the request is analogous to a:
   a. discriminative stimulus
   b. response
   c. positive reinforcer
   d. conditioned stimulus (CS)

7. A rat is reinforced for the first lever-pressing response that occurs, *on the average*, after 60 seconds. Which schedule is the rat on?
   a. FR
   b. VR
   c. FI
   d. VI

8. When the rat presses a lever, the mild electric shock on the cage floor is turned off. What procedure is being used?
   a. punishment
   b. escape
   c. discrimination training
   d. avoidance

9. A cue light comes on in the dog's shuttle box. It jumps the hurdle to the other side. What procedure is being used?
    a. punishment
    b. escape
    c. discrimination training
    d. avoidance

10. In Mowrer's explanation of avoidance, the cue stimulus acquires the capacity to elicit fear through the process of:
    a. operant conditioning
    b. classical conditioning
    c. generalization
    d. discrimination

11. The contingencies are as follows: if the response occurs, a stimulus is *presented*; if the response does not occur, the stimulus is not presented. Under this procedure the strength of the response *decreases*. What procedure is being used?
    a. positive reinforcement
    b. negative reinforcement
    c. punishment
    d. avoidance training

12. In terms of the traditional view of conditioning, research on conditioned taste aversion was surprising because:
    a. there was a very long delay between CS and UCS
    b. the dislike of a particular taste was operantly conditioned
    c. conditioning occurred to all stimuli present when the food was consumed
    d. the sense of taste seems to be relatively weak

13. Animal trainers (the Brelands) trained pigs to put coins in a piggy bank for a food reward. The animals learned the response but, instead of depositing the coins immediately in the bank, the pigs began to toss them in the air, drop them, push them on the ground, and so on. What had occurred that interfered with conditioning?
    a. conditioned taste aversion
    b. blocking
    c. instinctive drift
    d. S & L scandal

14. A stimulus paired with a UCS fails to establish a CR because it is redundant with an already established CS. What is involved?
    a. spontaneous recovery
    b. stimulus generalization
    c. instinctive drift
    d. blocking

15. Earlier learning viewpoints considered classical and operant conditioning to be automatic processes involving environmental events that did not depend at all on biological or cognitive factors. Research in which of the following areas casts doubt on this point of view?
    a. blocking and signal relations
    b. instinctive drift and conditioned taste aversion
    c. response-outcome relations
    d. all of the above

Answers: 1. b 2. b 3. d 4. c 5. a 6. a 7. d 8. b 9. d 10. b 11. c 12. a 13. c 14. d 15. d.

7 HUMAN MEMORY

REVIEW OF KEY IDEAS

ENCODING: GETTING INFORMATION INTO MEMORY

1. **List and describe the three basic human memory processes.**

   1-1. The three basic human memory processes are:

   (a) Putting the information in, a process called _encoding_.

   (b) Holding onto the information, a process called _storage_.

   (c) Getting the information back out, a process called _retrieval_.

   Answers: 1-1. (a) encoding (b) storage (c) retrieval.

2. **Compare and contrast the early and late selection theories of attention and the resolution of the debate.**

   2-1. If you are being introduced to a new person and you want to remember her name, it is first necessary to give *selective* _attention_ to this information. This requires _filtering_ out irrelevent sensory input. The debate between early and late selection theories of attention is an argument over when this filtering takes place, before or after _meaning_ is given to the arriving material.

   2-2. Below are research findings that support either early or late selection theories of attention. Tell which theory is supported by each example and why.
   (a) A person involved in a cocktail party conversation can usually hear his or her name being mentioned across the room. _late since meaning has been applied to the information_

   (b) Information from two messages delivered simultaneously to both ears at once (biaural listening) is more difficult to retain than if this same information is simultaneously sent such that the right ear hears one of the messages and the left ear hears the other (dichotic listening). _early since meaning has not been applied to the information_

2-3. Since research evidence, as well as casual observations, seems to support ___both___ theories, it thus appears that human beings have the capacity to decide ___where___ to place their attention filter.

Answers: 2-1. attention, filtering, meaning   2-2. (a) Late, since meaning has been applied to the information. (b) Early, since meaning has not been applied to the information.   2-3. both, where.

3. List and describe the three levels of information processing proposed by Craik and Lockhart (1972).

3-1. Craik and Lockhart propose three levels for encoding incoming information, with ever increasing retention as the depth of processing increases. In their order of depth these three levels are:

(a) ___structural___   (b) ___phonemic___   (c) ___semantic___

3-2. Below are three-word sequences. Tell which level of processing each sequence illustrates and why.
(a) cat IN tree ___semantic because we immediately give meaning to the words___

(b) car BAR czar ___phonemic because the words sound alike___

(c) CAN CAP CAR ___structural because the words look alike___

3-3. If this theory is correct, then we would expect most persons to best remember the sequence in ___cat in tree___. This is because the words in this sequence have greater ___meaning___ than do the other two sequences.

Answers: 3-1. (a) structural (b) phonemic (c) semantic   3-2. (a) Semantic because we immediately give meaning to the words. (b) Phonemic because the words sound alike. (c) Structural because the words look alike.   3-3. cat in tree, meaning.

4. Summarize the procedure, results, and implications of the Featured Study (Craik & Tulving, 1975) on depth of processing.

4-1. The major objective of the Featured Study was to test the hypothesis that the retention of stimulus words would increase as subjects moved from ___structural___ to ___phonemic___ to ___semantic___ encoding. It was also hypothesized that processing time would be longest for ___semantic___ encoding, next longest for ___phonemic___ encoding, and shortest for ___structural___ encoding. Subjects were shown a stimulus word and asked to make one of three different judgments about the word. In a third of the words the judgment required structural processing, in a third of the words phonemic processing, and in a third of the words semantic processing. The two dependent measures in this study were ___time to respond___ and ___ability to remember___.

4-2. Rank order the results of this study regarding time to respond:
Fastest response time ___structural___
Next fastest response time ___phonemic___
Slowest response time ___semantic___

4-3. Rank order the results of this study regarding retention rate of the words:
Greatest retention _semantic_
Next greatest retention _phonemic_
Lowest retention _structural_

4-4. Although these results supported the hypotheses that deeper levels of processing require a longer time for processing but are better remembered, further studies showed that: _it's possible to design a task in which structural encoding takes longer than semantic encoding._

Answers: 4-1. structural, phonemic, semantic, semantic, phonemic, structural, time to respond, ability to remember (retention rate) **4-2.** structural, phonemic, semantic **4-3.** semantic, phonemic, structural **4-4.** In some instances structural encoding may take longer than semantic encoding.

5. Discuss three techniques for enriching the encoding process.

5-1. Elaboration helps us to better remember the words RUN FAST CAT than the words WORK SLOW TREE. Why is this? _you can imagine a cat running fast._

5-2. According to Paivio's dual-coding theory, why is it easier to remember the word APPLE rather than the word PREVAIL? _apple refers to a concrete object — it is easier to form a visual image of the word apple, thus allowing for storage of both the word and image._

5-3. What is the general idea behind self-referent encoding? _self referent encoding involves deciding how or whether information is personally relevant — if so, we are more likely to remember information when it is relevant to ourselves_

Answers: 5-1. Because the words RUN FAST CAT allow us to make richer and more elaborate associations among them than do the other three (for example you can imagine a cat running fast). **5-2.** Because it is easier to form a visual image of the word APPLE, thus allowing for storage of both the word and image. **5-3.** We are more likely to remember information when it is relevant to ourselves.

STORAGE: MAINTAINING INFORMATION IN MEMORY

6. Describe the role of the sensory store in memory.

6-1. Sensory memory allows for retention of a very (large/small) amount of information for a very (brief/long) period of time. The retention time for vision is less than _one_ _second_, although for other senses such as hearing and touch it may last more than a second. In other words, sensory memory allows us to retain almost all incoming information long enough to allow for further processing. Thus sensory memory is a store for briefly retaining almost all incoming (processed/unprocessed) information.

Answers: 6-1. large, brief, one second, unprocessed.

7. **Describe the characteristics of short-term memory and contrast them with long-term memory.**

7-1. Indicate whether the following statements apply to short-term memory (STM) or long-term memory (LTM).

LTM (a) Has a virtually unlimited storage capacity.

STM (b) Has a storage capacity of seven plus or minus two items.

STM (c) Requires continuous rehearsal to maintain information in store for more than 20 or 30 seconds.

LTM (d) Stores information more or less permanently

STM (e) Chunking can help to increase the capacity of this system.

STM (f) Alan Baddeley has proposed three components of this memory system that make it a "working memory."

Answers: 7-1. (a) LTM (b) STM (c) STM (d) LTM (e) STM (f) STM.

8. **Summarize the evidence on the hypothesis that all memories are stored permanently in long-term memory (LTM).**

8-1. There are two views regarding the durability of information in LTM. One is that no information is ever lost and the other is that _some information is lost_ . Those who favor the "no-loss" view explain forgetting as a failure of _retrieval_ . The information is still there, we just can not get it out.

8-2. How do the some-loss proponents counter the following three lines of evidence cited by the no-loss proponents?
   (a) Flashbulb memories of previous events? _while some of our memories appear to be of the flashbulb variety, it doesn't mean that all of them need to be._

   (b) The remarkable recall of hypnotized subjects? _hypnotized subjects is often found to be incorrect._

   (c) Penfield's electrically triggered memories? _these electrically triggered memories were often incorrect and more resembled dreams or hallucinations than real events._

Answers: 8-1. some information is lost, retrieval 8-2. (a) While some of our memories appear to be of the flashbulb variety, it does not mean that all of them need to be. (b) Their recall of information is often found to be incorrect. (c) The memories were often incorrect and more resembled dreams or hallucinations than real events.

9. **Describe how verbal rehearsal relates to LTM storage and discuss the likely causes of the serial position effect.**

9-1. Perhaps the major way in which information is transferred from STM to LTM is through the use of _verbal_ _rehearsal_ . The longer information is retained in STM through verbal rehearsal, the (less/more) likely it is to be transferred to LTM.

9-2. Roughly sketch the serial position effect onto the figure below. Then label the area on the sketch with a P that shows the primacy effect and with an R that shows the recency effect.

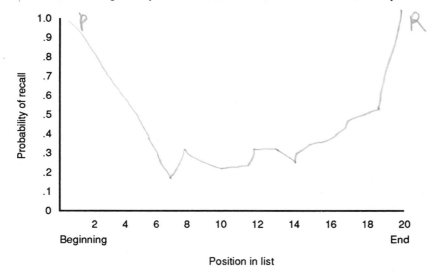

9-3. What appears to account for the primacy effect? words at the beginning get rehearsed more often.

9-4. What appears to account for the recency effect? words at the end still remain in short term memory

Answers: 9-1. verbal rehearsal, more   9-2. The curve you drew should be in the shape of a U. The primacy effect should be at the beginning (upper left side) and the recency effect at the end (upper right side).   9-3. Words at the beginning get rehearsed more often.   9-4. Words at the end still remain in STM.

10. Describe the use of various organizational frameworks in long-term memory.

10-1. Group the following words into two groups or categories:

rose   dog   grass   cat   tree   rat

You probably grouped the words into plants and animals, which is the general idea behind ___clustering___ . Thus clustering leads to forming categories (concepts) and in turn the categories are organized into ___conceptual___ *hierarchies*. For example, the categories of plants and animals can be placed under the higher category (hierarchy) of ___living___ things.

10-2. In addition to conceptual categories, it appears that LTM also stores information in terms of *semantic networks*. If you understand the idea behind semantic networks and its related idea of *spreading activation,* you should be able to answer the questions below.

Person A attends an urban university and frequently studies while riding a bus to and from school.

Person B attends a university located in a rural area and frequently studies outside in one of the many park-like areas surrounding the school.

(a) When asked to think of words associated with the word STUDY, which of the above persons is most likely to think of the word GRASS? ___B___

(b) Which person is most likely to think of the word TRAFFIC? ___A___

(c) Which person is most likely to think of the word PEACEFUL? ___B___

10-3. Finally, it appears that LTM also stores information in coherent clusters called ___schemas___. For

example, when you recall going to a restaurant or attending a concert you make use of a particular kind

of schema called a ___script___.

Answers: 10-1. clustering, conceptual, living   10-2. (a) person B (b) person A (c) person B   10-3. schemas, script.

RETRIEVAL: GETTING INFORMATION BACK OUT OF MEMORY

11. Describe how retrieval cues, context cues, and mood are related to retrieval.

11-1. In the following examples indicate whether retrieval cues, context cues, or mood are being used to retrieve information from long-term memory.
(a) In trying to recall the name of a high school classmate you get the feeling that his first name began with an L and begin saying names like Larry, Leroy, Lionel, etc. _retrieval cues_

(b) Or you may attempt to recall the high school classmate by imagining the history class in which he sat in the row next to you. _context cues_

(c) Or you may try to recall the name by trying to recapture the sadness you both experienced together upon hearing about the death of a fellow classmate. _mood_

Answers: 11-1. (a) retrieval cues (b) context cues (c) mood.

12. Summarize evidence demonstrating the reconstructive nature of memory.

12-1. Since we use schemas to move information in and out of long-term memory, it is not too surprising

that retrieved information may be altered by the schema. This is the general idea behind the

___reconstructive nature of memory___.

12-2. For example, Elizabeth Loftus found that subjects were much more likely to falsely recall seeing broken

glass on a videotaped scene when they were originally asked, "How fast were the cars going when they

(hit/smashed) into each other." In this case the word "smashed" resulted in a different

___schema___ than did the word "hit."

12-3. While research evidence clearly shows that schemas do cause alterations in memory, it is difficult to tell if the alterations were caused by reconstructive errors or constructive errors. Distinguish between these two kinds of errors.
Reconstructive errors — _reconstructive errors occur during the retrieval process_

Constructive errors — _constructive errors occur during the encoding and storage processes._

Answers: 12-1. reconstructive nature of memory   12-2. smashed, schema   12-3. Reconstructive errors occur during the retrieval process. Constructive errors occur during the encoding and storage processes.

FORGETTING: WHEN MEMORY LAPSES

13. **Describe the various measures of forgetting.**

13-1. Which of the three different methods of measuring forgetting is being illustrated in each of the following situations?
(a) You are asked to identify a suspect in a police lineup. *recognition*

(b) You time yourself while learning 20 new French words. After a week you find you have forgotten some of the words and you again time yourself while learning the list a second time. *relearning*

(c) You are asked to draw a floor plan of your bedroom from memory. *recall*

Answers: 13-1. (a) recognition (b) relearning (c) recall.

14. **Explain how "forgetting" may be a matter of ineffective encoding.**

14-1. Why are most people unable to recognize the correct penny shown at the beginning of this chapter in the text? *they never encoded the correct figure in their memories!*

14-2. What is another name for information loss due to ineffective coding of this kind? *pseudo forgetting*

14-3. Why is semantic coding better than phonemic coding for enhancing future recall of the material? *semantic coding will lead to deeper processing and more elaborate associations*

Answers: 14-1. They never encoded the correct figure in their memories. 14-2. pseudoforgetting 14-3. Semantic coding will lead to deeper processing and more elaborate associations.

15. **Compare and contrast decay and interference as potential causes of forgetting.**

15-1. Two other theories of forgetting propose additional factors that may be involved in retrieval failure. One theory holds that retrieval failure may be due to the impermanence of the memory storage itself. This is the notion behind the ___*decay*___ theory of forgetting. Decay theory is best able to explain retrieval failure in ___*long*___ ___*term*___ memory and to a lesser extent in short-term memory.

15-2. The other theory attributes retrieval failure to other information already in the memory or to information arriving at a later date. This is the notion behind the ___*interference*___ theory of forgetting. According to interference theory, the failure may be caused by interference from information already in the memory, a phenomenon called ___*proactive*___ *interference*, or the failure may be caused by interference occurring after the original memory was stored, a phenomenon called ___*retroactive*___ *interference*. Interference is most likely to occur when the materials being stored are very (similar/different).

Answers: 15-1. decay, sensory store 15-2. interference, proactive, retroactive, similar.

16. **Explain how forgetting may be due to factors in the retrieval process.**

16-1. Breakdowns in the retrieval process can occur when the encoding specificity principle is violated. This means there has been a mismatch between the ___retrieval___ *cue* and the ___memory___ *code*. A common instance of this violation is seen when one attempts to retrieve a semantically coded word with ___phonemic___ retrieval cues.

16-2. Retrieval failure may also occur when there is a poor fit between initial encoding processing and the processing required by the measure of retention. In other words, the two kinds of processing are not transfer-___appropriate___.

16-3. Sigmund Freud felt that some breakdowns in the retrieval process could be attributed to purposeful suppression of information by unconscious forces, a phenomenon called ___motivated___ forgetting.

Answers: 16-1. retrieval, memory, phonemic   16-2. appropriate   16-3. motivated.

IN SEARCH OF THE MEMORY TRACE: THE PHYSIOLOGY OF MEMORY

17. **Summarize evidence on the physiology of memory.**

17-1. Which of the following biochemical changes have been implicated in the physiology of memory?
(a) Alterations in synaptic transmission at specific sites.
(b) Induced changes in RNA.
(c) Inadequate synthesis of acetycholine.
(d) Alterations in protein synthesis.

17-2. Answer the following questions regarding the neural circuitry of memory.
(a) What neural changes were found in rats that learned to run a series of mazes?
increased growth of neuronal dendritic trees

(b) What caused a rabbit to loose its memory of a conditioned eye blink?
destruction of an area in the cerebellum

(c) What do localized neural circuits have to do with memory?
they may form the basis for specific memory traces.

17-3. Amnesia cases due to head injury provide clues about the anatomical basis of memory. There are two basic types of head-injury amnesia. When the memory loss is for events prior to the injury it is called ___retrograde___ amnesia. When the memory loss is for events following the injury it is called ___anterograde___ amnesia.

17-4. Damage to what three areas in the limbic system have been found to result in amnesia?
hippocampus, amygdala, thalamus

17-5. The limbic system also appears to play a role in the hypothesized consolidation process, which assumes that the consolidation of memories begins in the _____*limbic*_____ system. These memories are then stored in various areas of the _____*cerebral*_____ cortex.

Answers: 17-1. a, c, d   17-2. (a) increased growth of neuronal dendritic trees (b) destruction of an area in the cerebellum (c) They may form the basis for specific memory traces.   17-3. retrograde, anterograde   17-4. amygdala, hippocampus, thalamus   17-5. limbic, cerebral.

ARE THERE MULTIPLE MEMORY SYSTEMS?

18. **Distinguish between implicit versus explicit memory, declarative versus procedural memory, and episodic versus semantic memory.**

   18-1. Label the two following situations as to whether they are examples of implicit or explicit memory.

   (a) After studying for your history test you were able to easily recall the information during the exam. ___*explicit*___

   (b) While studying for your history exam you unexpectedly recall an incident from the previous summer. ___*implicit*___

   18-2. Another division of memory systems has been hypothesized for declarative memory and procedural memory. Identify these two divisions from their descriptions given below.

   (a) This memory system allows you to drive a car or play a piano with minimal attention.
   ___*procedural*___

   (b) This memory system allows you to explain how to drive a car or play a piano to a friend.
   ___*declarative*___

   18-3. It has been suggested that there is an apparent relationship between implicit memory and ___*procedural*___ memory and between explicit memory and ___*declarative*___ memory.

   18-4. It has also been hypothesized that declarative memory can be further subdivided into semantic and episodic memory. Identify these two kinds of memory from the following descriptions:

   (a) This kind of memory acts like an encyclopedia, storing all of the factual information you possess.
   ___*semantic*___

   (b) This kind of memory acts like an autobiography, storing all of your personal experiences.
   ___*episodic*___

Answers: 18-1. (a) explicit (b) implicit   18-2. (a) procedural (b) declarative   18-3. procedural, declarative 18-4. (a) semantic (b) episodic.

PUTTING IT IN PERSPECTIVE

19. **Explain how this chapter highlighted the subjectivity of experience and the multifactorial causation of behavior.**

19-1. The text mentions four major areas in which subjectivity may influence memory. See if you can remember them given the hint of the first letter of the two key words in each area.

S A *selective attention when observing events*

S S *depending of Schemas and scripts to organize memory*

R N *the reconstructive nature of memory*

M F *Motivated forgetting*

19-2. Since the memory of a specific event can be influenced by many factors operating in each of the three memory stores, it is obvious that memory, like most behavior, has _*multifactorial*_ _*causation*_.

Answers: 19-1. Selective Attention when observing events. Depending on Schemas and Scripts to organize memory. The Reconstructive Nature of memory. Motivated Forgetting. 19-2. multifactorial causation.

APPLICATION: IMPROVING EVERYDAY MEMORY

20. **Outline strategies by which everyday memory can be improved.**

20-1. Strategies for enhancing memory are called _*mnemonic*_ devices. Examples of strategies which do not employ visual images are listed below. See if you can identify which strategy is being employed in each illustration.

(a) Using the phrase, "My Very Excellent Mother Just Sells Nuts Under Protest," to remember the names and positions of the planets illustrates the use of an _*acrostic*_.

(b) Most persons can remember their own phone number because of extensive _*overlearning*_.

(c) It is wise to make use of "tip of the tongue" occurrences when attempting to retrieve information and thus take advantage of _*retrieval*_ cues.

(d) International Business Machines is easily identified by its _*acronym*_ IBM.

(e) Rather than merely underlining important material in a text, it is much better to subject this material to _*deep*_ *processing* so as to enrich understanding.

(f) Willie Nurd the bookworm studies much of the time, but he always takes breaks between study periods. Willie must realize the importance of _*distributed*_ _*practice*_.

(g) Since you are going to the store your roommate asks you to bring her a bar of Ivory soap, a box of Kleenex, and a Snickers bar. You then make up a story which begins, "On my way to the Ivory Coast to check on the latest shipment of Kleenex, I . . ." Here you're making use of a _*narrative*_ method as a mnemonic device.

20-2. Three techniques involving visual imagery can also serve as helpful mnemonic devices, the link method, the method of loci, and the keyword method. Identify them in the examples below.

(a) You want to remember the name of your bus driver, Ray Blocker, who has especially large forearms. You form an image of a man using his large arms to *block* light *rays* from his face. *Key word*

(b) You want to remember to buy bananas, eggs, milk, and bread. You visualize walking into your front door and tripping on a bunch of bananas. Stumbling forward into the hallway you notice broken eggs on the table... *loci*

(c) You imagine yourself using a banana to break eggs, which you then pour into a bowl of milk and bread. *link*

Answers: 20-1. mnemonic (a) acrostic (b) overlearning (c) retrieval (d) acronym (e) deep (f) distributed practice (g) narrative **20-2.** (a) keyword method (b) method of loci (c) link method.

REVIEW OF KEY TERMS

Anterograde amnesia
Attention
Biaural listening
Chunk
Clustering
Conceptual hierarchy
Consolidation
Decay theory
Declarative memory system
Dichotic listening
Dual-coding theory
Elaboration
Encoding
Encoding specificity principle
Episodic memory system
Explicit memory
Flashbulb memories
Forgetting curve
Implicit memory

Interference theory
Keyword method
Levels of processing theory
Link method
Long-term memory (LTM)
Long-term potentiation
Method of loci
Mnemonic devices
Mood-congruence effect
Motivated forgetting
Nonsense syllables
Overlearning
Primacy effect
Proactive interference
Procedural memory system
Recall
Recency effect
Recognition

Rehearsal
Relearning
Retention
Retrieval
Retroactive interference
Retrograde amnesia
Schema
Script
Self-referral encoding
Semantic memory system
Semantic networks
Sensory memory
Serial position effect
Short-term memory (STM)
State-dependent memory
Storage
Tip-of-the-tongue phenomenon
Transfer-appropriate processing

_____ 1. Putting coded information into memory.

_____ 2.   Maintaining coded information in memory.

_____ 3. Recovering information from memory stores.

_____ 4. The process of focusing awareness on a narrowed range of stimuli or events.

_____ 5. Listening to two separate auditory inputs sent simultaneously to both ears.

_____ 6. Listening to two separate auditory inputs sent simultaneously, but each is sent to only one ear.

_____ 7. The initial processing of information is similar to the type of processing required by the subsequent measure of retention.

_____ 8. Occurs when memory is better for information that is consistent with one's ongoing mood.

_____ 9. Memory which involves the intentional recollection of previous experiences.

_____ 10. A theory that proposes that deeper levels of processing result in longer lasting memory codes.

_____ 11. Involves linking a stimulus to other information at the time of encoding.

_____ 12. A theory that memory is enhanced by forming both semantic and visual codes since either can lead to recall.

_____ 13. Preserves information in the original sensory form for a very brief time.

_____ 14. A limited capacity memory store that can maintain unrehearsed information for 20 to 30 seconds.

_____ 15. The process of repetitively verbalizing or thinking about new information.

_____ 16. A group of familiar stimuli stored as a single unit.

_____ 17. An unlimited capacity memory store that can hold information over lengthy periods of time.

_____ 18. Unusually vivid and detailed recollections of momentous events.

_____ 19. Occurs when subjects show better recall of items at the beginning and end of a list than for items in the middle.

_____ 20. Occurs when items at the beginning of a list are recalled better than other items.

_____ 21. Occurs when items at the end of a list are recalled better than other items.

_____ 22. Memory for factual information.

_____ 23. Memory for actions, skills, and operations.

_____ 24. Memory made up of chronological, or temporally dated, recollections of personal experiences.

_____ 25. Memory that contains general knowledge that is not tied to the time when the information was learned.

_____ 26. The tendency to remember similar or related items in a group.

_____ 27. These consist of concepts joined together by links that show how the concepts are related.

_____ 28. A long lasting increase in neural excitability at synapses along a specific neural pathway.

_____ 29. An organized cluster of knowledge about a particular object or sequence of events.

_____ 30. A particular kind of schema that organizes what people know about common activities.

_____ 31. A temporary inability to remember something you know accompanied by the feeling that it's just out of reach.

_____ 32. Improved recall that is attributed to being in the same emotional state during encoding and subsequent retrieval.

_____ 33. Consonant-vowel-consonant letter combinations that do not correspond to words (NOF, KER, etc.).

_____ 34. A curve graphing retention and forgetting over time.

_____ 35. The proportion of material remembered.

_____ 36. The ability to remember information without any cues.

_____ 37. Requires the selection of previously learned information from an array of options (e.g., multiple-choice tests).

_____ 38. Requires the memorization of information a second time to determine how much time or effort is saved.

_____ 39. Attributes forgetting to the impermanence of memory storage.

_____ 40. Attributes forgetting to competition from other material.

_____ 41. Occurs when new information impairs the retention of previously learned information.

_____ 42. Occurs when previously learned information impairs the retention of new information.

_____ 43. States that the value of a retrieval cue depends on how well it corresponds to the memory code.

_____ 44. Involves purposeful suppression of memories.

_____ 45. A theoretical process involving the gradual conversion of information into durable memory codes stored in long-term memory.

_____ 46. The loss of memory for events that occurred prior to a brain injury.

_____ 47. The loss of memory for events that occur after a brain injury.

_____ 48. Strategies for enhancing memory.

_____ 49. The continued rehearsal of material after it has apparently been mastered.

_____ 50. Involves forming a mental image of items to be remembered in a way that connects them together.

_____ 51. A mnemonic device that involves taking an imaginary walk along a familiar path.

_____ 52. Involves associating a concrete word with an abstract word and generating an image to represent the concrete word.

_____ 53. A multi-level classification system based on common properties among items (e.g., cats, animals, living things).

_____ 54. Is apparent when retention is exhibited on a task that does not require intentional remembering.

_____ 55. The process of deciding how or whether information is personally relevant.

Answers: 1. encoding 2. storage 3. retrieval 4. attention 5. biaural listening 6. dichotic listening 7. transfer-appropriate processing 8. mood-congruence effect 9. explicit memory 10. levels of processing theory 11. elaboration 12. dual-coding theory 13. sensory memory 14. short-term memory (STM) 15. rehearsal 16. chunk 17. long-term memory (LTM) 18. flashbulb memories 19. serial position effect 20. primacy effect 21. recency effect 22. declarative memory system 23. procedural memory system 24. episodic memory system 25. semantic memory system 26. clustering 27. semantic networks 28. long-term potentiation 29. schema 30. script 31. tip-of-the-tongue phenomenon 32. state-dependent memory 33. nonsense syllables 34. forgetting curve 35. retention 36. recall 37. recognition 38. relearning 39. decay theory 40. interference theory 41. retroactive interference 42. proactive interference 43. encoding specificity principle 44. motivated forgetting 45. consolidation 46. retrograde amnesia 47. anterograde amnesia 48. mnemonic devices 49. overlearning 50. link method 51. method of loci 52. keyword method 53. conceptual hierarchy 54. implicit memory 55. self-referral encoding.

REVIEW OF KEY PEOPLE

Richard Atkinson & Richard Shiffrin   Hermann Ebbinghaus   Wilder Penfield
Gordon Bower   Elizabeth Loftus   George Miller
Fergus Craik & Robert Lockhart   Endel Tulving

_____ 1. Proposed three progressively deeper levels for processing incoming information.

_____ 2. Influential in the development of the model of three different kinds of memory stores (sensory, STM, and LTM).

_____ 3. Observed that electrical stimulation of the brain could elicit forgotten memories.

_____ 4. Proposed the idea that categorical information is organized into conceptual hierarchies.

_____ 5. Demonstrated that the reconstructive nature of memory can distort eyewitness testimony.

_____ 6. Used nonsense syllables to become famous for his forgetting curve.

_____ 7. One of his many contributions was the encoding specificity principle.

_____ 8. Proposed the concept of chunking for storing information in short-term memory.

Answers: 1. Craik & Lockhart   2. Atkinson & Shiffrin   3. Penfield   4. Bower   5. Loftus   6. Ebbinghaus   7. Tulving 8. Miller.

SELF-QUIZ

1. Which of the following is not one of the three basic human memory processes?
   a. storage
   b. retrieval
   c. decoding
   d. encoding

2. Which one of the three levels of processing would probably be employed when attempting to memorize the following three-letter sequences WAB WAC WAD?
   a. structural
   b. semantic
   c. phonemic
   d. chunking

3. Retrieval from long-term memory is usually best when the information has been stored at which level of processing?
   a. structural
   b. semantic
   c. phonemic
   d. chunking

4. According to Paivio's dual-coding theory:
   a. words are easier to encode than images
   b. abstract words are easier to encode than concrete words
   c. visual imagery may hinder the retrieval of words
   d. none of the above

5. Which of the memory stores can store the least amount of information?
   a. sensory store
   b. short-term memory
   c. long-term memory

6. Hypnotized subjects are generally able to achieve highly accurate retrieval of information from long-term memory. This statement is:
   a. true
   b. false

7. Information is primarily transferred from short-term memory to long-term memory through the process of:
   a. elaboration
   b. verbal rehearsal
   c. clustering
   d. sensory coding

8. In learning a list of 20 new Spanish words you are likely to experience:
   a. a primacy effect
   b. a recency effect
   c. a serial position effect
   d. all of the above

9. Interference is to forgetting as clustering is to:
   a. categories
   b. decay
   c. rehearsal
   d. recognition

10. When you attempt to recall the name of a high school classmate by imagining yourself back in the English class with her, you are making use of:
    a. retrieval cues
    b. context cues
    c. schemas
    d. recognition cues

11. Taking this particular self-test measures your:
    a. constructive errors
    b. reconstructive errors
    c. recall
    d. recognition

12. Ineffective coding of information may result in:
    a. the primacy effect
    b. the recency effect
    c. pseudoforgetting
    d. chunking

13. Decay theory is best able to explain the loss of memory in:
    a. sensory store
    b. long-term memory
    c. short-term memory
    d. both short-term and long-term memory

14. When you violate the encoding specificity principle you are likely to experience an inability to:
    a. encode information
    b. store information
    c. retrieve information
    d. none of the above

15. Evidence continues to grow that RNA may provide the chemical code for memory. This statement is:
    a. true
    b. false

16. It is very easy to recall the name of your high school because it has been subject to extensive:
    a. deep processing
    b. clustering
    c. chunking
    d. overlearning

    Answers: 1. c 2. a 3. b 4. d 5. b 6. b 7. b 8. d 9. a 10. b 11. d 12. c 13. a 14. c 15. b 16. d.

8 LANGUAGE AND THOUGHT

REVIEW OF KEY IDEAS

THE COGNITIVE REVOLUTION IN PSYCHOLOGY

1. **Describe the "cognitive revolution" in psychology.**

   1-1.   Answer the following questions regarding the cognitive revolution in psychology.
   (a) In what decade did this revolution get underway?

   (b) Why were earlier cognitive approaches abandoned?

   (c) What theoretical school openly opposed the cognitive approach?

   (d) What accounts for the success of this new cognitive revolution?

   Answers: 1-1. (a) The 1950s (b) They were too subjective (as opposed to being empirical or objective). (c) behaviorism (d) It uses empirical methods to study cognitive processes.

LANGUAGE: TURNING THOUGHTS INTO WORDS

2. **Summarize evidence on language acquisition in chimpanzees, including the Featured Study (Savage-Rumbaugh et al., 1986) on Kanzi.**

   2-1.   Indicate whether each of the following is true or false.

   _____ (a) Researchers have been able to teach chimpanzees to use symbols to communicate.

   _____ (b) Chimpanzees find it difficult to catch onto the rules of language.

   _____ (c) Language acquisition in chimpanzees appears to be very similar to language acquisition in children.

2-2. The Featured Study was a developmental account of how a chimp, Kanzi, learned to communicate with his caretakers.

(a) What were Kanzi's ages during the period of the study?

(b) How did Kanzi communicate with his caretakers?

(c) How did the caretakers communicate with each other and with Kanzi when in his presence?

(d) What previous experience with language did Kanzi have?

Answers: 2-1. (a) true (b) true (c) false 2-2. (a) 2 1/2 to 5 years (b) by touching geometric symbols representing words (c) in this same manner (d) passively watching his mother communicate with the caretakers.

3. Outline the key properties of language and use these to reevaluate the ape-language controversy.

3-1. Language is characterized by four properties: symbolic, semantic, generative, and structured. Identify each of these properties in the following statements.

(a) Applying rules to arrange words into phrases and sentences illustrates the _____

property of language.

(b) Using words or geometric forms to represent objects, actions, or events illustrates the

_____ property of language.

(c) Making different words out of the same letters, such as NOW and WON, illustrates the

_____ property of language.

(d) Giving the same meaning to different words, such as chat, katz, and cat, illustrates the

_____ property of language.

3-2. Which of these four properties of language did Kanzi appear to use?

Answers: 3-1. (a) structured (b) symbolic (c) generative (d) semantic 3-2. all four, but in a rudimentary form.

4. Describe the hierarchical structure of language.

4-1. Arrange the following parts of language into their correct hierarchical structure:

SENTENCES - SOUNDS - WORDS - MEANINGFUL UNITS - PHRASES

CHAPTER EIGHT

4-2. Identify the following parts (units) of language.

(a) With around 40 of these basic sounds you can say all of the words in the English language.

_____

(b) Phonemes are combined into these smallest units of meaning in a language, which may include root words as well as prefixes and suffixes. _____

(c) These rules specify how words can be combined into phrases and sentences. _____

Answers: 4-1. sounds - meaningful units - words - phrases - sentences   4-2. (a) phonemes (b) morphemes (c) syntax.

5. Outline the development of human language during the first year.

5-1. Answer the following question regarding the development of language during the first year of life.
(a) What are a child's three major vocalizations during the first 6 months of life?

(b) What gradually occurs during the babbling stage of language development?

(c) What is the range in months for the babbling stage of language development?

Answers: 5-1. (a) crying, laughing, and cooing (b) The babbling increasingly resembles spoken language. (c) 6 to 18 months.

6. Describe children's early use of single words and word combinations.

6-1. What does the text mean when it states that the receptive vocabulary of toddlers is much larger than their productive vocabulary?

6-2. Identify the following phenomenon observed in children's early use of language.

(a) What phenomenon is illustrated when a child calls all four-legged creatures "doggie"?

_____

(b) What phenomenon is illustrated when a child correctly communicates her desire to know where the family dog is simply by saying "doggie"? _____

(c) What phenomenon is illustrated when a child complains to her mother, "Doggie eat cookie"?

_____

(d) What phenomenon is illustrated when a child puns, "I love your I's"? _____

(e) Solve the following anagram that best describes how children acquire language skills.? FWSYLIFT

_____

Answers: 6-1. They can understand more spoken words than they can reproduce themselves.
6-2. (a) overextensions (b) holophrases (c) telegraphic speech (d) metalinguistic awareness (e) swiftly.

7. **Compare and contrast the behaviorist, nativist, and interactionist perspectives on the development of language.**

   7-1. Identify the following perspectives on the development of language.

   (a) This perspective places great emphasis on the role of reinforcement and imitation.

   _____

   (b) This perspective assumes that children make use of a language acquisition device (LAD) to acquire transformational rules, which enable them to easily translate between surface structure and deep structure. _____

   (c) This interactionist perspective argues that language development is tied to progress in thinking and general cognitive development. _____

   (d) This interactionist perspective argues that language development is directed to some extent by the social benefits children derive from interaction with mature language users. _____

   7-2. Which perspective places greatest emphasis on:

   (a) nurture _____

   (b) nature _____

   (c) nature interacting with nurture _____

   Answers: 7-1. (a) behaviorist (b) nativist (c) cognitive theories (d) social communication theories 7-2. (a) behaviorist (b) nativist (c) interactionist.

8. **Discuss whether language determines thought or thought determines language.**

   8-1. What is the major idea behind Benjamin Whorf's linguistic relativity hypothesis?

   8-2. What did Eleanor Rosch's experiment show when she compared the color recognition ability of English speaking people and Dani people, who have only two words for color?

   8-3. While language does not appear to determine the kinds of ideas people can think about, it does exert some influence over the way they approach an idea. This is the general idea behind the _____ of questions.

   Answers: 8-1. Language determines thought. 8-2. She found no difference in the ability to deal with colors. 8-3. framing.

PROBLEM SOLVING: IN SEARCH OF SOLUTIONS

9. **List and describe the three types of problems proposed by Greeno, placing the sample problems from Figure 8.5 in the appropriate categories.**

   9-1.   Greeno has proposed three types of problems. Identify each of these categories from their descriptions given below.
   (a) This type of problem requires the problem solver to discover the relations (structure) among the parts of the problem.

   (b) This type of problem requires the problem solver to arrange the parts in a way that satisfies some criterion.

   (c) This type of problem requires the problem solver to carry out a sequence of transformations in order to reach a specific goal.

   9-2.   Tell which type each of the following problems in Figure 8.5 exemplify.
   (a) The string and anagram problems.

   (b) The hobbits and orcs and the water jars problems

   (c) The series completion and the analogy problems.

   Answers: 9-1. (a) inducing structure (b) arrangement (c) transformation   9-2. (a) arrangement (b) transformation (c) inducing structure.

10. **Describe four common barriers to effective problem solving.**

   10-1.   Which of the barriers to effective problem solving (functional fixedness, unnecessary constraints, mental set, and irrelevant information) are you overcoming when you:
   (a) make a financial decision without first consulting your horoscope?

   (b) teach an old dog a new trick?

   (c) use a page of newspaper as a wedge to keep a door open?

   (d) ignore the advice that "This is the way we've always done it"?

   Answers: 10-1. (a) irrelevant information (b) mental set (c) functional fixedness (d) unnecessary constraints.

11. **List and describe five examples of general problem-solving strategies.**

   11-1.   The text describes five different problem-solving techniques, or _____. Which of

   these heuristics (means/ends analysis, form subgoals, work backward, search for analogies, change the

   representation of the problem) would be most applicable in solving the following problems?
   (a) While opening your car door you drop the keys. The keys hit your foot and bounce underneath the car,
   too far to reach. It has stopped raining so you close your unbrella and ponder how to get your keys.

   (b) You have accepted the responsibility for chairing the homecoming celebration at your school.

   (c) You are rebuilding the disk brake on the left front wheel of your car and cannot recall how two of the
   parts fit together. You also intend to rebuild the brake on the right front wheel.

   (d) As an entering freshman in college, you have already chosen a field of study and a specific graduate school
   you wish to attend. Now all you have to do is accomplish this goal.

   (e) You have agreed to become the compaign chairwoman of a friend who wants to run for student body
   president. Obviously your goal is to make your friend look like a good choice to students, but what heuristic
   would politicians often employ here.

   Answers: 11-1. heuristics (a) search for analogies (the umbrella can be used as a rake) (b) form subgoals (c) work
   backwards (see how the parts fit together in the right wheel) (d) means/ends analysis (e) change the representation of
   the problem (make the opponents look like a bad choice).

12. **Summarize how experts and novices differ in their problem solving.**

   12-1.   Psychologists have found several differences in the approaches taken by experts and novices when faced

   with similar problems. For example, master chess players are far better able to group chess pieces into

   familiar groups or patterns, a process called _____.

   12-2.   It has also been found that, in comparison to novices, experts are less likely to jump right into a

   complex problem. Rather, they will first make effective use of _____ an approach

   to a solution.

   12-3.   Finally, in comparison to novices, experts are much more likely to recognize analogies in problems and

   to categorize problems according to their (situations/solutions). In other words, they look beyond the

   surface aspects and focus on the _____ structures of problems

   Answers: 12-1. chunking   12-2. planning   12-3. solutions, deeper.

DECISION MAKING: CHOICES AND CHANCES

13. **Compare the additive and elimination by aspects approaches to selecting an alternative.**

13-1. The text describes two approaches to decision making. What is the major advantage of an additive strategy?

13-2. What is the major advantage of the elimination by aspects strategy?

Answers: 13-1. It allows attractive attributes to compensate for unattractive attributes (you don't have to throw out the baby with the bath water). 13-2. It allows for easier decision making when the task is complex and there are numerous alternatives.

14. **Explain the factors that individuals typically consider in risky decision making.**

14-1. What differentiates risky decision making from other kinds of decision making?

14-2. What is the most you can know when making a risky decision?

14-3. What two things must be known in order to calculate the expected value of making a risky decision?

14-4. How does the concept of subjective utility explain why some persons still engage in risky decision making when the expected value indicates the probability of a loss?

Answers: 14-1. The outcome is uncertain. 14-2. The probability of winning. 14-3. The average amount of money you could expect to win or loose with each play and the probability of a win or loss. 14-4. The personal worth of the outcome may outweigh the high probability of losing.

15. **Describe the availability and representativeness heuristics used to estimate subjective probabilities.**

15-1. Estimating the probability of an event on the basis of how often one recalls it has been experienced in the past is what Tversky and Kahneman call a(n) _____ heuristic.

15-2. When most people are asked if there are more words that begin with N or words that have N as the third letter, they apply the availability heuristic and guess incorrectly. Explain why they do this.

15-3. Estimating the probability of an event on the basis of how similar it is to a particular model or stereo-type of that event is what Tversky and Kahneman call a _____ heuristic.

15-4. "Steve is very shy. He has a high need for structure and likes detail. Is Steve more likely to be a salesperson or a librarian?" When most persons are given this problem they guess that he is a librarian even though there are many more salespersons than there are librarians. Explain why they do this.

Answers: 15-1. availability 15-2. Because they can immediately recall many more words that begin with N than words having N as the third letter. 15-3. representativeness 15-4. Because they employ the representativess heuristic and Steve fits the stereotype of a librarian.

PUTTING IT IN PERSPECTIVE

16. **Explain how this chapter highlighted three of the text's themes: the influence of heredity and the environment, the empirical nature of psychology, and the subjectivity of experience.**

16-1. Explain how the interactionist theory of language development illustrates the interaction between heredity and environment.

16-2. Explain why psychologists' study of higher mental processes, such as problem solving, illustrates the empirical nature of psychology.

16-3. How does the reframing of choice statements involved in decision making processes illustrate the subjectivity of experience?

Answers: 16-1. It accepts the behaviorist's position that environment is important and also the nativist's position that nature is important. 16-2. They had to develop empirical methods and measurements in order to study these elusive processes. 16-3. Choices that are objectively identical can subjectively seem very different.

UNDERSTANDING PITFALLS IN DECISION MAKING

17. **Describe some examples of flawed reasoning in decision making that reflect our use of the representativeness heuristic.**

17-1. State which example of flawed use of the representativeness heuristic is being described.
(a) The belief that a small sampling of cases can be as valid as a large sampling of cases.

(b) Estimating that the odds of two uncertain events happening together are greater than the odds of either event happening alone.

(c) The belief that a chance event increases if the event hasn't occurred recently.

(d) Inflating the probability of dramatic, vivid, but infrequent events.

(e) Failure to take base rate into account when estimating the probability of a given event.

18. **Describe our propensities to seek confirming information and overrate our confidence.**

18-1. What omission leads to the confirmation bias when making decisions?

18-2. How is this same phenomenon related to belief perseverance?

18-3. Answer the following true/false questions regarding the overconfidence effect.

_____ (a) We are much less subject to this effect when making decisions about ourselves as opposed to more worldly matters.

_____ (b) Scientists are not generally prone to this effect when making decisions about information in their own fields.

_____ (c) In the study of college students cited by the text it was observed that the gap between personal confidence and actual accuracy of decisions increased as the confidence level increased.

Answers: 18-1. Failure to seek out disconfirming evidence. 18-2. Disconfirming evidence is not given the same scrutiny as confirming evidence. 18-3. (a) false (b) false (c) true.

REVIEW OF KEY TERMS

Availability heuristic
Cognition
Compensatory decision models
Decision making
Deep structure
Fast mapping
Framing
Functional fixedness
Heuristic
Holophrases
Insight

Language
Language acquisition device (LAD)
Linguistic relativity
Mean length of utterances (MLU)
Means/ends analysis
Mental set
Metalinguistic awareness
Morphemes
Noncompensatory decision models
Overextensions

Overregularization
Phonemes
Problem solving
Psycholinguistics
Representativeness heuristic
Risky decision making
Surface structure
Syntax
Telegraphic speech
Trial and error

_____ 1. The study of the psychological mechanisms underlying the acquisition and use of language.

_____ 2. A collection of symbols, and rules for combining those symbols, that can be used to create an infinite variety of messages.

_____ 3. The smallest units of sound in a spoken language.

_____ 4. The smallest units of meaning in a language.

_____ 5. The rules that specify how words can be combined into phrases and sentences.

_____ 6. Using a word incorrectly to describe a wider set of objects or actions than it is meant to.

_____ 7. Single-word utterances that represent the meaning of several words.

_____ 8. Consists mainly of content words with articles, prepositions, and other less critical words omitted.

_____ 9. The ability to reflect on the use of language.

_____ 10. Basing the estimated probability of an event on the ease with which relevant instances come to mind.

_____ 11. Basing the estimated probability of an event on how similar it is to the typical prototype of that event.

_____ 12. The mental processes involved in acquiring knowledge.

_____ 13. The tendency to perceive an item only in terms of its most common use.

_____ 14. The sudden discovery of a correct solution to a problem following incorrect attempts.

_____ 15. Identifying differences that exist between the current state and the goal state and making changes that will reduce these differences.

_____ 16. A strategy for solving problems.

_____ 17. The process by which children map a word on an underlying concept after only one exposure to the word.

_____ 18. The average of youngsters' spoken statements (measured in morphemes).

_____ 19. Generalizing grammatical rules to irregular cases where they do not apply.

_____ 20. Decision making models allow for attractive attributes to compensate for unattractive attributes.

_____ 21. Decision making models that do not allow for some attributes to compensate for others.

_____ 22. Making decisions under conditions of uncertainty.

_____ 23. A hypothetical innate mechanism or process that facilitates the learning of language.

_____ 24. Persisting in using problem-solving strategies that have worked in the past.

_____ 25. The theory that one's language determines one's thoughts.

_____ 26. The active efforts to discover what must be done to achieve a goal that is not readily attainable.

_____ 27. Trying possible solutions sequentially and discarding those that are in error until one works.

_____ 28. Evaluating alternatives and making choices among them.

_____ 29. How issues are posed or how choices are structured.

_____ 30. The underlying meaning of a sentence or statement.

_____ 31. The word arrangement used in expressing a sentence or statement.

Answers: 1. psycholinguistics 2. language 3. phonemes 4. morphemes 5. syntax 6. overextensions
7. holophrases 8. telegraphic speech 9. metalinguistic awareness 10. availability heuristic 11. representativeness
heuristic 12. cognition 13. functional fixedness 14. insight 15. means/end analysis 16. heuristic 17. fast mapping
18. mean length of utterances (MLU) 19. overregularization 20. compensatory decision models 21. noncompensatory
decision models 22. risky decision making 23. language acquisition device (LAD) 24. mental set 25. linguistic relativity
26. problem solving 27. trial and error 28. decision making 29. framing 30. deep structure 31. surface structure.

REVIEW OF KEY PEOPLE

Noam Chomsky   Herbert Simon   Amos Tversky & Daniel Kahneman
Sue Savage-Rumbaugh   B. F. Skinner

_____ **1.** Won the Nobel Prize for his research on decision making and artificial intelligence.

_____ **2.** Proposed that children learn language through the established principles of learning.

_____ **3.** Proposed that children learn language through a biologically built-in language acquisition device.

_____ **4.** Performed research that showed people base probability estimates on heuristics that do not always yield reasonable estimates of success.

_____ **5.** Along with her colleagues she taught the chimp Kanzi to communicate in a way that made use of all the basic properties of language.

Answers: 1. Simon 2. Skinner 3. Chomsky 4. Tversky & Kahneman 5. Savage-Rumbaugh.

SELF-QUIZ

1. Which of the following explanations best explains the success of the cognitive revolution in psychology?
   a. the refining of introspection as a research method
   b. the development of empirical methods
   c. the development of computer analogies for human thinking
   d. both a and c

2. Which of the following represents the top of the hierarchy in the structure of language?
   a. meaningful units
   b. sentences
   c. phrases
   d. words

3. The word FAIRLY would be an example of a:
   a. morpheme
   b. phoneme
   c. syntactical unit
   d. none of the above

4. Children and chimpanzees do not appear to learn language in the same manner. This statement is:
   a. true
   b. false

5. When a child says that TUB and BUT are constructed of the same three letters she is showing an awareness of:
   a. morphemes
   b. phonemes
   c. metalinguistics
   d. syntax

6. The fact that children appear to learn rules, rather than specific word combinations, when acquiring language skills argues most strongly against which theory of language development?
   a. cognitive
   b. behaviorist
   c. nativist

7. Which of the following is not one of the basic properties of language?
   a. generative
   b. symbolic
   c. structured
   d. alphabetical

8. Which of the following heuristics would you probably employ if assigned the task of carrying out a school election?
   a. work backwards
   b. representativeness
   c. search for analogies
   d. form subgoals

9. Which one of Greeno's problems is exemplified by the anagram?
   a. arrangement
   b. inducing structure
   c. transformation
   d. chunking

10. Experts differ from novices in their problem solving in that they are more likely to make use of:
    a. planning
    b. chunking
    c. focusing on the deeper structures
    d. all of the above

11. People generally prefer a choice that provides an 80 percent chance of success over one that provides a 20 percent chance of failure. This illustrates the effect of:
    a. the availability heuristic
    b. the representativeness heuristic
    c. framing
    d. confirmation bias

12. When faced with having to choose among numerous alternatives, most persons will opt for:
    a. a noncompensatory decision model
    b. a compensatory decision model
    c. a means/ends analysis
    d. a subjective-utility model

13. What is the most you can know when making a risky decision?
    a. the amount you can win
    b. the amount you can loose
    c. both of the above
    d. none of the above

14. Most persons mistakenly believe that more people die from tornadoes than from asthma. This is because they mistakenly apply:
    a. a means/ends analysis
    b. a compensatory decision model
    c. an availability heuristic
    d. a representativeness heuristic

15. Failure to actively seek out contrary evidence may lead to:
    a. overestimating the improbable
    b. the conjunction fallacy
    c. the gambler's fallacy
    d. confirmation bias

16. Which of the following persons is known for his nativist theory of language development?
   a. Noam Chomsky
   b. B. F. Skinner
   c. Herbert Simon
   d. Amos Tversky

Answers: 1. b 2. b 3. d 4. a 5. c 6. b 7. d 8. d 9. a 10. d 11. c 12. a 13. d 14. c 15. d 16. a.

9 INTELLIGENCE AND PSYCHOLOGICAL TESTING

REVIEW OF KEY IDEAS

KEY CONCEPTS IN PSYCHOLOGICAL TESTING

1. **List and describe the principle categories of psychological tests.**

    1-1.   Most psychological tests can be placed into one of two very broad categories. These two categories are:
    _____ and _____.

    1-2.   There are three categories of mental abilities tests. Below are examples of each of these categories. Identify them.

    (a) The ACT and SAT tests you may have taken before entering college are examples of

    _____ tests.

    (b) The exams you frequently take in your introductory psychology class are examples of

    _____ tests.

    (c) Tests used to demonstrate general intellectual giftedness are examples of _____

    tests.

    1-3.   Personality tests allow an individual to compare himself or herself to other persons with respect to

    particular personality _____. Personality tests generally (<u>do/do not</u>) have right and

    wrong answers.

    Answers: 1-1. mental abilities tests, personality tests   **1-2.** (a) aptitude (b) achievement (c) intelligence
    1-3. characteristics, do not.

2. **Discuss the concepts of standardization and test norms.**

    2-1.   Administering the same test under the same conditions to a large group of persons who are representa-

    tive of the population you wish to measure is the general idea behind test _____.

2-2. In order to interpret a particular score on a test it is necessary to know how other persons score on this test. This is the general idea behind *test* _____. An easy method for providing comparisons of test scores is to convert the raw scores into _____ scores.

Answers: 2-1. standardization   2-2. norms, percentile.

3. Explain the meaning of test reliability and validity and how they are estimated.

3-1. The ability of a test to produce consistent results across subsequent measurements of the same persons is known as its _____. The ability of a test to actually measure what it claims to measure is known as its _____.

3-2. Readministering the same test to the same group of persons in a week or two following the original testing allows one to estimate the _____ of a test. If a test is highly reliable then a persons's scores on the two different administrations will be very similar. The amount of similarity can be assessed by means of the _____ *coefficient*.

3-3. There are three general kinds of validity. Identify each of these kinds from the descriptions given below.

(a) This kind of validity will tend to be high when, for example, scores on the ACT and SAT actually predict success in college. _____

(b) This kind of validity will be of particular importance to you when taking your exams for this class. It will be high if the exam sticks closely to the explicitly assigned material. _____

(c) This kind of validity is more vague than the other two kinds and refers to the ability of a test to measure abstract qualities, such as intelligence. _____

3-4. As with the estimation of reliability, the estimation of validity makes use of the

_____   _____.

Answers: 3-1. reliability, validity   3-2. reliability, correlation   3-3. (a) criterion-related validity (b) content validity (c) construct validity   3-4. correlation coefficient.

THE EVOLUTION OF INTELLIGENCE TESTING

4. **Summarize the contributions of Galton, Binet, Terman, and Wechsler to the evolution of intelligence testing.**

   4-1.   Identify each of the above men from the descriptions of their contributions given below.

   (a) This man developed the first useful intelligence test. His tests were used to predict success in school and scores were expressed in terms of mental age. _____

   (b) This man revised Binet's tests to produce the Stanford-Binet Intelligence Scale, the standard for all further intelligence tests. _____

   (c) This man began the quest to measure intelligence. He assumed that intelligence was mainly inherited and could be measured by assessing sensory acuity. _____

   (d) This man developed the first successful test of adult intelligence, the WAIS. He also developed new intelligence tests for children. _____

   (e) In developing his new intelligence tests, this man added many non-verbal items to his tests that allowed for the separate assessment of both verbal and non-verbal abilities. He also replaced the IQ score with one based on the normal distribution. _____

   Answers: 4-1. (a) Binet (b) Terman (c) Galton (d) Wechsler (e) Wechsler.

BASIC QUESTIONS ABOUT INTELLIGENCE TESTING

5. **List and describe the major functions of intelligence testing.**

   5-1.   The text lists three major functions of intelligence testing. List these functions below.

   Answers: 5-1. (In any order) screening and diagnosis, selection and placement, evaluation and research.

6. **Explain the meaning of an individual's score on a modern intelligence test.**

   6-1.   Answer the following questions regarding intelligence test scores.
   (a) In what manner is human intelligence assumed to be distributed?

   (b) What percentage of people have an IQ score below 100?

   (c) What would an IQ score of 130 mean?

   Answers: 6-1. (a) It forms a normal distribution. (b) 50% (c) Approximately 98% of the population is below this score or approximately 2% of the population is above this score.

7. **Describe the reliability and validity of modern intelligence tests.**

   7-1. Answer the following questions with respect to the reliability of modern intelligence tests.
         (a) What kind of reliability estimates (correlation coefficients) are found with most modern intelligence tests?

         (b) What might be a problem here with respect to an individual's test score?

   7-2. Answer the following questions with respect to the validity of modern intelligence tests.
         (a) What is the correlation between IQ tests and grades in school?

         (b) What is the correlation between IQ tests and the number of years of schooling that people complete?

         (c) What might be a general problem with assuming intelligence tests are a valid measure of general mental ability?

   Answers: 7-1. (a) They are in the low .90s. (b) Temporary conditions could lower the score.   7-2. (a) .50-.60 (b) .70s (c) They principally focus the academic/verbal intelligence and ignore other kinds of intelligence.

8. **Discuss the stability of IQ scores and how well they predict vocational success.**

   8-1. By what age do IQ scores become fairly good predictors of adolescent and adult intelligence?

   8-2. Is the ability of intelligence tests to predict vocational success much higher or much lower than their ability to predict academic success?

   8-3. What two kinds of intelligence that may be especially important for vocational success are not assessed by IQ tests?

   8-4. Intelligence tests are particularly poor in predicting success within a particular vocational group. Why is this?

   Answers: 8-1. seven or eight   8-2. much lower   8-3. practical intelligence and social intelligence   8-4. The range of test scores is so restricted.

EXTREMES OF INTELLIGENCE

9. **Describe how mental retardation is defined and divided into various levels.**

   9-1. In addition to having subnormal mental abilities (IQ scores of less than 70), what else is included in the definition of mental retardation?

9-2. There are four levels of mental retardation; mild, moderate, severe, and profound. Identify each of these levels from the descriptions given below:
(a) These persons have IQ scores below 20 and require total care.

(b) These persons have IQ scores between 50 and 70 and with some help may become self-supporting citizens.

(c) These persons have IQ scores between 35 and 50 and can be semi-independent in a sheltered environment.

(d) These persons have IQ scores between 20 and 35 and can help to contribute to their self-support under total supervision.

Answers: 9-1. They must show deficiencies in everyday living skills originating before age 18. 9-2. (a) profound (b) mild (c) moderate (d) severe.

10. Discuss the causes of mental retardation and programs for the retarded.

10-1. Although there are over 200 organic syndromes associated with retardation, including Downes syndrome, Phenylketonuria, and hydrocephalacy, organic causes only account for about _____ percent of retardation cases.

10-2. There are two general hypotheses as to the causes of the remaining 75 percent of retardation cases, most of which are diagnosed as mild. Identify these hypotheses from the descriptions given below.
(a) This hypothesis suggests that retardation is caused by a variety of unfavorable environmental variables.

(b) This hypothesis suggests that retardation results from subtle physiological effects that are difficult to detect.

10-3. In recent years treatment programs for the mentally retarded have been guided by the notion that retarded persons should be treated in the least restrictive and most normal environment possible. This notion is called the _____ *principle*. When this principle is applied to schools it is known as _____.

Answers: 10-1. 25 10-2. (a) environmental (b) biological 10-3. normalization, mainstreaming.

11. **Discuss the identification of gifted children, their personal characteristics, and programs for the gifted.**

11-1. Answer the following questions regarding gifted children.

(a) What is the range of minimum IQ scores necessary to be classified as gifted?

(b) What did Terman's long-term study of gifted children show with respect to the physical, social, and emotional development of these gifted children?

(c) What three factors must intersect and be present to an exceptional degree in order to produce the rarest form of giftedness according to Renzulli?

(d) What two educational interventions are sometimes available to gifted children?

Answers: 11-1. (a) 130 to 145 (b) They were above average in all three areas. (c) intelligence, motivation, creativity (in any order) (d) curriculum *enrichment* and grade *acceleration*.

HEREDITY AND ENVIRONMENT AS DETERMINANTS OF INTELLIGENCE

12. **Summarize evidence from twin studies and adoption studies on whether heredity affects intelligence and discuss the concept of heritability.**

12-1. Below are the median correlations for the intelligence of four different groups of children: siblings reared together, fraternal twins reared together, identical twins reared apart, and identical twins reared together. Match the group with the appropriate correlation.

.85 _____   .58 _____

.68 _____   .44 _____

12-2. What do the above correlations tell us about the role of heredity on intelligence?

12-3. What relationship has been found between the intelligence of children adopted out at birth and their biological parents?

12-4. What does it mean when it is said by some that the heritability ratio is 80% for human intelligence?

12-5. Why can you not use a heritability ratio to explain a particular individual's intelligence?

Answers: 12-1. (.85) identical twins reared together, (.68) identical twins reared apart, (.58) fraternal twins reared together, (.44) siblings reared together 12-2. That heredity plays a significant role in intelligence. 12-3. There is a significant correlation in intelligence. 12-4. The variation in intelligence in a particular group is estimated to be 80% due to heredity, leaving 20% for environmental factors. 12-5. It is a group statistic and may give misleading results when applied to particular individuals.

13. **Summarize evidence from research on adoption, environmental deprivation or enrichment, and home environment showing how experience shapes intelligence.**

13-1. Complete the statements below that list three findings from adoption studies indicating that environment influences intelligence.

(a) There is a positive correlational relationship between the intelligence of adopted children and their

_____.

(b) Siblings reared together are more alike than siblings _____.

(c) Unrelated children reared together show a significant positive relationship with respect to

_____.

13-2. What effects on intelligence have been found among children reared in deprived environments?

13-3. What effects on intelligence have been found among children moved from deprived environments to more enriched environments?

13-4. What relationship has been found between the intellectual quality of home environment and the intelligence of children?

Answers: 13-1. (a) foster parents (b) reared apart (c) their intelligence   13-2. There is a gradual decrease in intelligence across time.   13-3. There is a gradual increase in intelligence across time.   13-4. They are significantly correlated.

14. **Using the concept of reaction range, explain how heredity and the environment interact to affect intelligence.**

14-1. The notion behind the concept of reaction range is that heredity places an upper and lower

_____ on how much an individual can vary with respect to a characteristic such as

intelligence. The reaction range for human intelligence is said to be around _____

IQ points.

14-2. This means that a child with an average IQ of 100 can vary between 90 and 110 IQ points, depending

on the kind of _____ he or she experiences.

14-3. The major point here is that the limits for intelligence are determined by _____

factors, and the movement within these limits is determined by _____ factors.

Answers: 14-1. limit, 20-25   14-2. environment   14-3. genetic or hereditary, environmental.

15. **Discuss proposed explanations for observed cultural differences in IQ scores and describe the Featured Study on interracial adoption.**

   15-1. Three explanations for the cultural differences in IQ scores are listed below. Tell what each of these explanations means.
   (a) Jensen's heritability explanation.

   (b) Cultural disadvantage.

   (c) Cultural bias in IQ tests.

   15-2. Answer the following questions regarding Scarr and Weinberg's study of interracial adoption and IQ.
   (a) What were the average IQ scores of the black children adopted by the white families?

   (b) What is the estimated IQ scores for black children living in the Twin Cities area?

   (c) What general conclusion can be drawn from this study?

   Answers: 15-1. (a) The cultural differences are due to heredity. (b) The cultural differences are due to environmental factors. (c) IQ tests are biased in favor of persons from white middle-class backgrounds. **15-2.** (a) 106 to 110 (b) 90 (c) Black children living in economically advantaged homes did not display IQ deficits.

NEW DIRECTIONS IN THE ASSESSMENT AND STUDY OF INTELLIGENCE

16. **Describe three new trends in the assessment and study of intelligence.**

   16-1. Answer the following questions regarding new trends in the assessment and study of intelligence.
   (a) One trend is that two kinds of tests are replacing intelligence tests. What kinds of tests are these?

   (b) A second trend revolves around what is happening to the search for Spearman's *g*. What is going on here?

   (c) A third trend concerns the search for biological correlates of intelligence. Most work here seeks to find correlations between reaction time and IQ. What have been the results so far?

   Answers: 16-1. (a) achievement and aptitude tests (b) It is being replaced by the search for specific mental abilities. (c) The correlations are too low to be of any practical significance.

17. Describe Sternberg's and Gardner's theories of intelligence.

17-1. Sternberg's triarchic theory proposes that intelligence is composed of three basic parts. Match these parts with their individual functions:

_____ Contextual subtheory

_____ Experiential subtheory

_____ Componential subtheory

(a) Emphasizes the role played by society.
(b) Emphasizes the cognitive processes underlying intelligence.
(c) Emphasizes the interplay between intelligence and experience.

17-2. Sternberg also theorizes that the componential subtheory is composed of three divisions. Match these divisions with their appropriate function:

_____ Metacomponents

_____ Performance components

_____ Knowledge-acquisition components

(a) Involved in learning and storing information.
(b) The executive processes that govern approaches to problems.
(c) Carry out the instruction of the metacomponents.

17-3. Gardner has proposed seven relatively distinct human intelligences. What does his research show with respect to a *g* factor among these separate intelligences?

Answers: **17-1.** contextual (a), experiential (c), componential (b) **17-2.** metacomponents (b), performance components (c), knowledge-acquisition components (a) **17-3.** There does not appear to be a *g* factor; rather people display a mixture of intermediate abilities.

PUTTING IT IN PERSPECTIVE

18. Discuss how the chapter highlighted the idea that psychology evolves in a sociohistorical context and the idea that heredity and environment jointly influence behavior.

18-1. Below are four examples of the sociohistorical context of psychology and four examples of how psychologists study the joint influence of heredity and environment. Use SH to indicate sociohistorical context and HE to indicate heredity and environment interactions.

_____ (a) Twin studies

_____ (b) The increasing use of standardized testing

_____ (c) The Cyril Burt affair

_____ (d) Adoption studies

_____ (e) The concept of reaction range

_____ (f) Greater interest on how we use intelligence

_____ (g) Family environment studies

_____ (h) The greater emphasis on specific abilities

Answers: **18-1.** (a) HE (b) SH (c) SH (d) HE (e) HE (f) SH (g) HE (h) SH.

MEASURING AND UNDERSTANDING CREATIVITY

19. **Discuss popular ideas about the nature of creativity.**

    19-1.   Popular notions about creativity would have us believe that creative ideas arise from nowhere, occur in a burst of insight, are not related to hard work, and are unrelated to intelligence. What does the text say about these notions?

    Answers: 19-1. They are all false.

20. **Describe creativity tests and summarize how well they predict creative achievement.**

    20-1.   Most tests of creativity attempt to asses (<u>conventional/divergent</u>) thinking, such as: List as many uses as you can for a book. Creativity scores are based on the _____ of alternatives generated and the originality and _____ of the suggested alternatives.

    20-2.   Creativity tests are rather (<u>good/mediocre</u>) predictors of creativity in the real world. One reason for this is that they attempt to treat creativity as a (<u>specific/general</u>) trait, while research evidence seems to show it is related to quite _____ domains.

    Answers: **20-1.** divergent, number, usefulness (utility)   **20-2.** mediocre, general, specific.

21. **Discuss associations between creativity and personality, intelligence, and mental illness.**

    21-1.   What four personality characteristics are rather consistently found to be related to creativity?

    21-2.   What is the intelligence level of most highly creative people?

    21-3.   What form of mental illness appears to be associated with creative achievement?

    Answers: **21-1.** autonomy, independence, self-confidence, nonconformity   **21-2.** average to above average   **22-3.** mood disorders.

REVIEW OF KEY TERMS

Achievement tests
Aptitude tests
Construct validity
Content validity
Covergent thinking
Creativity
Criterion-related validity
Crystallized intelligence
Deviation IQ scores
Divergent thinking

Eugenics
Factor analysis
Fluid intelligence
Heritability ratio
Intelligence quotient (IQ)
Intelligence tests
Mental age
Mental retardation
Normal distribution

Percentile score
Personality tests
Psychological tests
Reaction range
Reliability
Standardization
Test norms
Test-retest reliability
Validity

_____ 1. A standardized measure of a sample of a person's behavior.

_____ 2. Tests that measure general mental ability.

_____ 3. Tests that measure various personality traits.

_____ 4. Tests that assess talent for specific kinds of learning.

_____ 5. Tests that gauge the mastery and knowledge of various subject areas.

_____ 6. The development of uniform procedures for administering and scoring tests, including the development of test norms.

_____ 7. Data that provides information about the relative standing of a particular test score.

_____ 8. Number indicating the percentage of people who score above or below a particular test score.

_____ 9. The measurement consistency of a test.

_____ 10. Estimated by comparing subjects' scores on two administrations of the same test.

_____ 11. The ability of a test to measure what it was designed to measure.

_____ 12. The degree to which the content of a test is representative of the domain it is supposed to measure.

_____ 13. The degree to which the scores on a particular test correlate with scores on an independent criterion (test).

_____ 14. The degree to which there is evidence that a test measures a hypothetical construct.

_____ 15. The idea of controlling reproduction so as to gradually improve hereditary characteristics in a population.

_____ 16. A score indicating the mental ability typical of a chronological age group.

_____ 17. Mental age divided by chronological age and multiplied by 100.

_____ 18. A symmetrical, bell-shaped curve that describes the distribution of many physical and psychological attributes.

_____ 19. Scores that translate raw scores into a precise location in the normal distribution.

_____ 20. Subnormal general mental ability accompanied by deficiencies in everyday living skills originating prior to age 18.

_____ 21. An estimate of the percentage of variation in a trait determined by genetic inheritance.

_____ 22. Genetically determined limits on intelligence.

_____ 23. Method that uses the correlation among many variables to identify closely related clusters.

_____ 24. The ability to apply acquired knowledge and skills to problem solving.

_____ 25. Includes reasoning ability, memory capacity, and speed of information processing.

_____ 26. The generation of ideas that are original, novel, and useful.

_____ 27. Thinking that attempts to narrow down a list of alternatives to a single best solution.

_____ 28. Thinking that attempts to expand the range of alternatives by generating many possible solutions.

Answers: 1. psychological tests 2. intelligence tests 3. personality tests 4. aptitude tests 5. achievement tests 6. standardization 7. test norms 8. percentile score 9. reliability 10. test-retest reliability 11. validity 12. content validity 13. criterion-related validity 14. construct validity 15. eugenics 16. mental age 17. intelligence quotient (IQ) 18. normal distribution 19. deviation IQ scores 20. mental retardation 21. heritability ratio 22. reaction range 23. factor analysis 24. crystallized intelligence 25. fluid intelligence 26. creativity 27. convergent thinking 28. divergent thinking.

REVIEW OF KEY PEOPLE

Alfred Binet   Arthur Jensen   Lewis Terman
Sir Cyril Burt   Sandra Scarr   David Wechsler
Sir Francis Galton   Robert Sternberg

_____ 1. Developed the Stanford-Binet Intelligence Scale.

_____ 2. Developed the first successful test of adult intelligence.

_____ 3. Postulated a cognitive triarchic theory of intelligence.

_____ 4. Used nonexistent data to support the view that intelligence is primarily inherited.

_____ 5. Proposed a reaction range model for human intelligence.

_____ 6. Developed the first useful intelligence test.

_____ 7. Postulated a heritability explanation for cultural differences in intelligence.

_____ 8. Began the quest to measure intelligence.

Answers: 1. Terman 2. Wechsler 3. Sternberg 4. Burt 5. Scarr 6. Binet 7. Jensen 8. Galton.

SELF-QUIZ

1. This self-test you are now taking is an example of:
   a. an aptitude test
   b. an achievement test
   c. an intelligence test
   d. a criterion-related test

2. Which of the following statistics is generally used to estimate reliability and validity?
   a. the correlation coefficient
   b. the standard deviation
   c. the percentile score
   d. the median

3. What kind of validity do tests such as the SAT and ACT particularly strive for?
   a. content validity
   b. construct validity
   c. absolute validity
   d. criterion-related validity

4. Spearman's g infers that:
   a. most kinds of intelligence are highly related.
   b. most kinds of intelligence are not highly related.
   c. intelligence is highly correlated with personality characteristics.
   d. intelligence is primarily inherited.

5. With respect to modern intelligence tests:
   a. reliability is generally higher than validity.
   b. validity is generally higher than reliability.
   c. reliability and validity are about the same.
   d. I have no idea what you are talking about.

6. If the heritability ratio for intelligence is 80%, this means that for you as an individual 80% of your intelligence is determined by heredity and 20% is determined by your environment. This statement is:
   a. true
   b. false

7. Perhaps the strongest evidence for a heredity factor for intelligence comes from studies of:
   a. unrelated children reared together.
   b. deprived home environments.
   c. enriched home environments.
   d. none of the above.

8. If the reaction range concept of human intelligence is correct, then a child with exactly normal intelligence will probably not exceed an IQ of:
   a. 100
   b. 110
   c. 120
   d. 130

9. Which of the following retarded groups can often pass for normal as adults?
   a. mild
   b. moderate
   c. profound
   d. both a and b

10. What percentage of mental retardation cases have been definitely linked to organic causes?
    a. approximately 25%
    b. approximately 50%
    c. approximately 75%
    d. approximately 90%

11. Terman's long-term study of gifted children found that they tended to excel in:
    a. physical development
    b. social development
    c. emotional development
    d. all of the above

12. Which of the following groups shows the highest correlation with respect to intelligence?
    a. fraternal twins reared together
    b. fraternal twins reared apart
    c. identical twins reared apart
    d. both a and c

13. The search for biological correlates of intelligence are beginning to prove quite fruitful. This statement is:
    a. true
    b. false

14. What is the role of metacomponents in Sternberg's triarchic theory of intelligence?
    a. learning and storing information
    b. carrying out instructions
    c. giving instructions
    d. all of the above

15. What form of mental illness has been frequently found to be associated with outstanding creative ability?
    a. anxiety disorders
    b. mood disorders
    c. schizophrenia
    d. antisocial personality

16. Most tests of creativity emphasize:
    a. convergent thinking
    b. divergent thinking
    c. both of the above
    d. none of the above

Answers: 1. b 2. a 3. d 4. a 5. a 6. b 7. d 8. b 9. a 10. a 11. d 12. c 13. b 14. c 15. b 16. b.

CHAPTER NINE

10 MOTIVATION AND EMOTION

REVIEW OF KEY IDEAS

MOTIVATIONAL THEORIES AND CONCEPTS

1. **Compare and contrast the instinct, sociobiology, drive, and incentive theoretical perspectives on motivation.**

   1-1. Review the sections on the four motivational theories. Then check your understanding by placing the name of the appropriate theory (instinct, sociobiology, drive, or incentive) in the blanks below.

   _____ Cannot easily account for behavior which *increases* tension.

   _____ Unlearned, uniform in expression, universal within the species.

   _____ Motivation to pursue a goal or object depends on the *value* of the object and one's *expectancy* of success at obtaining it.

   _____ Emphasizes evolution and species survival value more than the other theories.

   _____ Emphasizes homeostasis, the pressure to return to a state of equilibrium.

   _____ Emphasizes environmental factors in motivation.

   _____ Actions result from attempts to reduce internal states of tension.

   _____ Has proposed a genetic basis for human sex role differences.

   _____ Emphasizes "pull" from the environment (as opposed to "push" from internal states).

   Answers: 1-1. drive, instinct, incentive, sociobiology, drive, incentive, drive, sociobiology, incentive.

2. **Distinguish between biological and social needs and describe the hierarchy of needs proposed by Maslow.**

   2-1. Most theories distinguish between _____ needs, such as hunger and thirst, and

   _____ needs, which are acquired through _____ or the process

   of socialization. Most biological needs have evolutionary significance and are required for the

   _____ of the group or individual.

2-2. While there are relatively few _____ needs, an individual may theoretically acquire an unlimited number of _____ needs.

2-3. Are such motives as aggression and nurturance social needs or biological needs? Explain.

2-4. Write the names of Maslow's hierarchical levels of needs in the blanks at the right of the pyramid. Start with (a) at the lowest level.

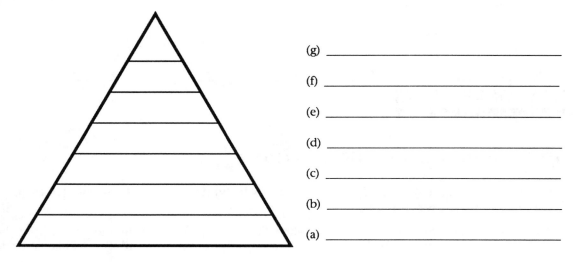

(g) _____

(f) _____

(e) _____

(d) _____

(c) _____

(b) _____

(a) _____

2-5. When, or in what circumstance, does a higher level of need become activated?

2-6. How do needs toward the top of the pyramid differ from those near the bottom?

2-7. Maslow asserted that our highest growth need is our need for self-actualization. What is the need for self-actualization?

Answers: 2-1. biological, social, learning, survival 2-2. biological, social 2-3. Theorists disagree, and these motives have been classified in both categories. The distinction between biological and social needs is a useful one but not always clear-cut. 2-4. (a) physiological needs (b) safety and security needs (c) love and belongingness needs (d) esteem needs (e) cognitive needs (f) aesthetic needs (g) need for self-actualization 2-5. A higher level is activated only when a lower level is satisfied. For example, needs for achievement and recognition are generally activated only after needs for love and belongingness are satisfied. 2-6. The closer a need is to the top of the pyramid, the more it is socially based; the closer to the bottom, the more it is biologically based. 2-7. the need to express one's full potential (i.e., to "be all that you can be," although Maslow didn't have in mind joining the Army).

THE MOTIVATION OF HUNGER AND EATING

3. Summarize evidence on the role of biological factors in the regulation of hunger.

3-1. (Because it is often difficult to recall biological terminology, you may want to review the section on biological factors before proceeding.) Three major biological factors are involved in hunger regulation: the brain, blood _____, and _____. Within the brain the major structure implicated has been the _____.

3-2. The two areas of the hypothalamus associated with hunger level are the _____ hypothalamus (LH) and the _____ nucleus of the hypothalamus (VMH).

3-3. Different things happen when these areas are electrically stimulated as opposed to when they are destroyed or lesioned. For example, when the lateral hypothalamus is electrically stimulated, animals will tend to (start /stop) eating. When the LH is lesioned, however, the animals will (start /stop) eating.

3-4. Summarize the effects of stimulation and lesioning of the hypothalamus by writing either "start eating" or "stop eating" in the blanks at the right.

Lateral, electrical stimulation _____

Lateral, lesioning _____

Ventromedial nucleus, electrical stimulation _____

Ventromedial nucleus, lesioning _____

3-5. Of course, food intake has an effect on body size and weight. Starvation is likely to be the result for rats with a lesioned _____ hypothalamus, while obesity is the result for rats that have their _____ hypothalamus destroyed.

3-6. While the LH and VMH are implicated in hunger, they are no longer considered to be simple on-off switches. Other factors that have strong effects on hunger and food intake are blood _____ and _____.

3-7. Much of the food we consume is converted into _____, a simple sugar that is an important source of energy. Manipulations that lower glucose tend to _____ hunger; raising glucose levels generally decreases hunger. Based on this evidence, Mayer proposed that neurons in the _____ called _____ monitor glucose levels and contribute to the experience of hunger. More recent research has suggested that rather than being in the brain, glucose-sensitive neurons may be in the _____ and may communicate to the brain through the vagus nerve.

3-8. For cells to extract glucose from the blood, the hormone insulin must be present. Injections of insulin (in nondiabetics) will produce a(n) _____ in the level of sugar in the blood, with the result that the person experiences a(n) _____ in the sensation of hunger. In addition to insulin, some investigators have suggested that another hormone, abbreviated CCK, is related to (increasing/decreasing) the experience of hunger.

Answers: 3-1. sugar (glucose), hormones, hypothalamus 3-2. lateral, ventromedial 3-3. start, stop 3-4. start eating, stop eating, stop eating, start eating 3-5. lateral, ventromedial 3-6. glucose (sugar), hormones 3-7. glucose, increase, brain, glucostats, liver 3-8. decrease, increase, decreasing.

4. **Summarize evidence on the role of environmental factors in the regulation of hunger.**

4-1. Although we have some innate taste preferences, it is also clear that _____ affects some of our food choices and even influences the amounts that we eat.

4-2. In one study an artificial sweetener was substituted in people's diets without their knowledge. If only physiological mechanisms regulated eating behavior, we would expect increased eating to compensate for the caloric loss, yet most subjects (did/did not) increase food consumption. Thus, learning seems to influence both our taste preferences and the _____ we consume.

4-3. Some people may experience hunger or begin to eat as a function of simply looking at the clock; the clock says, in effect, "Time to eat," and they begin eating. Thus, food-related _____ in our environment, such as the taste of food, the availability or sight of food, and the _____ of day, may influence food consumption.

4-4. Besides affecting eating habits and providing cues to eating, the environment may also provide unpleasant or frustrating events that produce emotional _____, a factor that may also trigger eating in many people. Although stress and increased eating are linked, recent evidence suggests that an important factor may be heightened physiological _____ produced by stress rather than the stress itself.

Answers: 4-1. learning (the environment) 4-2. did not, amounts 4-3. cues, time 4-4. stress, arousal.

5. **Discuss the contribution of food-related cues, genetic predisposition, and set point to obesity.**

5-1. Have you ever smelled fresh apple pie (or some other tempting odor) only to suddenly realize that you were hungry? If so, you, like most of us, have experienced the power of external cues. Describe Schachter's theory about the differences between obese and nonobese people's sensitivity to external cues.

5-2. Judith Rodin, one of Schachter's students, found that people sensitive to external food cues tend to secrete insulin, which may reduce blood _____ and increase _____. What does Rodin's research suggest about the theory that eating in some people is caused by *external* cues?

5-3. What has Rodin concluded about the link between sensitivity to external cues and obesity?

5-4. It is by now clear that many more factors besides responsivity to external cues are responsible for body weight regulation. In fact, a strong genetic factor has been implicated in weight. In the space below summarize the results of Stunkard et al.'s (1986) important study on the relationship between children's weight and the weights of their biological and their adoptive parents.

5-5. Basal or resting metabolism accounts for about two-thirds of an individual's energy output. What has research found with regard to differences between obese and non-obese in metabolic rates?

5-6. The concept of set point may help explain why body weight remains so stable. The theory proposes that each individual has a "natural" body weight determined in large part by the *number* of

_____ _____ that an individual happens to have. Although

the number of fat cells in the body may increase through persistent overeating, the number is usually

(very stable/highly variable) throughout one's lifetime.

5-7. The larger the (number/size) of fat cells, the higher the set point. When a person diets, fat cells decrease

in _____ but not in _____.

5-8. Dieting or weight gain produces a change in the _____ of the fat cells but not, in

most cases, the _____ of fat cells. Thus, maintenance of body weight below one's

"natural" weight, or _____ _____, is difficult, as is mainte-

nance above one's set point.

Answers: 5-1. Schachter thought that obese people are especially sensitive to external cues (such as the taste, sight, and smell of food) and not very sensitive to internal, physiological cues of hunger. Thus, while normal-weight people eat as a function of internal cues, the obese, Schachter thought, eat when exposed to external cues.   5-2. glucose (sugar), hunger. Since insulin produces an internal signal, it is difficult to argue that the eating occurs simply because of external cues.   5-3. Rodin asserts that the link between obesity and sensitivity to external cues is weaker than Schachter had proposed. Rodin has found that many obese people are not especially responsive to external cues and that many thin or normal-weight people are responsive to such cues.   5-4. These investigators found that in terms of body weight adopted children resemble their biological parents more than they resemble their adoptive parents. 5-5. No differences have been found.   5-6. fat cells, very stable   5-7. number, size, number   5-8. size, number, set point.

SEXUAL MOTIVATION AND BEHAVIOR

6. Describe the impact of hormones and pheromones in regulating animal and human sexual behavior.

6-1. Hormones are clearly linked to sexual behavior in lower animals. With regard to human sexual behavior, however, the effect of hormones is considerably (greater/less) than is the case with lower animals.

6-2. The principal class of female hormones are called _____. The principal class of males sex

hormones are termed _____.

6-3. Although the relationship is relatively weak, some studies have found an association between testosterone, a key androgen, and sexual activity among human (<u>males/females/both</u>). The presence of estrogen in human beings (<u>has/has not</u>) been found to be correlated with sexual activity.

6-4. What is a pheromone?

6-5. Is there any evidence that pheromones affect *sex drive* in human beings and other higher primates? What aspects of human behavior do pheromones seem to affect? Describe the study involving sweat and menstrual synchronization.

Answers: 6-1. less 6-2. estrogens, androgens, both sexes 6-3. testosterone, is not 6-4. A pheromone is a chemical secreted by one animal that affects the behavior of other animals. 6-5. There is no evidence that pheromones affect the human sex drive. There is evidence that pheromones affect the menstrual cycles, however: Women who live together tend to have synchronized ovulatory cycles. One study found that a solution of alcohol and sweat taken from some women tended to produce synchronized cycles when rubbed on the lips of other women.

7. Discuss the role of attraction to a partner in animal and human sexual behavior.

7-1. Sexual interest in a potential partner may be affected by (a) the so-called _____

effect, which refers to the preference for a variety of sexual partners; (b) the tendency for many animal

species to be _____ of partners on the basis of the physical (and other)

_____ of a potential partner; and (c) the subtle or not so subtle expression of sexual

interest, or sexual _____, from a potential partner.

7-2. While there are wide individual differences among both males and females, men appear to be more motivated by the desire for (<u>physical/emotional</u>) gratification in sexual relations and women by (<u>physical/emotional</u>) gratification.

7-3. What are thought to be the causes of the gender differences in motives for sexual behavior referred to above?
a. They involve primarily socialization or learning.
b. They involve primarily biological factors.
c. The causes are unknown; some theorists interpret the differences in terms of biology and others in terms of environment.

Answers: 7-1. (a) Coolidge (b) selective, characteristics (c) overtures 7-2. physical, emotional 7-3. c.

8. Summarize the evidence on the impact of erotic materials on human sexual behavior.

8-1. Discuss research findings on the reaction of men and of women to erotic materials in terms of:
(a) reported dislike of the material.

(b) physiological responses.

(c) sexual activity.

8-2. In the Zillman and Bryant studies described, male and female undergraduate subjects were exposed to relatively heavy doses of pornography over a period of weeks. What effect did this have on:
(a) attitudes about sexual practices.

(b) satisfaction with their sexual partners.

8-3. *Aggressive* pornography usually depicts violence against women.
(a) What laboratory evidence indicates that viewing aggressive pornography affects aggression against women?

(b) What is the effect of viewing aggressive pornography on attitudes toward rape?

Answers: 8-1. (a) Women are more likely than men to report disliking erotic materials. (b) Women and men appear to be equally physiologically responsive to erotic materials. (c). For a few hours immediately after exposure, the likelihood of sexual activity occurring is somewhat increased. 8-2. (a) Attitudes about sexual practices became more liberal; for example, both males and females came to view premarital and extramarital sex as more acceptable. (b) Subjects became less satisfied with their partners in terms of physical appearance and sexual performance. 8-3. (a) Some studies have found that pornography depicting violence against women increases male subjects' aggressive behavior toward women. In these laboratory studies, aggression is defined as willingness to deliver electric shock to other subjects. (b) Exposure to aggressive pornography appears to make sexual coercion or rape seem less offensive.

9. **Explain how personality and age influence individual differences in sex drive.**

9-1.   (a) How are individual differences in personality characteristics related to sex drive?

(b) How does age affect sex drive?

Answers: 9-1. (a) Extraverts tend to be more sexually active than introverts; people who experience a lot of guilt about sexual urges tend to be less sexually active than those who do not. (b) Sexual activity tends to decline from middle age on, although the decreases are not as great as younger people assume.

10. **Outline the four phases of the human sexual response.**

10-1.   Write the names of the four phases of the human sexual response in the order in which they occur. (Hint: I just made up a mnemonic device that's hard to forget. The first letter of each phase name produces EPOR, which happens to be ROPE spelled backwards.)

_____   _____

_____   _____

10-2.   In the blanks below write the first letter of each phase name that correctly labels the descriptions below.

_____ Rapid increase in arousal (respiration, heart rate, blood pressure, etc.).

_____ Vasocongestion of blood vessels in sexual organs; lubrication in female.

_____ Continued arousal but at a slower place.

_____ Tightening of the vaginal entrance.

_____ Pulsating muscular contractions and ejaculation.

_____ Subsidence of physiological changes produced by arousal.

_____ Includes a refractory period for men.

Answers: 10-1. (a) excitement (b) plateau (c) orgasm (d) resolution   10-2. E, E, P, P, O, R, R.

AFFILIATION: IN SEARCH OF BELONGINGNESS

11. **Describe the affiliation motive and the need for intimacy.**

11-1.   Most human beings seek the company of others, a need referred to as the _____

motive.

11-2.   Bowlby, among others, has asserted that the need to affiliate is largely (innate/acquired). Most theorists, however, believe that the need for affiliation is primarily a (social/biological) need.

Answers: 11-1. affiliation   11-2. innate, social.

12. **Discuss how individual differences in the need for affiliation influence affiliation behavior.**

12-1. Need for affiliation may be measured by a test known as the Thematic Apperception Test, or

_____ for short. This test involves asking subjects to write or tell

_____ in response to pictures of people in various scenes.

12-2. Certain *themes* emerge from the TAT stories that may be scored to show the strengths of various needs or motives. How do people who score high on need for affiliation differ from those who score low?

12-3. People seem not only to want interaction with others but to want a particular kind of interaction

marked by warm, personal, and open communication. This type of affiliative need is referred to as the

_____ motive and is scored separately from the affiliation motive. People whom

others describe as warm and who tend to be self-disclosing are more likely to score (high/low) on the

intimacy scale, while those characterized as self-centered and domineering tend to score (high/low).

Answers: 12-1. TAT, stories   12-2. They tend to show affiliative behaviors—like joining groups or visiting with friends or worrying about being accepted by others   12-3. intimacy, high, low.

ACHIEVEMENT: IN SEARCH OF EXCELLENCE

13. **Discuss how individual differences in the need for achievement influence achievement behavior.**

13-1. What procedure is used to measure individual subjects' need for achievement?

13-2. High scores on tests of achievement motivation are correlated with particular traits or behaviors. List a few of these in the space below.

Answers: 13-1. The procedure is the same as that used for the affiliation and intimacy motives. Subjects tell stories about TAT pictures, which are then scored in terms of need for achievement.   **13-2.** Hard work, persistence, willingness to delay gratification, preference for competitive occupations, etc.

14. **Explain how situational factors and fear of failure affect achievement strivings.**

14-1. According to Atkinson's elaboration of McClelland's views, achievement-oriented behavior is deter-

mined not only by achievement motivation but by the _____

_____ of success and the _____ that success will occur.

14-2. As the difficulty of a task increases, the _____ of success at the task decreases and the _____ value of the task increases. Thus, when both the incentive value and probability of success are weighed together, people with a high need for achievement would tend to select tasks of (<u>extreme/moderate</u>) difficulty.

14-3. In addition to including success in the equation, Atkinson indicates that fear of failure must be factored in. Thus, pursuit of achievement is affected by these six variables: need for _____ and fear of _____; perceived probability of _____ and perceived probability of _____; and the _____ values of both success and of failure.

14-4. The motivation to avoid failure may either stimulate achievement or inhibit achievement. Explain.

Answers: 14-1. incentive value, probability   14-2. probability, incentive, moderate   14-3. achievement, failure; success, failure; incentive   14-4. One may achieve to avoid failure in a particular area; thus, fear of failure may lead to achievement. On the other hand, one could also avoid failure by not pursuing a particular goal; thus, fear of failure could lead to lack of achievement.

THE ELEMENTS OF EMOTIONAL EXPERIENCE

15. List and describe the three components of emotion.

15-1. The word *cognition* refers to thoughts, beliefs, or conscious experience. When faced with a large spider (or having to make a speech in public) you might say to yourself, "I'm terrified." That's cognition, and your evaluative reaction is clearly (<u>subjective/objective</u>). Thus, one component of emotion is the _____ component, which consists of your _____ feelings.

15-2. The second component of emotion is the bodily reaction or _____ component, which includes primarily actions of the _____ nervous system. Your encounter with a spider might be accompanied by changes in heart rate, breathing, or blood pressure or by increased electrical conductivity of the skin known as the _____ skin response (GSR).

15-3. Confronted by an enormous spider you may scream or jump. These *actions* represent the _____ component of emotions. We communicate our emotions not only verbally but through _____ behavior, much of which is shown in facial expressions.

15-4. Lie detectors don't actually detect lies, they detect bodily changes that reflect the _____ component of emotion. Research has found that lie detectors are inaccurate about _____ of the time.

CHAPTER TEN

15-5.   What evidence is there that the facial expressions that accompany different emotions are largely innate?

THEORIES OF EMOTION

16.   **Compare and contrast the James-Lange and Cannon-Bard theories of emotion and explain how Schachter reconciled these conflicting views in his two-factor theory.**

16-1.   For each of the following statements indicate the theory described.

(a) The subjective experience of emotion is caused by different patterns of autonomic arousal.

_____

(b) General autonomic arousal causes one to look for an explanation or label; thus, the subjective

experience of emotion is caused both by arousal and by cognition. _____

(c) Emotions originate in subcortical brain structures. _____

(d) Ralph observes that his heart pounds whenever Mary is around, so he figures he must be in love.

_____

16-2.   In what sense does Schachter's theory reconcile the James-Lange and Cannon-Bard theories?

17.   **Summarize the procedure, results, and implications of the Featured Study (Schachter & Singer, 1962) on emotions as labels for arousal.**

17-1.   How did the study attempt to manipulate arousal independently of cognitions?

17-2. How did the study attempt to manipulate cognitions
(a) in terms of the subjects' immediate environment?

(b) in terms of instructions to subjects?

17-3. What were the results and conclusions? In what respect were the results somewhat weak?

Answers: 17-1. Some subjects were injected with adrenaline (which causes general autonomic arousal) and some with a placebo. 17-2. (a) Subjects waited with an accomplice of the experimenter who acted in a euphoric manner for some subjects and angrily for others. (b) Some subjects were correctly informed about the effects of adrenaline and others were misinformed (told to expect no effects or told incorrect side effects). 17-3. The misinformed groups tended to be more euphoric (or more angry) than the correctly informed group; thus, cognition clearly has an important role in emotion. The problem with the study is that in the majority of the comparisons no significant differences were found between the placebo and misinformed adrenaline conditions. If arousal is so important for emotion, why would the placebo group be about as emotional as the specifically aroused (adrenaline) group?

18. Summarize the evolutionary perspective on emotion.

18-1. What good does it do to get angry? Perhaps this emotion is of less use in our modern world, but from

an evolutionary perspective anger might well have some _____ value in preparing

an organism for aggression and defense.

18-2. Evolutionary theorists view emotions primarily as (innate/learned) reactions that have been passed on because of their survival value. They also believe that emotions originate in subcortical areas, parts of the brain that evolved before the cortical structures associated with higher mental processes. In the view of the evolutionary theorists, then, emotion is largely (dependent on/ independent of) thinking.

18-3. How many basic, inherited emotions are there? The evolutionary writers assume that the wide range of

emotions we experience are blends or different levels of about _____ innate or

prewired primary emotions.

Answers: 18-1. survival (adaptive) 18-2. innate, independent of 18-3. eight to ten.

PUTTING IT IN PERSPECTIVE

19. **Explain how this chapter highlights three of our organizing themes: (a) psychology's theoretical diversity, (b) the joint influence of heredity and environment, and (c) the multiple causes of behavior.**

   19-1. Indicate which of the text's themes fit the following examples by writing the appropriate initials in the blanks: TD for theoretical diversity, HE for heredity and environment, and MC for multiple causation.

   (a) Achievement behavior is affected by achievement motivation, the likelihood of success, the likelihood of failure, and so on. _____

   (b) Some psychologists believe that learning habits are a major factor in obesity; others emphasize set point. _____

   (c) Body weight seems to be influenced by set point, blood glucose, and inherited metabolism. It is also affected by eating habits and acquired tastes. _____ and _____

   (d) Schachter and Singer viewed emotion as a combination of physiological arousal and cognition; the evolutionary theorists believe that emotions are innate. _____

   Answers: 19-1. (a) MC (b) TD (c) HE, MC (d) TD.

APPLICATION: UNDERSTANDING HUMAN SEXUALITY

20. **Summarize information provided on key factors in rewarding sexual relationships.**

   20-1. Each of the following statements is based on one of the five key factors that promotes rewarding sexual relationships. Indicate whether the statements are true or false.

   _____ A college text or course is usually an excellent source of information on human sexuality.

   _____ Many sexual problems are derived from guilt associated with a value system that views sex as immoral or depraved.

   _____ Talking about what one likes, asking questions, and in general communicating about sex with one's partner is important in a sexual relationship.

   _____ It is normal for individuals to fantasize about imaginary or former lovers during sexual encounters.

   _____ It is normal for couples to disagree about how frequently to have sex.

   Answers: 20-1. true, true, true, true, true.

21. **Describe some common sexual dysfunctions and summarize advice provided on coping with these problems.**

   21-1. Fill in the following information regarding erectile difficulties.
   (a) Older, pejorative name:

   (b) Most common cause:

   (c) Estimated proportion of cases involving organic causes:

   (d) Possible treatment:

21-2. Fill in the following information regarding premature ejaculation.
(a) Possible cause:

(b) Possible treatments:

21-3. Fill in the following information regarding orgasmic difficulties.
(a) Older, pejorative name for orgasmic difficulties in women:

(b) Possible causes:

(c) Possible treatments:

Answers: 21-1. (a) impotence (b) anxiety, especially connected with sexual performance (c) one-quarter (d) sensate focus (verbally guided pleasuring with gradual removal of performance prohibitions) 21-2. (a) early sexual experience that emphasized rapid climax (b) slowing down the tempo of intercourse; sensate focus exercises that enhance ejaculatory self-control 21-3. (a) frigidity (in women) (b) guilt, negative attitudes about sex, anxiety about achieving orgasm, etc. (c) restructuring of values, sensate focus.

REVIEW OF TERMS

Achievement motive
Affiliation motive
Androgens
Aphrodisiac
Basal metabolic rate
Drive
Emotion
Erectile difficulties
Estrogens
Galvanic skin response (GSR)
Glucose

Glucostats
Hierarchy of needs
Homeostasis
Incentive
Insulin
Intimacy motive
Lie detector
Motivation
Need for self-actualization
Orgasm
Orgasmic difficulties

Pheromone
Polygraph
Premature ejaculation
Refractory period
Sensate focus
Set point
Sex therapy
Sexual dysfunction
Sociobiology
Vasocongestion

_____ 1. Goal-directed behavior that may be affected by needs, wants, interests, desires, and incentives.

_____ 2. A general theory of motivation that emphasizes evolution and the survival value of social motives.

_____ 3. A state of physiological equilibrium or balance.

_____ 4. An internal state of tension that motivates the organism to reduce the tension and return to homeostasis.

_____ 5. An external goal that motivates behavior.

_____ 6. A systematic arrangement of needs according to priority.

_____ 7. The need to fulfill one's potential.

_____ 8. Blood sugar.

_____ 9. Neurons that are sensitive to glucose.

_____ 10. A hormone secreted by the pancreas needed for extracting glucose from the blood.

_____ 11. The body's rate of energy output at rest.

_____ 12. The theoretical natural point of stability in body weight.

_____ 13. The principal class of female sex hormones.

_____ 14. The principal class of male sex hormones.

_____ 15. A chemical secreted by one animal that affects the behavior of another animal.

_____ 16. Substance purported to increase sexual desire.

_____ 17. Engorgement of the blood vessels.

_____ 18. Sexual climax.

_____ 19. A time following orgasm during which males are unresponsive to sexual stimulation.

_____ 20. The motive to associate with others.

_____ 21. The need to have warm, close exchanges with others marked by open communication.

_____ 22. The need to master difficult challenges and to excel in competition with others.

_____ 23. An increase in the electrical conductivity of the skin related to an increase in sweat gland activity.

_____ 24. A reaction that includes cognitive, physiological, and behavioral components.

_____ 25. The technical name for the "lie detector."

_____ 26. The informal name for polygraph, an apparatus that monitors physiological aspects of arousal (e.g., heart rate, GSR).

_____ 27. An impairment in sexual functioning that causes subjective distress.

_____ 28. Persistent inability to achieve or maintain an erection adequate for sexual intercourse.

_____ 29. Climax in men occurring too quickly.

_____ 30. Difficulty in achieving orgasm.

_____ 31. Professional treatment of sexual dysfunctions.

_____ 32. A sexual exercise involving pleasurable touching, verbal feedback, and performance restrictions.

Answers: 1. motivation 2. sociobiology 3. homeostasi 4. drive 5. incentive 6. hierarchy of needs 7. need for self-actualization 8. glucose 9. glucostats 10. insulin 11. basal metabolic rate 12. set point 13. estrogens 14. androgens 15. pheromone 16. aphrodisiac 17. vasocongestion 18. orgasm 19. refractory period 20. affiliation motive 21. intimacy motive 22. achievement motive 23. galvanic skin response (GSR) 24. emotion 25. polygraph 26. lie detector 27. sexual dysfunction 28. erectile difficulties 29. premature ejaculation 30. orgasmic difficulties 31. sex therapy 32. sensate focus.

REVIEW OF KEY PEOPLE

John Atkinson
Walter Cannon
Paul Ekman
William James

Abraham Maslow
William Masters & Virginia Johnson
David McClelland

Henry Murray
Judith Rodin
Stanley Schachter

_____ 1. Proposed that emotions arise in subcortical areas of the brain.

_____ 2. Compiled an influential catalogue of common social needs; also devised the TAT.

_____ 3. Proposed a hierarchy of needs; stressed the need for self-actualization.

_____ 4. Proposed that eating on the part of obese people is controlled by external cues; devised the two-factor theory of emotion.

_____ 5. Found that external cues may elicit insulin secretions and that the obese are not especially sensitive to external cues.

_____ 6. Did the ground-breaking work on the physiology of the human sexual response.

_____ 7. Is responsible for most of the early research on achievement motivation.

_____ 8. Emphasized additional factors in an elaboration of McClelland's theory of achievement motivation .

_____ 9. In a series of cross-cultural studies found that people can identify about seven basic emotions from facial expressions.

_____ 10. Thought emotion arose from the perception of one's autonomic arousal.

Answers: 1. Cannon 2. Murray 3. Maslow 4. Schachter 5. Rodin 6. Masters & Johnson 7. McClelland 8. Atkinson 9. Ekman 10. James.

SELF-QUIZ

1. Which of the following is unlearned, uniform in expression, and universal within a particular species?
   a. incentive
   b. drive
   c. instinct
   d. motivation

2. In Maslow's hierarchy of needs, which of the following needs would have to be satisfied before the need for self-actualization became activated?
   a. physiological needs
   b. safety and security needs
   c. esteem needs
   d. all of the above

3. What happens when a rat's lateral hypothalamus is lesioned?
   a. It starts eating.
   b. It looks for a sexual partner.
   c. It stops eating.
   d. It loses bladder and bowel control.

4. What is the effect of insulin on blood glucose?
   a. Glucose level increases.
   b. Glucose level decreases.
   c. Glucose changes to free fatty acids.
   d. CCK increases.

5. Which of the following is thought to be a major determinant of set point?
   a. number of fat cells
   b. size of fat cells
   c. amount of exercise
   d. skill at tennis

6. Estrogens are found in:
   a. males
   b. females
   c. both males and females
   d. androids

7. For which of the following groups are the gonadal hormones, the estrogens and androgens, the major factor in sexual motivation and activity?
   a. many lower animals
   b. human males
   c. human females
   d. all of the above

8. A chemical secreted by one animal that affects the behavior of another animal is known as a(n):
   a. androgen
   b. affiliatrogen
   c. hormone
   d. pheromone

9. What is the name of the sexual phase during which orgasm occurs?
   a. excitement
   b. plateau
   c. orgasm
   d. resolution

10. Which of the following tend to be more sexually active?
    a. extraverts
    b. introverts
    c. erotophobes
    d. glucostats

11. What test is generally used to measure need for achievement?
    a. the TAT
    b. the GSR
    c. the Rorschach
    d. the MMPI

12. Evidence regarding facial expression in different cultures and observation of the blind suggest that:
    a. Schachter's two-factor theory is correct.
    b. facial expression of emotion is to a large extent innate.
    c. emotions originate in the cortex.
    d. learning is the major factor in explaining basic facial expressions.

13. According to Schachter's theory of emotion:
    a. Different emotions are represented by different autonomic reactions.
    b. Emotions originate in subcortical brain structures.
    c. Fear produces a desire to avoid affiliation.
    d. Both arousal and cognition are needed to produce emotion.

14. Whether or not achievement behavior will occur depends on one's need for achievement, fear of failure, and the probabilities and incentive values of success and failure on a specific task. Whose theory does this statement represent?
    a. McClelland
    b. Atkinson
    c. Cannon
    d. James

15. Which of the following is true?
    a. Fantasizing during sexual encounters is generally evidence of repressed conflicts.
    b. Talking rather than acting diminishes sexual satisfaction.
    c. Premature ejaculation is usually caused by unconscious hostility.
    d. Orgasmic difficulties often derive from negative attitudes about sex.

Answers: 1. c 2. d 3. c 4. b 5. a 6. c 7. c 8. d 9. c 10. a 11. a 12. b 13. d 14. b 15. d.

11 HUMAN DEVELOPMENT ACROSS THE LIFE SPAN

REVIEW OF KEY IDEAS

PROGRESS BEFORE BIRTH: PRENATAL DEVELOPMENT

1. **Outline the major events of the three phases of prenatal development.**

1-1. Each box below represents one month in the typical pregnancy; each short line on top represents one week. Indicate the beginning and end of each phase of prenatal development by placing the appropriate letters from the diagram in the blanks below.

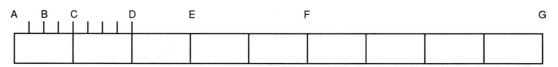

(a) The germinal stage begins at birth and ends at point ___B___.

(b) The embryonic stage begins at point ___B___ and ends at point ___D___.

(c) The fetal stage begins at point ___D___ and ends at point ___G___.

1-2. List the names of the three phases of prenatal development in the order in which they occur. In the parentheses at the right indicate the age ranges encompassed by each stage.

(a) ___germinal___ (1st 2 weeks)

(b) ___embryonic___ (2 weeks - 2 mos)

(c) ___fetal___ (2 mos - birth)

1-3. Match the letter identifying each stage in the previous question with the descriptions below.

___a___ The placenta begins to form.

___b___ At the end of this stage the organism begins to have a human appearance; it is about an inch in length.

___a___ The zygote implants in the fallopian tubes.

___c___ Muscles and bones develop and physical movements occur.

___b___ Most major birth defects probably have their origins in this stage.

Answers: 1-1. (a) B (b) B, D (c) D, G   1-2. (a) germinal (birth to two weeks) (b) embryonic (two weeks to two months) (c) fetal (two months to nine months)   1-3. a, b, a, c, b.

2. **Summarize the impact of environmental factors on prenatal development.**

   2-1. Indicate whether the following statements concerning environmental factors and fetal development are true or false.

   _T_ Severe malnutrition increases the risk of birth complications and neurological deficits.

   _F_ Studies consistently indicate that moderate malnutrition does not have a harmful effect on infant development.

   _F_ Few if any drugs consumed by a pregnant woman are able to pass through the placental barrier.

   _F_ Recent studies indicate that moderate drinking during pregnancy produces no risk for the developing fetus.

   _T_ Heavy drinking of alcohol by a pregnant woman may produce microencephaly, heart defects, and retardation in her child.

   _T_ Smoking during pregnancy is related to increased risk of miscarriage and other birth complications.

   _T_ The placenta screens out many but not all infectious diseases.

   _T_ Genital herpes is transmitted primarily during the birth process, when newborns come into contact with their mothers' lesions.

   _T_ Aids is transmitted primarily during the birth process, when newborns come into contact with their mothers' blood cells.

   Answers: 2-1. true, false, false, false, true, true, true, true, true.

THE WONDROUS YEARS OF CHILDHOOD

3. **Summarize the evidence on the perceptual abilities of infants.**

   3-1. Have you ever noticed that newborn babies don't seem to see very well? Why is that?
   visual acuity of ~20/500 — blurred

   3-2. What is accommodation? At about what age does accommodation occur?
   accomodation involves changing the eye's focus by adjusting the curvature of the lens. Becomes adequate at about 4 mos.

   3-3. By about what age does the newborn's visual acuity improve to about 20/100? _6 mos_
   To 20/20? _4 yrs._

   3-4. According to the visual cliff studies, at about what age are most infants capable of perceiving depth?
   6 mos.

   3-5. Which is more fully developed at birth, hearing or vision?
   hearing

   3-6. At about what age does the infant begin to visually recognize its mother's face? At about what age does the child recognize its mother's voice? _about 3 months. within 1st week_

   3-7. What is auditory localization? When do children show an ability to localize?
   ability to detect the direction a sound is coming from. @birth.

3-8. The vision and hearing of newborns have been more extensively studied than the other senses. What do available data indicate about early development of the remaining senses?

other senses seem to develop reasonably early

Answers: **3-1.** Because the newborn, with a visual acuity of about 20/500, *doesn't* see very well; it sees blurred images. **3-2.** Accommodation involves changing the eye's focus by adjusting the curvature of the lens. Accommodation becomes adequate at about 4 months of age. **3-3.** 6 months, age 4 **3-4.** about 6 months **3-5.** hearing **3-6.** about 3 months, within the first week **3-7.** Localization is the ability to detect the direction a sound is coming from. Children show some localization immediately after birth. **3-8.** The other senses (taste, smell, and touch) seem to develop reasonably early.

4. Describe the two general trends in motor development and identify the process underlying this development.

4-1. In the space below list the two trends referred to and define or describe each.

cephalocaudal trend : *head to foot*

proximodistal trend : *center outward*

4-2. The process that underlies the two trends in motor development is maturation. What is maturation? (Be very specific.) *maturation — developmental changes that occur in an organism as a result of genetic, as opposed to environmental, factors.*

Answers: **4-1.** Cephalocaudal trend: the tendency of children to gain motor control of the upper body before the lower body. Proximaldistal trend: the tendency to gain control of the torso before the limbs. **4-2.** Maturation refers to developmental changes that occur in an organism as a result of *genetic*, as opposed to environmental, factors.

5. Summarize the findings of Thomas and Chess's longitudinal study of infant temperament.

5-1. Thomas and Chess identified three basic temperaments, described below. Place the names of these temperamental styles in the appropriate blanks.

(a) Happy, regular in sleep and eating, adaptable, not readily upset. *easy*

(b) Less cheery, less regular in sleep and eating, slower in adapting to change, more wary of new experiences, moderate in reactivity. *slow to warm up*

(c) Glum, erratic in sleep and eating, resistant to change, irritable. *difficult*

5-2. Approximately what percentage of the children are easy? *40* Slow-to-warm-up? *15*

Difficult? *10* What percentage seems to consist of mixtures of the three basic categories?

35

5-3. What is the major result and conclusion from the Thomas and Chess study?

a child's temperment at 3 mos. tended to be a good predictor of his or her temperment at 10 yrs. of age. → children's temperment tends to be generally stable over time, which suggests that temperment has a strong biological basis.

Answers: 5-1. (a) easy (b) slow-to-warm-up (c) difficult   5-2. 40%, 15%, 10%, 35%   5-3. A child's temperament at 3 months tended to be a good predictor of his or her temperament at 10 years of age. Thus, children's temperament tends to be generally stable over time, which suggests that temperament has a strong biological basis.

6. Summarize theory and research on infant-mother attachment.

6-1. One theory of mother-infant attachment is the early behavioral idea that an infant's attraction to its mother derives from the association between the mother and food. According to this point of view, attachment is (learned/innate), and the mother becomes a ___*conditioned*___ reinforcer.

6-2. The simple conditioning theory of attachment was long ago discarded as a result of the Harlows' famous studies with rhesus monkeys. These studies demonstrated that when infant monkeys were frightened they clung to the "substitute mothers" that (fed them/were soft). Even though they had been reinforced by the wire mothers, the infant monkeys had formed stronger attachments to the (terrycloth/wire) mothers.

6-3. A second theory which emerged as a result of the Harlows' findings is Bowlby's notion that there is a biological basis for mother-infant attachment. According to this view, infants emit certain behaviors that automatically trigger affectionate and protective responses in adults. Such infant behaviors include ___*Smiling*___, cooing, clinging, and so on. Both the infant's behaviors and the adult's responses to them are assumed to be in large part (learned/innate).

6-4. Research by Ainsworth and her colleagues indicates that attachments between mothers and their infants tend to fall into three categories: *secure* attachments, which pose (intense/minimal) problems for infant and mother; *anxious-ambivalent* attachments, a pattern in which children become extremely ___*Anxious*___ when separated from their mothers; and *avoidant* attachments, a condition in which children seek (very little/too much) contact with their mothers.

6-5. The best conclusion from the research on attachment described in this section is that:
a. Attachment is determined by the responsiveness or sensitivity of the mother.
b. Attachment is determined by the behavior and temperament of the infant (e.g., smiling, crying, babbling).
c. Both of the above.
d. Neither of the above.

Answers: 6-1. learned, conditioned   6-2. were soft, terrycloth   6-3. smiling, innate   6-4. minimal, anxious, very little   6-5. c. The main point is that infants, as well as mothers, differ widely in the the traits which they bring to the relationship; degree of attachment is determined by a mutual interplay between the behaviors of the infant and those of the mother.

7. Outline Erikson's stages of childhood personality development and summarize the strengths and weaknesses of Erikson's theory.

7-1. Erikson's theory is clearly derived from Freudian psychoanalytic theory. Freud asserted that there are five childhood stages that determine the adult's personality. In contrast, Erikson proposed that there are ___8___ stages that influence personality across an individual's (childhood/entire lifespan).

7-2. Erikson described four childhood stages and four adult stages. In the spaces below write the names of the crises that mark the four childhood stages and indicate in the parentheses the approximate ages at which they are supposed to occur.

(a) _____ vs. _____ ( )

(b) _____ vs. _____ ( )

(c) _____ vs. _____ ( )

(d) _____ vs. _____ ( )

7-3. Below are descriptions of several individuals. In what childhood stage would they have acquired these characteristics, according to Erikson? Use the letters from the above question to indicate the appropriate stage.

_____ Jack has trouble performing competently in the world of work and is not a productive member of society.

_____ Kristi seems extremely insecure and suspicious of everyone.

_____ Larry never did get along with his siblings and parents; as an adult he feels guilty and lacks self-confidence.

_____ From an early age Maureen's parents never seemed satisfied with what she did. Maureen has been plagued by self-doubts and has never become truly independent.

7-4. As you may have noted in responding to the previous item, a weakness of Erikson's theory is that it attempts to account for very (few/many) aspects of personality. Thus, the theory cannot explain the enormous individual _____ between people.

Answers: 7-1. 8, entire lifespan 7-2. (a) trust vs. mistrust (first year) (b) autonomy vs. shame and doubt (second year) (c) initiative vs. guilt (third through sixth years) (d) industry vs. inferiority (age 6 to adolescence) 7-3. d, a, c, b 7-4. few, differences.

8. **Outline Piaget's stages of cognitive development and summarize the strengths and weaknesses of Piaget's theory.**

8-1.   The diagram below represents Piaget's four main stages of development. Write the names of the stages in the appropriate blanks.

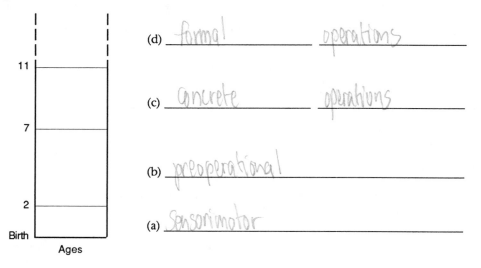

(d) _formal operations_

(c) _Concrete operations_

(b) _preoperational_

(a) _Sensorimotor_

8-2.   The stages of development are marked by changes in children's thinking processes brought about by two major processes. If the child interprets a new experience in terms of an *existing* mental structure, then _assimilation_ is operating. On the other hand, if the child interprets an experience by *changing* his thinking strategy, then the child has used _accomodation_.

8-3.   Following is a list of characteristics of children's thinking during various stages. Identify the stage by placing the correct letter (from the diagram above) in the blanks.

_a_   At the end of this stage the child is able to think symbolically (e.g., in terms of mental images).

_a_   At the beginning of this stage the child's behavior is dominated by reflexes and the ability to coordinate sensory input and movement.

_c_   The child understands conservation but cannot handle hierarchical classification.

_d_   The child's thought processes are abstract and systematic.

_a_   Object permanence occurs toward the end of this stage.

_a_   During the first part of this stage, "Out of sight out of mind" might describe the child's reaction to hidden objects.

_b_   When water is poured from a wide beaker into a taller beaker, children say there is now more water in the taller beaker.

_b_   The child demonstrates a lack of understanding of conservation.

_b_   The child shows the shortcomings of centration, irreversibility, egocentrism, and animism.

_d_   The child is mentally able to undo an action and focus on more than one feature of a problem at the same time.

8-4. Two rows of marbles, with the same number of marbles in each row, are placed on a table as follows:

Row A: •   •   •   •   •   •   •   •

Row B: •   •   •   •   •   •   •   •

One row is then spread out so that it takes up more space:

Row A: •   •   •   •   •   •   •   •

Row B: •   •   •   •   •   •   •   •

(a) Suppose that this demonstration was presented to a *preoperational* child. If the preoperational child is asked which row now has more marbles, which row would the child point to? ___A___

(b) The preoperational child has not yet mastered the principle that physical quantities remain constant in spite of changes in their shape or, in this case, arrangement. What is the name of this principle? ___conservation___

8-5. Some research has demonstrated that certain aspects of Piaget's theory may be incorrect in detail. For example, there is some evidence that object permanence and some aspects of conservation may develop (earlier/later) than Piaget had thought.

8-6. Piaget also had little to say about individual ___differences___ in development or about the so-called ___mixing___ of stages in which elements of an earlier stage may appear in a later one. Nonetheless, Piaget's place in history as the great child psychologist is intact. The strength of Piaget's theory is the brilliance and novelty of his approach and the wealth of ___research___ that it has inspired.

Answers: 8-1. (a) sensorimotor (b) preoperational (c) concrete operations (d) formal operations 8-2. assimilation, accommodation 8-3. a, a, c, d, a, a, b, b, b, d 8-4. (a) A (b) conservation 8-5. earlier 8-6. differences, mixing, research.

9. Describe how the information processing approach has contributed to our understanding of cognitive development.

9-1. The information processing approach has been especially useful in accounting for developmental changes in *attention* and in *memory*. The length of time that an individual can focus on a particular task is known as attention ___span___.

9-2. Preschool children have a very short attention span that increases with age. Children also gradually improve in their ability to filter out irrelevant input and to focus their attention ___selectively___.

9-3. Memory also improves throughout childhood, primarily through the use of three strategies which tend to be adopted at different ages. Following are examples of these strategies. Label each and indicate the age at which it first tends to appear.

(a) Nancy tries to remember how to spell the word *friend* for a spelling test. She repeats over and over to herself, "F-R-I-E-N-D": ___rehearsal___. Children start using this technique at around age ___5___.

(b) Ralph wants to recall the names, in order, of Piaget's stages. He comes up with this mnemonic: Some Psychologists Can't Forget (S, P, C, F). He also tries to think of the meaning of the stage names and create new examples which illustrate each one: ___elaboration___. Individuals start using this technique at around ___adolescence___.

(c) Sue is trying to remember the names of various types of trees. She organizes them into three groups: those with leaves, those with needles, and those with flowers: ___organization___. Individuals start using this technique at around ___9-10___.

Answers: 9-1. span   9-2. selectively   9-3. (a) rehearsal, 5 (b) elaboration, adolescence (c) organization, 9 or 10.

10. Outline Kohlberg's stages of moral development and summarize the strengths and weaknesses of Kohlberg's theory.

10-1. Kohlberg's theory includes three levels, each with two stages. Indicate which of the three moral levels is described by each of the following statements.

Acts are considered wrong because they are punished or right because they lead to positive consequences. _____

Individuals at this level conform very strictly to society's rules, which they accept as absolute and inflexible. _____

This level is characterized by situational or conditional morality, such that stealing might be considered wrong in one circumstance but right in another. _____

10-2. Research has found that children (do/do not) tend to progress through Kohlberg's stages in the order that he indicated. In addition, moral reasoning (does/does not) tend to be associated with moral behavior. For example, as children get older, stages 1 and 2 reasoning tend to decrease while stages 3 and 4 reasoning tend to _____.

10-3. Two major criticisms of Kohlberg's theory are described. First, there tends to be a "_____" of stages in which characteristics of several stages may appear at once. For example, an individual might demonstrate conditional morality for some problems but stick to conventional thinking for others. Second, the theory does not address the issue of possible _____ differences. Thus far, research has found (very little/a great deal of) evidence for the existence of gender differences in morality.

Answers: 10-1. preconventional, conventional, postconventional   10-2. do, does, increase   10-3. mixing, gender, very little.

11. **Describe developmental trends in altruism and aggression and explain how both are shaped by heredity, parental modeling, and media role models.**

11-1. (Altruism/Aggression) tends to increase with age. (Altruism/Aggression) tends, in general, to decrease with age.

11-2. Type of aggression also changes with age. Younger children display more instrumental aggression, aggression directed toward obtaining some _____. Older children display more _____ aggression, aggression directed toward hurting someone rather than accomplishing an objective. As individuals age their aggression also tends to become less physical and more _____.

11-3. Which gender tends to be more aggressive, boys or girls?
a. girls
b. boys
c. neither; boys at some ages and girls at other ages

11-4. What specific evidence from twin studies indicates that aggression and altruism are influenced by heredity?

11-5. In addition to children's genetic inheritance, children learn from observing their parents and from observing role models in the mass media. What is the name of the learning process involved? _____ _____ Do the children learn both altruism and aggression in this manner? _____ Which seems to be modeled more frequently in the media, altruism or aggression? _____

Answers: 11-1. Altruism, Aggression 11-2. goal (object), hostile, verbal 11-3. b 11-4. On measures of both altruism and aggression, identical twins were more similar to each other than were fraternal twins. 11-5. observational learning, yes, aggression.

12. **Summarize the procedure, results, and implications of the Featured Study (Eron et al., 1983) on the effects of exposure to media violence.**

12-1. In the Eron et al. (1983) study, two groups of children were measured at the beginning of the study and followed longitudinally over a period of time. The experimental design is illustrated in the following diagram, which shows when each group was measured. Write in the missing grade levels in the parentheses.

Grade level

	When first measured	When measured later
Group 1	first	(_____)
Group 2	(_____)	(_____)

12-2. How did the researchers assess the amount of television the children watched?

12-3. How did they assess the degree of aggressiveness of the children?

12-4. Indicate true or false For each of the following statements.

_____ The correlations between amount of violent TV viewed and aggressiveness were significant but relatively small in magnitude.

_____ In contrast to the researcher's earlier study, the correlations occurred for girls as well as boys.

_____ Taken together this and other studies provide evidence that media violence is causally related to aggressive behavior.

Answers: 12-1. Group 1: first and third; Group 2: third and fifth   12-2. They asked the children to indicate TV watching on a self-report questionnaire.   12-3. They used peer ratings from the children's classmates.   12-4. All three are true.

THE TRANSITION OF ADOLESCENCE

13. Describe the major events of puberty and discuss the effects of unusually early or late maturation.

13-1. Puberty is a time of rapid _____ ,which includes sudden increases in both height and weight and shifts in body proportions. In addition to developing the capacity for reproduction, adolescents develop features not directly related to reproduction, such as facial hair in males and breasts in females. These features are termed _____ _____ characteristics.

13-2. Girls generally begin puberty at about age _____ and boys at about age _____. Those individuals who mature much earlier or much later than their peers may feel especially uncomfortable about their looks, and these negative feelings may persist into adulthood. This is particularly true of girls who mature (early/late) and boys who mature (early/late).

Answers: 13-1. growth, secondary sex   13-2. 11, 13, early, late.

14. Evaluate the assertion that adolescence is a time of instability and turmoil in light of current evidence on adolescent suicide.

14-1. Imagine that you are at a social gathering. The subject of adolescent stress comes up, and someone says, "It's such a turbulent period, it's no wonder that so many adolescents commit suicide." Suicide at any age is disturbing, but you disagree that adolescence is either so turbulent or characterized by such a large number of suicides, and you describe the following two or three research findings to back up your assertions:

14-2. Of course, even though adolescent suicide may not be of the incidence that some may have thought, there is still reason for concern with regard to (1) the increase in suicides among young people and (2) the number of attempted suicides. In the space below give the data that back up these two assertions.

Answers: 14-1. (1) The suicide rate for adolescents (ages 15–19 in the study referred to) is lower than it is for any older age group. (2) Fewer than 1% of adolescents even attempt suicide. (3) Studies indicate that a majority of adolescents encounter no more stress than is likely to occur in other periods of life. 14-2. (1) Suicide among young people ages 15–24 increased 183% between 1960 and 1982. (2) Deaths by suicide occur in a ratio of about 1 in 8 attempts in the general population but perhaps 1 in 100 attempts among adolescents. Thus, the epidemic may be in suicide attempts rather than in suicides.

15. Explain why the struggle for a sense of identity is particularly intense during adolescence and discuss some common patterns of identity formation.

15-1. Adolescence is clearly a period of change, so it is readily understandable that adolescents tend to focus on identity. The changes that tend to produce concern with identity include (1)

_____ changes that accompany the growth spurt, (2) changes in

_____ processes (i.e., the beginning of formal operational thought), and (3)

concern with what one will become, what one will eventually take on as a _____.

15-2. Marcia (1966, 1980) has described four orientations that people may adopt in attempting to resolve the identity crisis. These are not stages that people pass through in an orderly manner but statuses which they may adopt on either a relatively permanent or temporary basis. One possible status is simply to take on the values and roles prescribed by one's parents; this is termed _____. While this may temporarily resolve the crisis, in the long run the individual may not be comfortable with the adopted identity. A second orientation involves a period of experimentation with various ideologies and careers and a delay in commitment to any one; this is termed _____. If the experimentation and lack of commitment become permanent, the individual is said to be in a status of _____ _____. On the other hand, if the consideration of alternatives leads to conviction about a sense of self, one takes on the status referred to as

_____ _____.

Answers: 15-1. physical, cognitive, vocation (career)   15-2. foreclosure, moratorium, identity diffusion, identity achievement.

THE EXPANSE OF ADULTHOOD

16. **Summarize the evidence on the stability of personality and the prevalence of the mid-life crisis and outline Erikson's stages of development and adulthood.**

16-1. Do people change throughout their lifetime? Or does personality tend to remain the same? Current research seems to support the conclusion that:
   a. personality is stable across one's lifetime
   b. personality changes across one's lifetime
   c. both of the above
   d. neither of the above

16-2. How can you account for the conflicting results about stability of personality? Explain how it is possible that personality appears both to stay the same over time and to change dramatically.

16-3. Two influential studies conducted in the 1970s asserted that people experience a period of emotional

turmoil some time between age 35 and 45, a transitional phase known as the _____

_____ .

16-4. The midlife crisis, described as a period of reappraisal and assessment of time left, was thought by the original writers (Gould and Levinson) to be a transitional phase which affected (<u>a minority/most</u>) adults. More recently, other investigators have found that the midlife crisis characterizes (<u>a minority/most</u>) of adults.

16-5. The difference between Gould and Levinson's conclusions and those of the more recent researchers may have to do with the difference in methods used. Explain.

16-6. In the spaces below write the names of the crises that mark Erikson's three stages of adulthood. In the parentheses indicate the approximate period of adulthood during which the crises are supposed to occur.

   (a) _____ vs. _____ (   )

   (b) _____ vs. _____ (   )

   (c) _____ vs. _____ (   )

16-7. Following are descriptions of the crises occurring in each of the above stages. Indicate the stages by placing the appropriate letters in the blanks.

   _____ Concern for helping future generations versus a self-indulgent concern for meeting one's own desires.

   _____ Concerned with finding meaning in the remainder of one's life versus preoccupation with earlier failures and eventual death.

   _____ Concerned with whether one can successfully develop intimacy with others as opposed to a manipulative strategy in which others are viewed as means to an end.

Answers: 16-1. c   16-2. Some personality traits (e.g., extraversion-introversion) appear to be quite stable; others (e.g., masculinity-femininity) tend to change as people grow older.   16-3. midlife crisis   16-4. most, a minority   16-5. Gould and Levinson used interview and case study methods, methods which are less objective than those used in the more recent research by McCrae and Costa.   16-6. (a) intimacy vs. isolation (early adulthood) (b) generativity vs. self-absorption (middle adulthood) (c) integrity vs. despair (aging years)   16-7. b, c, a.

17. **Describe typical transitions in family relations during the adult years.**

17-1. People emerge from families and most eventually form new families. The transition period during which people are single and therefore "between families" has been prolonged in recent years. Mention two or three factors that may account for the delay in marriage.

17-2. While the first few years of married life tend to be quite happy, a source of tension in recent years for the newly married concerns different expectations in an era of changing gender roles. What do men mean by equality in marriage, what do women mean by the term, and what is the evidence about task sharing?

17-3. What event in the family cycle tends to cause the first drop in marital satisfaction? Do parents report regretting their decision? When does marital satisfaction tend to start climbing back?

17-4. Indicate true or false for the following statements.

_____ New parents who overestimated the benefits and underestimated the costs of having children tend to experience more stress at the birth of the first child.

_____ Couples who have high levels of intimacy tend not to experience intense stress at the birth of the first child.

_____ Mothers are generally more adversely affected by conflicts with their adolescent children than are fathers.

_____ The period when offspring leave home tends to be stressful for parents.

Answers: 17-1. Factors that may be relevant to delaying marriage include: new career options for women, increased educational requirements for jobs, increased emphasis on personal autonomy, and, in general, an increased societal acceptance of the status of remaining single. 17-2. In one recent survey, half the men were unable to define equality in marriage and the other half defined it in psychological terms. Women defined it more concretely—in terms of sharing tasks and responsibilities. The evidence indicates that women are still doing the bulk of the housework in America even when employed outside the home. 17-3. At the birth of the first child, marital satisfaction, defined in terms of the percentage of husbands and wives reporting that their marriage was going well, declines. Despite this fact, most parents report no regret about having children. Marital satisfaction tends to increase when children leave home. 17-4. true, true, true, false.

18. **Discuss patterns of career development in both men and women.**

18-1. Donald Super breaks career development into five major stages. The *growth* stage, which occurs in childhood, involves fantasizing and thinking about job possibilities. List the remaining four stages and the approximate ages at which they occur in the spaces below.

_____ ( )

_____ ( )

_____ ( )

_____ ( )

18-2. Following are descriptions of events which may occur during the four stages after the growth stage. Place the name of the stage described in the appropriate blanks.

_____	Person is likely to receive support and guidance from a mentor.
_____	Future job moves almost always take place within the same occupational area.
_____	The individual may try out various work experiences; shifts occur if the first are not gratifying.
_____	The concern is with retaining achieved status rather than improving it.
_____	Energy may shift from work to the family or leisure activities.
_____	Involves preparation to leave the work place.

18-3. Most of the research findings summarized above are based on men. Although it was originally believed that findings relating to career development would apply equally well to women, evidence has indicated that they do not. How does the pattern of career paths of women differ from that of men?

18-4. Which of the following are factors that contribute to the less direct career paths of women? Place a T next to statements that are likely factors, an F next to those that are not.

_____ Women are more likely than men to interrupt their careers for child rearing or other family reasons.

_____ For affirmative action reasons, women tend to be advanced early in their careers to positions for which they are not qualified.

_____ Women tend to subjugate their career goals to those of their husbands'.

_____ Women are less likely than men to enjoy the benefits of mentoring (e.g., "old boy" network).

_____ Women face discrimination, especially at upper management levels (the "glass ceiling").

Answers: **18-1.** Exploration, establishment, maintenance, decline **18-2.** establishment, establishment, exploration, maintenance, maintenance, decline **18-3.** The career paths of women are frequently much less directly upward in a systematic pattern. Instead, the phases seem to be almost random. **18-4.** T, F, T, T, T

19. Describe the physical and cognitive changes associated with aging.

19-1. As we age, our physical and cognitive characteristics change. Indicate which traits show an increase and which show a decrease by placing checkmarks in the appropriate blanks.

	Increases	Decreases
Physical changes		
Proportion of body fat:	_____	_____
Overall weight:	_____	_____
Number of brain neurons:	_____	_____
Visual acuity:	_____	_____
Ability to see close:	_____	_____
Hearing:	_____	_____
Cognitive changes		
Memory:	_____	_____
Speed of learning:	_____	_____
Speed of memory retrieval:	_____	_____
Speed of solving problems:	_____	_____

19-2. Despite the decline in physical and cognitive capacities, aging is not so bad as it may at first seem. The increase in body fat is largely (cosmetic/debilitating) rather than functional, and the loss of visual and hearing acuity may be compensated for with glasses and hearing aids. With regard to loss of brain cells, it's not so much a matter of "who needs 'em" as that the gradual loss appears to have (little/a strong) effect on functioning. Women's reaction to menopause varies a great deal, but the evidence in general is that menopause is accompanied by (very strong/very little) emotional distress. Memory loss with aging is, in general, (modest/intense) and (is/is not) universal. Speed at problem solving (increases/decreases) with age, but ability at problem solving when time is not a factor (stays the same/decreases).

Answers: 19-1. All of the characteristics decrease with the exception of body fat and overall weight, which increase (except that overall weight may decrease somewhat after the mid-50s). 19-2. cosmetic, little, very little, modest, is not, decreases, stays the same.

PUTTING IT IN PERSPECTIVE

20. Explain how this chapter highlighted the interaction of heredity and environment.

20-1. Shyness, or inhibitedness, evidently has a genetic basis, but whether the characteristic persists depends on the environment. The behavior of a mother toward a child is affected both by her own inherited characteristics and by the behavior of the child; in turn, the behavior of the child is the result of its genetic inheritance and of the mother's behavior toward it. Thus, behavior is the result not of heredity or environment operating alone but of an _____ between the two factors.

20-2. One form of mental retardation results from phenylketonuria, an inherited inability to metabolize a common amino acid found in milk. When fed milk, children born with phenylketonuria become mentally retarded. Is this type of retardation an inherited disorder? Or is it caused by the environment?

20-3. This chapter has been concerned with changes in human behavior across the life span. The theme being stressed here is that these changes result from an *interaction* of heredity and environment. In your own words, explain how the interaction operates.

Answers: 20-1. interaction 20-2. This disorder might at first seem to be inherited, since there is a genetic trait involved. But the retardation does not occur if the infant is not fed milk products, which involves the environment. The point is that this disorder, like behavior in general, cannot be attributed solely to nature *or* to nurture: It is a function of an *interaction* between the two. 20-3. The interaction of heredity and environment refers to the fact that we are a product of both factors. It means more than that, however. Heredity and environment don't operate separately. Interaction means that the genetic factors affect the operation of the environment and that environmental factors affect genetic predispositions. The influence of one factor *depends on* the effects of the other.

APPLICATION: UNDERSTANDING GENDER DIFFERENCES

21. Summarize evidence on gender differences in behavior and discuss the significance of these differences.

21-1. Which sex tends to show more or to score higher on tests of the following traits or abilities? Check the appropriate column.

	Males	Females	Neither
Cognitive			
verbal skills	_____	_____	_____
mathematical skills	_____	_____	_____
visual-spatial skills	_____	_____	_____
Social			
aggression	_____	_____	_____
sensitivity to nonverbal cues	_____	_____	_____
susceptibility to influence	_____	_____	_____
emotionality	_____	_____	_____

21-2. There is an enormous overlap between the genders with regard to these traits. Many females are much more aggressive than the average male, for example, and many males are more sensitive to nonverbal cues than the average female. The differences referred to above are _____ differences, differences between averages. It is also important to note that the size of the gender differences is relatively _____; sex accounts for only about 1% to 6% of the variation among people.

Answers: 21-1. Males as a group are higher on mathematical and visual-spatial skills, females on verbal skills. Males are more aggressive, while females are better at picking up nonverbal cues and tend to be slightly more susceptible to social influence. The sexes don't seem to differ on emotionality.   21-2. group, small.

22. Explain how biological and environmental factors contribute to existing gender differences.

22-1. Money and his colleagues reported that androgenized females tend to prefer male playmates and to show traditionally "masculine" interests in male toys and vigorous outdoor activities. Androgenized females are girls who were exposed to high levels of _____ during _____ development. Such studies are of interest because they suggest that gender differences, or sex role behavior, may in part be a function of (biological/environmental) factors. There are, however, alternative explanations for these findings, one of which has to do with the way parents of androgenized girls may have treated their children. Describe this alternative explanation.

22-2. There is also some evidence suggesting that males depend more heavily on the left hemisphere for verbal processing and the right for spatial processing than is the case with females. In other words, males may tend to exhibit more cerebral _____ than females. Results on this subject have been mixed, however, and even if males do have more cerebral specialization, it would be difficult to explain how that would account for gender differences.

22-3. Whether or not biology affects gender roles, it is clear that environment does so. For example, our parents and peers will tend to operantly condition "sex-appropriate" behaviors by _____ some behaviors and _____ others.

22-4. Parents or peers might tease a young boy who attempts to play with dolls. Teasing, name calling, or other forms of disapproval would be an example of _____, a consequence that seems to be used (<u>less/more</u>) commonly than reward in socializing gender roles.

22-5. Children learn through rewards and punishments, the process of _____ conditioning, and they also acquire information by seeing what others do, the process of _____ learning. Children tend to imitate the behavior of the (<u>same sex/opposite sex</u>) models they observe.

22-6. Children adopt gender roles because they are rewarded for doing so and because they see role models engaging in those behaviors. In addition, as the cognitive theorists point out, children are active participants in their own gender-role socialization. Once they discover around ages 5 to 7 that being a boy or being a girl is a _____ condition, they want to engage in "sex-appropriate" behaviors, to do boylike or girllike things. This process is referred to as _____-socialization.

22-7. Whether through operant conditioning, observational learning, or self-socialization, the major forces for gender role socialization occur in three main aspects of the child's environment, in their _____, in _____, and in the _____.

Answers: 22-1. androgen, prenatal, biological. Because the children exposed to heavy amounts of androgen prenatally had masculine genitals, their families may not have treated them the same way that they would have treated nonandrogenized children. Thus, the differences in behavior could have been due to the family environment rather than hormones. 22-2. specialization 22-3. rewarding, punishing 22-4. punishment, more 22-5. operant, observational, same sex 22-6. permanent, self 22-7. families, schools, media.

REVIEW OF KEY TERMS

Accommodation
Aggression
Altruism
Animism
Assimilation
Attachment
Centration
Cephalocaudal trend
Cognitive development
Conservation
Cross-sectional study
Development
Developmental norms
Egocentrism
Embryonic stage

Fetal alcohol syndrome
Fetal stage
Gender
Gender differences
Gender roles
Gender stereotypes
Germinal stage
Irreversibility
Longitudinal study
Maturation
Mentor
Meta-analysis
Motor development
Object permanence

Placenta
Prenatal period
Proximodistal trend
Puberty
Secondary sex characteristics
Senile dementia
Separation anxiety
Sex
Social clock
Socialization
Stage
Temperament
Visual cliff
Zygote

_____ 1. The sequence of age-related changes that occurs as a person progresses from conception to death.

_____ 2. The period of pregnancy, extending from conception to birth.

_____ 3. The first two weeks after conception.

_____ 4. The structure that connects the circulation of the fetus and the mother but that blocks passage of blood cells.

_____ 5. The second stage of prenatal development, lasting from two weeks after conception until the end of the second month.

_____ 6. The third stage of prenatal development, lasting from two months after conception through birth.

_____ 7. A collection of congenital problems associated with a mother's excessive use of alcohol during pregnancy.

_____ 8. An experimental apparatus that includes a glass platform extending over a several-foot drop.

_____ 9. Developmental changes in muscular coordination required for physical movement.

_____ 10. The head-to-foot direction of motor development.

_____ 11. The center-outward direction of motor development.

_____ 12. The average ages at which people display certain behaviors and abilities.

_____ 13. Characteristic mood, energy level, and reactivity.

_____ 14. A study in which one group of subjects is observed over a long period of time.

_____ 15. A study in which groups that differ in age are compared at a single period of time.

_____ 16. Emotional distress displayed by an infant when separated from a person with whom it has formed an attachment.

_____ 17. Culturally constructed distinctions between femininity and masculinity.

_____ 18. Widely held beliefs about females' and males' abilities, personality traits, and social behavior.

_____ 19. Development of thinking, reasoning, remembering, and problem solving.

	20.	Interpreting new experiences in terms of mental structures already available.
_____	21.	Altering existing mental structures to explain new experiences.
_____	22.	A mental capacity that involves recognizing that objects continue to exist even when they are no longer visible.
_____	23.	Piaget's term for the awareness that physical quantities remain constant in spite of changes in their shape or appearance.
_____	24.	The Piagetian term for the tendency to focus on just one feature of a problem and neglect other important features.
_____	25.	The inability to cognitively visualize reversing an action.
_____	26.	Thinking characterized by a limited ability to share another person's viewpoint.
_____	27.	Someone with a senior position in an organization who serves as a role model, tutor, and advisor to a younger worker.
_____	28.	The attribution of lifelike qualities to inanimate objects.
_____	29.	A developmental period during which certain behaviors and capacities occur.
_____	30.	The biologically based categories of male and female.
_____	31.	Any behavior, either physical or verbal, that is intended to hurt someone.
_____	32.	Concern with the welfare of others, cooperation, and helping of others.
_____	33.	A close, emotional bond of affection between an infant and its caregiver.
_____	34.	Physical features associated with gender that are not directly needed for reproduction.
_____	35.	The period of early adolescence marked by rapid physical growth and the development of reproductive maturity.
_____	36.	A person's notion of a developmental schedule that specifies what he or she should have accomplished by certain points in life.
_____	37.	Developmental changes that reflect one's genetic blueprint rather than environment.
_____	38.	A one-celled organism created by the process of fertilization, the union of sperm and egg.
_____	39.	Behavioral differences between females and males.
_____	40.	A statistical procedure for combining data from different studies to estimate the size of a particular variable's effects.
_____	41.	The acquisition of norms, roles, and behaviors expected of people in a particular group.
_____	42.	Expectations concerning what is the appropriate behavior for each sex.
_____	43.	An abnormal deterioration in mental faculties that accompanies aging in about 15% of people over age 65.

Answers: 1. development 2. prenatal period 3. germinal stage 4. placenta 5. embryonic stage 6. fetal stage 7. fetal alcohol syndrome 8. visual cliff 9. motor development 10. cephalocaudal trend 11. proximodistal trend 12. developmental norms 13. temperament 14. longitudinal study 15. cross-sectional study 16. separation anxiety 17. gender 18. gender stereotypes 19. cognitive development 20. assimilation 21. accommodation 22. object permanence 23. conservation 24. centration 25. irreversibility 26. egocentrism 27. mentor 28. animism 29. stage 30. sex 31. aggression 32. altruism 33. attachment 34. secondary sex characteristics 35. puberty 36. social clock 37. maturation 38. zygote 39. gender differences 40. meta-analysis 41. socialization 42. gender roles 43. senile dementia.

REVIEW OF KEY PEOPLE

Mary Ainsworth
John Bowlby
Erik Erikson

Harry & Margaret Harlow
Lawrence Kohlberg

Jean Piaget
Alexander Thomas & Stella Chess

_____ 1. Conducted a major longitudinal study in which they identified three basic styles of children's temperament.

_____ 2. Used cloth and wire "substitute mothers" to study attachment in infant rhesus monkeys.

_____ 3. Theorized that there are critical periods in human infants' lives during which attachments must occur for normal development to take place.

_____ 4. Partitioned the life span into eight stages, each of which is accompanied by a psychosocial crisis.

_____ 5. Pioneered the study of children's cognitive development.

_____ 6. Developed a stage theory of moral development.

_____ 7. Described three categories of infant-mother attachment.

Answers: 1. Thomas & Chess 2. Harlow & Harlow 3. Bowlby 4. Erikson 5. Piaget 6. Kohlberg 7. Ainsworth .

SELF-QUIZ

1. Which prenatal period begins at the second week and ends at the second month of pregnancy?
   a. germinal stage
   b. embryonic stage
   c. fetal stage
   d. none of the above

2. In which prenatal stage do most major birth defects probably have their origins?
   a. germinal stage
   b. embryonic stage
   c. fetal stage
   d. none of the above

3. Which of the following senses seems to be weakest in the newborn?
   a. vision
   b. hearing
   c. smell
   d. touch

4. Maturation refers to developmental changes that occur in an organism as a result of:
   a. accommodation and assimilation
   b. genetic factors
   c. environmental factors
   d. parental and peer pressures

5. What is the major conclusion from Thomas and Chess's longitudinal study of temperament?
    a. Children's temperaments tend to go through predictable stages.
    b. The temperament of the child is not a good predictor of the temperament of the adult.
    c. Opposites attract.
    d. Children's temperaments tend to be consistent over the years.

6. The crisis occurring in the first year, according to Erikson, is one involving:
    a. trust versus mistrust
    b. initiative versus guilt
    c. industry versus inferiority
    d. all of the above

7. During which stage in Piaget's system is the child able to understand conservation but unable to handle hierarchical classification?
    a. sensorimotor
    b. preoperational
    c. concrete operations
    d. formal operations

8. A child in the early sensorimotor period is shown a ball, which she watches intensely. The ball is then hidden under a pillow. What will the child do?
    a. ask, "Where is the pillow?"
    b. stare at the pillow but not pick it up
    c. move the pillow and pick up the ball
    d. ignore the pillow, as if the ball didn't exist

9. Which of the following developed a stage theory of moral development?
    a. Piaget
    b. Kohlberg
    c. Gould
    d. Bowlby

10. Aggressiveness in human beings seems to be caused by:
    a. watching aggressive acts on TV
    b. biological (genetic) factors
    c. parental modeling
    d. all of the above

11. Suicide among adolescents ages 15-19 occurs:
    a. at a much higher level than in any older age group
    b. at a slightly higher level than in any older age group
    c. at a lower level than in any older age group
    d. at the same level as the 20-24 age group

12. Which of the following factors tends to be accompanied by a drop in ratings of marital satisfaction?
    a. childlessness during early married life
    b. the birth of the first child
    c. the first child's departure for college
    d. when the last child leaves home

13. Females tend to score slightly higher than males on tests of:
    a. verbal ability
    b. mathematical ability
    c. visual-spatial ability
    d. none of the above

14. Females exposed to high levels of androgen during prenatal development tend to have:
    a. masculine interests and preferences for male playmates
    b. androgenized genitals
    c. both of the above
    d. neither of the above

15. Once children discover that their gender is permanent, they are likely to want to engage in behavior that is "sex appropriate" as defined by the culture. This process is referred to as:
    a. operant conditioning
    b. observational learning
    c. self-socialization
    d. none of the above

Answers: 1. b 2. b 3. a 4. b 5. d 6. a 7. c 8. d 9. b 10. d 11. c 12. b 13. a 14. c 15. c.

12 PERSONALITY: THEORY, RESEARCH, AND ASSESSMENT

REVIEW OF KEY IDEAS

THE NATURE OF PERSONALITY

1. **Define the construct of personality in terms of consistency and distinctiveness.**

   1-1.   I can always tell when my colleague across the hall has finished for the day because I hear squeaking as he carefully moves his computer table under his bookcase. And I know what follows: He closes his books, sorts the papers on his desk into two piles, and slides the pens and pencils into his desk drawer. When I'm done, on other hand, I telegraph very little. The time comes, I step on the button that turns off my computer, and I am out the door leaving my generally messy desk behind. The fact that my colleague and I differ in this respect illustrates the central feature of the concept of personality termed _distinctiveness (behavioral differences)_. The fact that my colleague engages in the same behaviors almost every day illustrates the feature termed _consistency (stability)_.

   1-2.   In other words, personality involves the stability of an individual's behavior across time, the feature of _consistency_, and differences among people reacting to the same situation, the feature of _distinctiveness_.

   Answers: 1-1. distinctiveness (behavioral differences), consistency (stability)   1-2. consistency, distinctiveness.

2. **Explain what is meant by a personality trait and describe proposed systems for organizing traits.**

   2-1.   Consistent tendencies to behave in particular ways, which may be described by a series of adjectives (such as anxious, excitable, shy, aggressive, etc.), are termed personality _traits_.

2-2. There are an enormous number of traits words that could be used to describe people, and several systems have been devised in attempt to classify these terms. For example, Gordon Allport distinguished between three levels of traits: ___*cardinal*___ traits, which characterize almost all of a person's behavior (but are displayed by very few people); ___*central*___ traits, the five or ten dominant traits possessed by most people; and ___*secondary*___ traits, the less consistent dispositions that occur in some situations but not others.

2-3. Cattell has proposed another classification scheme for personality traits, derived from the statistical procedure of factor analysis, which reduces Allport's list of trait words to 16 ___*source*___ traits. These traits are basic dimensions of personality from which all other traits are supposed to derive.

2-4. One characteristic of science is its preference for parsimony, and McCrae and Costa have come up with yet a simpler model involving only ___*five*___ factors.

Answers: 2-1. traits 2-2. cardinal, central, secondary 2-3. source 2-4. 5.

PSYCHODYNAMIC PERSPECTIVES

3. **List and describe the three components into which Freud divided the personality and indicate how these are distributed across three levels of awareness.**

3-1. Below is a schematic illustration of the three Freudian structures of personality. Label each.

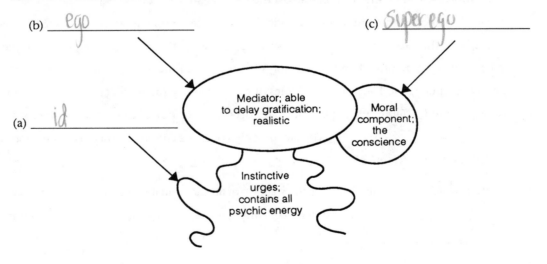

(b) ___*ego*___

(c) ___*Super ego*___

(a) ___*id*___

3-2. Freud superimposed the levels of consciousness on the psychic structures. The following illustration makes clear that two of the structures exist at all three levels while one is entirely unconscious. Label the levels.

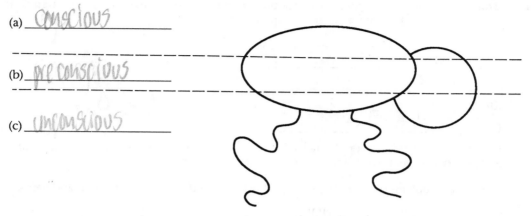

(a) _Conscious_

(b) _preconscious_

(c) _unconscious_

Answers: 3-1. (a) id (b) ego (c) superego   3-2. (a) conscious (b) preconscious (c) unconscious. (The diagram shows that the ego emerges from the id and that the superego grows out of the ego.)

4. Explain the preeminence of sexual and aggressive conflicts in Freud's theory and describe the operation of defense mechanisms.

4-1. Freud believed that most of our conflicts center in _sexual_ and _aggressive_ urges. Conflicts relating to these areas were preeminent in his mind because (1) they are subject to subtle social norms and are a source of confusion, and (2) they are more apt to be _frustrated_ than other urges.

4-2. Following is a list of the defense mechanisms. Match each with the correct description by placing the appropriate letters in the blanks.

A. rationalization	_f_	A return to an earlier less mature stage of development.
B. repression	_g_	Forming an imaginary or real alliance with a person or group; becoming like them.
C. projection	_a_	Creating false but reasonable-sounding excuses.
D. displacement	_b_	Pushing distressing thoughts into the unconscious.
E. reaction formation	_c_	Attributing ones own thoughts, feelings, or conflicts to another.
F. regression	_e_	Taking on an emotion the exact opposite of the way one really feels.
G. identification	_d_	Diverting emotional feelings from their original source to a substitute target.

4-3. Using the list from the previous question match the defense mechanisms with the following examples.

_e_ After John and Marsha break up, John says he hates Marsha; this statement helps him defend against his real feelings of affection.

_c_ "Society is filled with perverts," says the preacher; but later evidence suggests that he is the one with the sexual conflicts.

_f_ In reaction to the stress of entering college, Alice started acting like a grade-school kid.

_g_ Bruce acts like John Wayne, and he owns tapes of all the Duke's movies.

_d_ Mary is angry at her mother, so she kicks her baby brother.

Answers: 4-1. sexual, aggressive, frustrated (or thwarted, unfulfilled)   4-2. F, G, A, B, C, E, D   4-3. E, C, F, G, D.

5. **Outline Freud's psychosexual stages of development and their theorized relations to adult personality.**

5-1. List Freud's stages of psychosexual development, in the order in which they are supposed to occur, in the blanks below. Place the ages in the parentheses.

(a) _oral_ (0-1)

(b) _anal_ (1-3)

(c) _phallic_ (3-6)

(d) _latency_ (6-12)

(e) _genital_ (puberty onward)

5-2. The following behaviors or personality characteristics are supposed to result from fixation at a particular psychosexual stage. Place the names of the correct stages in the blanks.

(a) She has problems with anger control, is hostile toward people in authority, and defies any attempt at regulation of her behavior. _anal_

(b) He eats too much, drinks too much, and smokes. _oral_

(c) He has occasional outbursts of hostility toward his mother that he is hard pressed to understand or explain, and he can't seem to develop relationships with women. _phallic_

5-3. The Oedipus complex occurs during the _phallic_ stage, between the ages of _3_ and _5_. This complex theoretically involves an erotically tinged attraction toward the (same sex/opposite sex) parent and a strong hostility toward the (same sex/opposite sex) parent. Resolution of the Oedipus complex involves (increasing/stopping) both the child's erotic attraction and the child's hostility.

Answers: 5-1. (a) oral (first year) (b) anal (second year) (c) phallic (ages 3 through 5) (d) latency (age 5 to puberty) (e) genital (puberty on) 5-2. (a) anal (b) oral (c) phallic 5-3. phallic, 3, 5, opposite sex, same sex, stopping.

6. **Summarize the revisions of Freud's theory proposed by Jung and Adler.**

6-1. Freud devised the theory and method of treatment termed *psychoanalysis*. To differentiate his approach from Freud's, Jung called his theory _analytical_ _psychology_. Like Freud, Jung emphasized the unconscious determinants of personality. Unlike Freud, he proposed that the unconscious consists of two layers, a _personal_ unconscious and a _collective_ unconscious. The personal unconscious is similar to Freud's unconscious, but it has less emphasis on sexuality. The collective unconscious is a repository of inherited, ancestral memories, which Jung termed _archetypes_.

6-2. Jung's major contribution to psychology is considered by many to be his description of two major personality types: _introverts_, quiet, reserved people who tend to be preoccupied with their own internal world of thoughts; and _extraverts_, outgoing people who are more concerned with the external world of others.

6-3. For Freud, the driving energy behind the human personality was sexuality; for Jung it may have been the collective unconscious. For Adler, it was striving for _superiority_ and the attempt to overcome childhood feelings of inferiority. Efforts to overcome imagined or real inferiorities involve _compensation_ through development of one's abilities. While Adler considered compensation to be a normal mechanism, he saw _overcompensation_ as an abnormal attempt to conceal feelings of inferiority.

6-4. Adler is associated with the term _inferiority_ _complex_, an exaggerated feeling of inadequacy supposedly caused by parental pampering or neglect in early childhood. To a greater extent than either Freud or Jung, Adler emphasized the effects of the social context on personality development. For example, he thought that _birth order_ _____ (that is, whether one is an only child, first-born, second-born, etc.) had a major effect on personality. Although the concept created considerable interest, birth order has turned out to be a (weaker/ stronger) and (more/less) consistent factor than he had supposed.

Answers: 6-1. analytical psychology, personal, collective, archetypes 6-2. introverts, extraverts 6-3. superiority, compensation, overcompensation 6-4. inferiority complex, birth order, weaker, less.

7. Summarize the strengths and weaknesses of the psychodynamic approach to personality.

7-1. Psychoanalytic formulations have had a major impact on the field of psychology. List the three contributions discussed in your text.
① unconscious forces can influence behavior
② internal conflict often plays a key role in generating psychological distress
③ early childhood experiences can influence adult personality

7-2. Psychoanalytic formulations have also been extensively criticized. After each of the following statements list the particular criticism, from the discussion in your text, that the statement represents.

(a) Freud proposed that females develop weaker superegos and that they have a chronic sense of inferiority caused by penis envy. _Sexism_

(b) Although he discussed some characteristics associated with the psychosexual stages, Freud didn't really specify which events, occurring during which childhood stages, produce which sets of personality traits. _poor testability_

(c) Support for the theories has been provided solely by clinical case studies and by clinical intuition. _inadequate evidence_

Answers: 7-1. the discovery that unconscious forces can influence behavior, that internal conflict may generate psychological distress, and that early childhood experiences influence the adult personality 7-2. (a) sexism (b) poor testability (c) inadequate evidence.

BEHAVIORAL PERSPECTIVES

8. **Discuss how Skinner's principles of operant conditioning can be applied to the structure and development of personality.**

   8-1.   Which of the following processes plays an important part in Skinner's ideas about human behavior?
   a. mental conflict
   b. the mind
   c. free will
   d. none of the above

   8-2.   According to Skinner, much of our behavior is affected by reinforcement, punishment, or extinction—in other words, by the environmental ___consequences___ that follow our behavior. Thus, someone behaves aggressively (i.e., has an aggressive personality trait), for example, because he or she has been ___punished___ for behaving aggressively.

   8-3.   Skinner recognizes that there are individual differences and that people behave consistently over time, but the differences and consistencies occur because of what's going on in an individual's (mind/environment).

   8-4.   Thus, personality is not mental, but environmental, according to Skinner. Nor do people change their minds; their environment changes. Skinner makes a strong case for the point of view of environmental ___determinism (causation)___, which holds that our behavior is caused primarily by environmental factors.

   Answers: 8-1. d   8-2. consequences, reinforced   8-3. environment   8-4. determinism (causation).

9. **Describe Bandura's social-learning theory and compare it to Skinner's viewpoint.**

   9-1.   In what respect is Bandura's point of view similar to Skinner's?
   Bandura's point of view is similar to Skinner's in that Bandura believes that personality is largely shaped through learning and that behavior is determined by the environment.

   9-2.   Three of the major differences between Bandura's and Skinner's viewpoints involve the following concepts. Carefully define and explain these concepts and indicate how they represent a difference from Skinner's position.
   (a) reciprocal determinism: refers to the point of view that not only does environment determine behavior (Skinner) but that behavior determines environment; behavior, environment, and mental processes all mutually affect one another.

   (b) observational learning: is the process through which we learn behaviors by observing the consequences of someone else's (ie. a model's) behavior. For example, we learn not only by being reinforced (Skinner) but by observing someone else being reinforced.

   (c) self-efficacy: is our belief in our ability to perform certain behaviors. this belief affects whether we undertake those behaviors and how well we perform them. Skinner makes no allowance for mentalistic concepts such as self-efficacy

9-3. According to Bandura who do we imitate, and in what circumstances?

we tend to imitate models whom we see being reinforced (even though we experience the reinforcement vicariously rather than directly.

Answers: 9-1. It is similar in that Bandura believes that personality is largely shaped through learning and that behavior is determined by the environment. 9-2. (a) Reciprocal determinism refers to the point of view that not only does environment determine behavior (Skinner) but that behavior determines environment; behavior, environment, and mental processes all mutually affect one another. (b) Observational learning is the process through which we learn behaviors by observing the consequences of someone else's (i.e., a model's) behavior. For example, we learn not only by being reinforced (Skinner) but by observing someone else being reinforced. (c) Self-efficacy is our belief in our ability to perform certain behaviors. This belief affects whether we undertake those behaviors and how well we perform them. Skinner makes no allowance for mentalistic concepts such as self-efficacy. 9-3. We tend to imitate models whom we see being reinforced (even though we experience the reinforcement vicariously rather than directly).

10. Identify Mischel's major contribution to personality theory and indicate why his ideas have generated so much controversy.

10-1. Mischel's major contribution to personality theory is his contention that human behavior is determined to a much greater extent by the ___situation___ than by ___personality___.

10-2. Why is this such a controversial idea for personality theory?

the notion is controversial because the definition of personality involves the word consistency.

Answers: 10-1. situation (situational factors), personality (personality traits). 10-2. The notion is controversial because the very definition of personality involves the word consistency. Mischel's findings suggest that behavior is not very consistent, that it is largely determined by an ever-changing situation.

11. Summarize the strengths and weaknesses of the behavioral approach to personality.

11-1. The major strengths of the behavioral approach have been its commitment to empirical ___research___, which keeps it open to new findings and ideas, and its identification of important ___environmental___ determinants of behavior.

11-2. The major weaknesses of the behavioral approach, according to its critics, have been its overdependence on research involving ___animal___ subjects, its failure to integrate ___biological___ factors into the theories, and its ___fragmented___ view of personality.

Answers: 11-1. research, environmental (situational) 11-2. animal, biological (genetic), fragmented.

HUMANISTIC PERSPECTIVES

12. **Explain how humanism was a reaction against both the behavioral and psychodynamic approaches and discuss the assumptions of the humanistic view.**

12-1. The humanistic movement reacted against (a) the behavioral approach because of its mechanistic view and emphasis on _____animal_____ behavior and (b) the psychodynamic approach because of its emphasis on _____primitive_____ drives.

12-2. In addition, humanistic psychology objected to both movements because of their emphasis on _____determinism_____, or absolute causation, and what they perceived as a failure to recognize the _____unique_____ qualities of human behavior.

12-3. Humanistic psychology emphasizes the (similarities/**differences**) between human beings and the other animal species; believes we (are controlled by/**can rise above**) our biological heritage; asserts that we are largely (**rational**/irrational) creatures; and stresses a subjective, _____phenomenological_____ approach, which asserts that one must appreciate people's subjective impressions as opposed to the realities of the situation.

Answers: 12-1. animal, primitive (animalistic) 12-2. determinism, unique 12-3. differences, can rise above, rational, phenomenological.

13. **Identify the single structural construct in Rogers's person-centered theory and summarize his view of personality development.**

13-1. Recall that Freud viewed personality in terms of three structures, the id, ego, and superego. What is the single structure in Rogers's theory? Define that term.
the self or self-concept — it consists of the beliefs one has about oneself — one's self perceptions.

13-2. Although Mr. J. tends to be a submissive and somewhat lazy person (and that is the way his friends, family, and co-workers describe him), he views himself as hard-working and dynamic, a leader both on the job and at home.
(a) What is Mr. J.'s self-concept? *he is hard-working, dynamic, and a leader*

(b) Is his self-concept congruent or incongruent? *incongruent*

(c) According to Rogers, what parental behavior may have led to this incongruence? *conditional love or acceptance*

(d) According to Rogers, what parental behavior would have resulted in Mr. J.'s achieving congruence rather than incongruence? *unconditional love/acceptance*

13-3. Define the following Rogerian concepts.
(a) conditional love: *affection given conditionally — the child/person must live up to another's expectation in order to receive love*
(b) unconditional love: *affection given without condition — full acceptance of the person that is not dependent on what they are or do*

Answers: 13-1. The self or self-concept; it consists of the beliefs one has about oneself—one's self-perceptions. 13-2. (a) that he is hard-working, dynamic, and a leader (b) incongruent (c) conditional love or acceptance (d) unconditional love or acceptance   13-3. (a) affection given conditionally, the condition being that the child or adult must live up to another's expectations (b) affection given without conditions, full acceptance of the person that is not dependent on what he or she is or does.

14. Explain what Maslow meant by self-actualization and summarize his findings on the characteristics of self-actualizing people.

14-1.   In a few words, what did Maslow mean by self-actualization? *fulfilling one's potential*

14-2.   Suppose a woman had the talent and ambition to be a mathematician but followed a more practical course and became a nurse instead. What is the status of her need for self-actualization and her mental health, according to Maslow? *she isn't self actualized, she is not as healthy as she could be.*

14-3.   Which of the following characteristics did Maslow ascribe to self-actualized people? Place Y in the blank if the description applies, N if it does not.

   Y   Spontaneous.

   N   Relates better to fantasy than reality.

   Y   Sensitive to others' needs.

   Y   Has more profound emotional experiences than others.

   N   Uncomfortable being alone.

   Y   Not dependent on others for approval.

   Y   Enjoys strong friendships, which are few in number.

Answers: 14-1. the need to fulfill one's potential   14-2. She is not self-actualized, so she is not as healthy as she could be.   14-3. Y, N, Y, Y, N, Y, Y.

15. Summarize the strengths and weaknesses of the humanistic approach to personality.

15-1.   Three contributions from humanistic psychology are discussed in the text. First, the humanistic movement called attention to __*subjective (personal)*__ factors, such as beliefs and expectancies. Second, the movement emphasized the notion of the __*self*__, one's view of oneself. Third, it stressed the issue of what constitutes a __*normal (healthy)*__, as opposed to an abnormal, personality.

15-2.   Critics have also identified several weaknesses of the humanistic formulations. Match the weaknesses listed below with the statements by placing the appropriate letters in the blanks.
   A. poor testability
   B. unrealistic view of human nature
   C. inadequate evidence

   C   Humanistic psychologists tend to scorn research, so little experimental support for their views has emerged.

   b   Even without research, some of the descriptions, such as those of self-actualized personalities, have an idealized, perfectionistic ring.

   a   Humanistic ideas are frequently difficult to define, so research on some concepts is difficult or impossible.

Answers: 15-1. subjective (personal, cognitive), self (self-concept), normal (healthy)   15-2. C, B, A.

BIOLOGICAL PERSPECTIVES

16. **Describe Sheldon's and Eysenck's biological theories of personality.**

16-1. Following is a list of physical characteristics. Which Sheldon body type is each associated with? Identify the body type by placing the appropriate letters in the blanks below.

A. thin   Endomorph: _b_ _e_

B. fat   Mesomorph: _c_ _f_

C. muscular   Ectomorph: _a_ _d_

D. frail

E. soft

F. strong

16-2. Match the personality characteristics with the Sheldon body type by placing the appropriate letters in the blanks below.

A. inhibited   Endomorph: _h_ _d_ _g_

B. domineering   Mesomorph: _b_ _f_ _i_

C. intellectual   Ectomorph: _a_ _c_ _e_

D. sociable

E. fearful

F. energetic

G. affectionate

H. relaxed

I. competitive

16-3. The major flaw in Sheldon's procedures was that Sheldon himself, who was, of course, familiar with his own theory of body types, was the one who made the personality ratings. Thus, there was no double blind (Chapter 2), and the research probably suffered from ___experimenter___ bias. Sheldon's findings (have/(have not)) been supported by subsequent research.

16-4. According to Eysenck, individual differences in personality can be understood in terms of a heirarchy of traits. At the top of the heirarchy are three fundamental higher traits: ___extraversion___, ___neuroticism___, and ___psychoticism___.

16-5. Eysenck asserts that a major factor in personality involves the ease with which people can be ___conditioned___, either operantly or classically. Eysenck believes that differences in conditionability, like personality differences in general, are to a large extent a function of (environmental/(genetic)) factors.

16-6. Conditionability, in turn, is related to extraversion-introversion. Eysenck has indicated that (extraverts/(introverts)) have higher levels of physiological arousal, which make ((extraverts)/introverts) more readily conditioned.

16-7. Why would it be that people who are more easily conditioned tend to be introverts?

17. **Summarize the Featured Study (Tellegen et al., 1988) on personality similarity in twins and other research on heritability of personality.**

    17-1.   Which of the following groups were included in the featured study?
        a. identical twins reared together
        b. identical twins reared apart
        c. fraternal twins reared together
        d. fraternal twins reared apart
        e. all of the above

    17-2.   The most important and conclusive result of this study was the finding that the personalities of

        _____ were more similar than those of _____.
        a. identical twins reared together
        b. identical twins reared apart
        c. fraternal twins reared together
        d. fraternal twins reared apart

    17-3.   Approximately what percentage of the variance was assumed to be caused by genetic factors?
        a. 5% to 10%
        b. 10% to 22%
        c. 20% to 43%
        d. 40% to 58%

    17-4.   How important a determinant of personality was family environment, according to the results of this study?
        a. of very little importance
        b. of great importance, but not as important as heredity
        c. more important than heredity

    17-5.   The recent twin studies are likely to have a major impact on the way psychologists think about the causes of human behavior. Why are the results so important and so surprising?

theories of development and personality have tended to stress the importance of the environment, especially the family environment; the recent twin studies find heredity to be very important and family environment to be of little importance. Thus, the results are contrary to the expectations most of us and contrary to much of the theorizing in the field of personality.

18. **Summarize the the strengths and weaknesses of the biological approach to personality.**

18-1. Generally, parents are blamed for kids' personalities. I recently asked a friend of mine why she thought a mutual acquaintance of ours was so obnoxious. She said, "Well, raised with such crazy parents, what would you expect?" I said, "Is that an argument for environment or heredity?" That is one of the benefits of the twin studies: They put data in place of speculation. But what are some of the weaknesses of this research? Specifically, comment on the weaknesses of the following:
(a) heritability ratios: *Heritability ratios are rough estimates that will vary, depending on sampling and other factors.*

(b) separation of nature and nurture: *nature & nurture interact and thus cannot really be separated.*

(c) a biological theory: *there are many comprehensive theories of personality that attempt to account for the entire range of human behavior. There is no such comprehensive biological theory of personality.*

Answers: 18-1. (a) Heritability ratios are rough estimates that will vary, depending on sampling and other factors. (b) Nature and nurture *interact* and thus cannot really be separated. (c) There are many comprehensive theories of personality that attempt to account for the entire range of human behavior. There is no such comprehensive biological theory of personality.

CONTEMPORARY EMPIRICAL APPROACHES TO PERSONALITY

19. **Discuss the meaning and significance of locus of control.**

19-1. Locus of control seems to be an important and fairly stable personality trait that actually predicts behavior. Indicate which of the following statements describe internals and which describe externals by placing an I or an E in the blanks.

   _e_ They believe that their successes and failures are due to fate or luck.

   _e_ They are more likely to develop psychological disorders.

   _e_ They are more likely to experience anxiety and depression.

   _I_ They believe that the consequences of their behaviors are due to their actions or abilities.

   _I_ They are more likely to have high academic achievement.

   _I_ They are more likely to give up smoking.

   _I_ They are more likely to take up an exercise program.

19-2. In the space below give a brief, general definition of the concept *locus of control.*
locus of control is a generalized expectancy about the degree to which individuals control their outcomes.

Answers: 19-1. E, E, E, I, I, I, I   19-2. extent to which people believe that their actions affect outcomes (i.e., successes and failures). People with an internal locus of control believe that their actions strongly affect outcomes; people with an external locus of control believe that outcomes are controlled by external events, namely luck or fate.

20. **Discuss the meaning of sensation seeking and identify the characteristics of high sensation seekers.**

20-1. Sensation seekers are individuals who prefer high levels of sensory stimulation. In each pair of items that follow, circle the characteristic that best describes sensation seekers as opposed to sensation avoiders.

risk-taking _____ risk-avoiding
nonconforming _____ conforming
extraverted _____ introverted
impulsive _____ cautious
sexually adventurous _____ sexually conservative
like spicy foods _____ like bland foods

20-2. Sensation seeking seems to be a fairly potent personality characteristic that may influence the course of romantic relationships. Do people tend to prefer partners who are similar to themselves in sensation seeking, or do opposites attract with regard to this characteristic?

people prefer partners who are similar to themselves in sensation seeking

Answers: 20-1. All the items on the left should be circled. 20-2. As is the case with personality traits in general, people prefer partners who are similar to themselves in sensation seeking.

21. **Explain what is meant by self-monitoring and discuss the effects of self-monitoring on interpersonal relationships.**

21-1. Describe the characteristics of people who are high in self-monitoring with regard to the following situations:

(a) impression management: *adjust behavior to create desired impression*

(b) control of facial expressions: *good actors - able to control facial expressions to feign emotion when useful.*

(c) spotting deception: *good a spotting deceptive impression management in others.*

(d) dating and sexual relationships: *high self monitors date a greater variety of partners, less emotional commitment.*

21-2. To review locus of control, sensation seeking, and self-monitoring, match the specific trait with the behavioral descriptions by placing the correct letters in the blanks.
A. internal locus of control
B. external locus of control
C. high sensation seeking
D. low sensation seeking
E. high self-monitoring
F. low self-monitoring.

___C___ Last summer Ralph decided on the spur of the moment to sell his car and spend two months traveling by foot in India. Ralph's hobbies include sky-diving and gambling.

___b___ Floyd never seems to get the breaks in life. He feels somewhat depressed and hopes that fate will be kind to him. He is certain that there is nothing he can do to change the position he is in.

___e___ Margie figures she knows what people want, and she very successfully adjusts her personality to fit the occasion or the person she is with. She is good at faking emotion and also good at detecting deception in others. She is promiscuous, avoids emotional commitments, and finds the prospect of long-term relationships offensive.

___f___ Alice usually doesn't try to hide her feelings and isn't very good at it when she does try. She prefers close relationships with the opposite sex to playing the field. She isn't especially gullible, but she also isn't really good at figuring out when people are trying to deceive her.

___a___ Ruppert had a considerable amount of difficulty on the first test in his advanced calculus course, which surprised him since he generally did well in school. So, after going over the problems that he missed he adopted a different study strategy.

___d___ Jan hates it when her boyfriend drives too fast, and she refuses to go skiing with him because she thinks it's too dangerous.

Answers: 21-1. (a) able to adjust behavior to create desired impression (b) good actors: able to control facial expressions to feign emotion when useful (c) good at spotting deceptive impression management in others (d) more partners, less emotional commitment   21-2. C, B, E, F, A, D.

PUTTING IT IN PERSPECTIVE

22. **Explain how this chapter highlights two of our unifying themes: (a) psychology's theoretical diversity and (b) psychology evolves in a sociohistorical context.**

22-1. To some degree different theories of personality attempt to explain different facets of behavior, so in some cases the theories don't confront each other. On the other hand, there is considerable disagreement between theories on certain basic issues. For example, as shown in the illustrated comparison in your text, the Freudian, behavioral, and biological perspectives accept the notion of determinism while the ___humanistic___ perspective does not; and, the biological perspective and to some extent the psychoanalytic viewpoint stress genetic inheritance while the ___behavioral___ perspective stresses the environment.

22-2. There has also been some blending of theories: Eysenck's approach combines a ___biological___ perspective with behavioral concepts, and social learning theory combines behavioral concepts with ___cognitive___ processes.

22-3. With regard to the sociohistorical context, it is clear that psychology has affected our culture. For example, the surrealistic art movement was clearly influenced by ___psychoanalytic___ psychology, and the debate on the effects of media violence has been influenced by ___social learning___ theory.

22-4. In turn, culture has affected psychology. For example, it seems quite likely that the sexually repressive climate of Victorian Vienna caused Freud to emphasize the _sexuality_ of human behavior; and it is clear, from Freud's own description, that World War I influenced his development of the second Freudian instinct, the _aggression_ instinct. Thus, psychology evolves in a _sociohistorical_ context.

Answers: **22-1.** humanistic, behavioral **22-2.** biological (genetic, hereditary), cognitive (modeling, observational learning) **22-3.** psychoanalytic, social learning **22-4.** sexuality, aggression, sociohistorical.

APPLICATION: UNDERSTANDING PERSONALITY ASSESSMENT

23. Outline the four principal uses of personality tests.

23-1. List the four principal uses of personality tests in the blanks next to the correct descriptions.

(a) _psychological research_   Measuring personality traits in empirical studies.

(b) _counseling_   Advising people on career plans and decisions.

(c) _personnel selection_   Choosing employees in business and government.

(d) _clinical diagnosis_   Assessing type of psychological disorder a person may have.

Answers: **23-1.** (a) psychological research (b) counseling (c) personnel selection (d) clinical diagnosis.

24. Describe the MMPI and 16 PF personality tests and summarize the strengths and weaknesses of self-report inventories.

24-1. The MMPI and 16 PF personality inventories are (projective/self-report) tests. Both tests are also used to measure (single/multiple) traits.

24-2. Identify which test, the MMPI or 16 PF, is described by each of the following.

_16 PF_   Originally designed to assess the normal personality.

MMPI   Originally designed to diagnose psychological disorders.

_16 PF_   Consists of 187 items.

MMPI   Contains 567 items.

MMPI   Includes four validity scales to help detect deception.

24-3. The major strength of self-report inventories, in comparison with simply asking a person what they are like, is that self-report inventories provide a more precise and more (objective/personal) measure of personality.

24-4. The major weakness of self-report inventories is that they are subject to several sources of error, including the following. (1) Test-takers may intentionally fake responses, that is, may engage in deliberate _deception_. (2) While not realizing it, people may answer questions in ways to make themselves "look good," the _social desirability_ bias. (3) In addition, some people tend either to agree or to disagree with nearly every statement on a test, a source of error involving _response_ sets.

Answers: **24-1.** self-report, multiple **24-2.** 16 PF, MMPI, 16 PF, MMPI, MMPI **24-3.** objective **24-4.** deception, social desirability, response.

25. **Describe the projective hypothesis and summarize the strengths and weaknesses of projective tests.**

25-1. If you've ever looked at clouds and described the images you see, you've done something like what is done in projective testing. If you have further assumed that the images reflect something about your personality, then you've bought the notion behind the projective hypothesis. The projective hypothesis is the idea that people will tend to ___*project*___ their characteristics onto ambiguous stimuli, so that what they see reveals something about their personalities and problems.

25-2. Two major projective tests are the Rorschach, a series of ___*ink blots*___, and the TAT, a series of simple ___*pictures (scenes)*___.

25-3. The advantages of projective tests are that (1) since the way the tests are interpreted is not at all obvious, it is difficult for people to engage in intentional ___*deception*___; and (2) projective tests may help tap problems or aspects of personality of which people are ___*unconscious*___.

25-4. The major weaknesses of projective tests concerns their consistency or ___*reliability*___ and their accuracy or ___*validity*___. It should be noted, however, that when users agree on a systematic scoring procedure, (no/some) projective tests have shown adequate reliability and validity .

Answers: 25-1. project 25-2. inkblots, pictures (scenes) 25-3. deception, unconscious (unaware) 25-4. reliability, validity, some.

REVIEW OF KEY TERMS

Archetypes
Behaviorism
Cardinal trait
Central trait
Collective unconscious
Compensation
Conscious
Defense mechanisms
Displacement
Ego
Extraverts
Fixation
Humanism
Id
Identification
Incongruence
Introverts

Locus of control
Model
Need for self-actualization
Observational learning
Oedipal complex
Personal unconscious
Personality
Personality trait
Phenomenological approach
Pleasure principle
Preconscious
Projection
Psychodynamic theories
Psychosexual stages
Rationalization
Reaction formation

Reality principle
Reciprocal determinism
Regression
Repression
Secondary trait
Self-actualizing persons
Self-concept
Self-efficacy
Self-esteem
Self-monitoring
Self-report inventories
Sensation seeking
Social interest
Striving for superiority
Superego
Unconscious

_____ 1. An individual's unique constellation of consistent behavioral traits.

_____ 2. A characteristic that represents a durable disposition to behave in a particular way in a variety of situations.

_____ 3. A dominant trait that permeates nearly all of a person's behavior.

_____ 4. Prominent, general dispositions found in anyone.

_____ 5. Less consistent dispositions that surface in some situations but not in others.

_____ 6. All the diverse theories, descended from the work of Sigmund Freud, that focus on unconscious mental forces.

_____ 7. The primitive, instinctive component of personality that operates according to the pleasure principle.

_____ 8. The id's demands for immediate gratification of its urges.

_____ 9. The decision-making component of personality that operates according to the reality principle.

_____ 10. The ego's delay of gratification of the id's urges until appropriate outlets and situations can be found.

_____ 11. The moral component of personality that incorporates social standards about what represents right and wrong.

_____ 12. Consists of whatever you are aware of at a particular point in time.

_____ 13 Contains material just beneath the surface of awareness that can be easily retrieved.

_____ 14. Contains thoughts, memories, and desires that are well below the surface of conscious awareness.

_____ 15. The series of largely unconscious Freudian reactions that protect a person from unpleasant emotions such as anxiety or guilt.

_____ 16. The defense mechanism which pushes distressing thoughts and feelings into the unconscious or keeps them from emerging into consciousness.

_____ 17. Attributing your own thoughts, feelings, or motives to another.

_____ 18. Creating false but plausible excuses to justify unacceptable behavior.

_____ 19. Diverting emotional feelings (usually anger) from their original source to a substitute target.

_____ 20. Behaving in a way that is exactly the opposite of one's true feelings.

_____ 21. Reverting to immature patterns of behavior.

_____ 22. Bolstering self-esteem by forming an imaginary or real alliance with some person or group.

_____ 23. Developmental periods with a characteristic sexual focus that leave their mark on adult personality.

_____ 24. A failure to move forward from one stage to another as expected.

_____ 25. Characterized by erotically tinged desires for one's opposite-sex parent and hostility toward one's same-sex parent.

_____ 26. Jungian concept referring to the structure holding material that is not in one's awareness because it has been repressed or forgotten.

_____ 27. A storehouse of latent memory traces inherited from our ancestral past.

_____ 28. Emotionally charged images and thought forms that have universal meaning.

_____ 29. People who tend to be preoccupied with the internal world of their own thoughts, feelings, and experiences.

_____ 30. People who tend to be interested in the external world of people and things.

_____ 31. A universal drive to adapt, to improve oneself, and to master life's challenges.

	32.	Efforts to overcome imagined or real inferiorities by developing one's abilities.
_____	33.	An innate sense of kinship and belongingness with the human race.
_____	34.	A theoretical orientation based on the premise that scientific psychology should study only observable behavior.
_____	35.	The assumption that internal mental events, external environmental events, and overt behavior all influence one another.
_____	36.	Learning that occurs when an organism's responding is influenced by the observation of others.
_____	37.	A person whose behavior is observed by another.
_____	38.	Our belief about our ability to perform behaviors that should lead to expected outcomes.
_____	39.	A theoretical orientation that emphasizes the unique qualities of humans, especially their freedom and potential for personal growth.
_____	40.	Approach that assumes we have to appreciate individuals' personal, subjective experiences to truly understand their behavior.
_____	41.	A collection of beliefs about one's own nature, unique qualities, and typical behavior.
_____	42.	The degree of disparity between one's self-concept and one's actual experience.
_____	43.	The need to fulfill one's potential.
_____	44.	People with exceptionally healthy personalities, marked by continued personal growth.
_____	45.	A generalized expectancy about the degree to which we control our outcomes.
_____	46.	A generalized preference for high or low levels of sensory stimulation.
_____	47.	The degree to which people attend to and control the impression they make on others in social interactions.
_____	48.	A person's overall assessment of her or his personal adequacy or worth.
_____	49.	Personality tests that ask people a series of questions about their characteristic behavior.

Answers: 1. personality 2. personality trait 3. cardinal trait 4. central trait 5. secondary trait 6. psychodynamic theories 7. id 8. pleasure principle 9. ego 10. reality principle 11. superego 12. conscious 13. preconscious 14. unconscious 15. defense mechanisms 16. repression 17. projection 18. rationalization 19. displacement 20. reaction formation 21. regression 22. identification 23. psychosexual stages 24. fixation 25. Oedipal complex 26. personal unconscious 27. collective unconscious 28. archetypes 29. introverts 30. extraverts 31. striving for superiority 32. compensation 33. social interest 34. behaviorism 35. reciprocal determinism 36. observational learning 37. model 38. self-efficacy 39. humanism 40. phenomenological approach 41. self-concept 42. incongruence 43. need for self-actualization 44. self-actualizing persons 45. locus of control 46. sensation seeking 47. self-monitoring 48. self-esteem 49. self-report inventories.

REVIEW OF KEY PEOPLE

Alfred Adler
Gordon Allport
Albert Bandura
Raymond Cattell
Hans Eysenck

Sigmund Freud
Carl Jung
Abraham Maslow
Walter Mischel
Carl Rogers

Julian Rotter
B. F. Skinner
Mark Snyder
Marvin Zuckerman

_____ 1. One of the first theorists to make systematic distinctions between traits in terms of their importance.

_____ 2. The founder of psychoanalysis.

_____ 3. Developed the theory called analytical psychology and anticipated the humanists' emphasis on personal growth and self-actualization.

_____ 4. Founder of an approach to personality named individual psychology.

_____ 5. Modern behaviorism's most prominent theorist, recognized for his theories on operant conditioning.

_____ 6. A contemporary behavioral theorist who elaborated the concept of observational learning.

_____ 7. His chief contribution to personality theory has been to focus attention on the extent to which situational factors govern behavior.

_____ 8. One of the fathers of the human potential movement, he called his approach a person-centered theory.

_____ 9. The humanist who developed a theory of self-actualization.

_____ 10. Proposed that conditionability and introversion-extraversion are largely genetically determined.

_____ 11. The prominent social learning theorist who described the locus of control as a personality dimension.

_____ 12. The biologically oriented theorist who first described the personality trait of sensation seeking.

_____ 13. Described the trait of self-monitoring.

Answers: 1. Allport 2. Freud 3. Jung 4. Adler 5. Skinner 6. Bandura 7. Mischel 8. Rogers 9. Maslow
10. Eysenck 11. Rotter 12. Zuckerman 13. Snyder.

1. Personality traits are characterized by:
   a. consistency and distinctiveness
   b. charm and wit
   c. change as a function of the situation
   d. lack of individual differences

2. Which of the following are among the basic issues around which personality theories have been constructed?
   a. determinism versus free will
   b. consciousness versus the unconscious
   c. nature versus nurture
   d. all of the above

3. Which of the following is entirely unconscious, according to Freud?
   a. the id
   b. the ego
   c. the superego
   d. the archetype

4. Although Osmo at an unconscious level has great hatred for Cosmo, he says he likes Cosmo and, to the outside world, gives all the appearance of liking him. Which defense mechanism is Osmo using?
   a. regression
   b. reaction formation
   c. projection
   d. rationalization

5. The Oedipal complex occurs during the:
   a. oral stage
   b. anal stage
   c. phallic stage
   d. genital stage

6. Which of the following concepts did Carl Jung develop?
   a. archetypes
   b. the collective unconscious
   c. introversion-extraversion
   d. all of the above

7. Which of the following did Adler emphasize in his theory of personality?
   a. striving for superiority
   b. castration anxiety
   c. introversion-extraversion
   d. all of the above

8. Much of the behavior that we call personality results from reinforcement and observational learning, according to:
   a. Jung
   b. Skinner
   c. Bandura
   d. Adler

9. Which of the following accepts a deterministic view of human behavior?
   a. the psychoanalytic approach
   b. the biological approach
   c. the behavioral approach
   d. all of the above

10. According to Rogers, what causes incongruence?
    a. an inherited sense of irony
    b. conditional acceptance or affection
    c. unconditional acceptance or affection
    d. unconditioned stimuli

11. Suppose I had the desire and potential to be a violinist but became, instead, a psychologist. What is wrong with me, according to Maslow?
    a. I suffer from incongruence.
    b. I suffer from irony.
    c. I have not achieved self-actualization.
    d. I am directed toward overcoming inferiority.

12. According to Eysenck, differences in personality result in large part from differences in:
    a. introversion-extraversion
    b. genetic inheritance
    c. conditionability
    d. all of the above

13. Recent studies of the personalities of identical and fraternal twins are surprising and important because they indicate that:
    a. personality is in large part genetically determined
    b. environment is more important than heredity
    c. birth order is critical in personality formation
    d. monads and archetypes can be accounted for genetically

14. Sally believes that whatever happens to her, be it good or bad, is largely a matter of luck or fate. Sally has:
    a. an internal locus of control
    b. an external locus of control
    c. high self-monitoring
    d. a sensation seeking tendency

15. Amanda is extraverted, impulsive, and risk-taking, and she likes fast cars, spicy food, and adventurous men. She is also nonconforming, especially in the sense that she will not adapt her personality to the person she happens to be with. Amanda is high on:
    a. external locus of control
    b. self-monitoring
    c. sensation seeking
    d. illegal substances

Answers: 1. a 2. d 3. a 4. b 5. c 6. d 7. a 8. c 9. d 10. b 11. c 12. d 13. a 14. b 15. c.

13 STRESS, COPING, AND HEALTH

REVIEW OF KEY IDEAS

THE NATURE OF STRESS

1. **Define stress and discuss the relationship between the severity of stress and its effects.**

   1-1. The text defines stress as any circumstances that threaten or are *perceived* to threaten one's well-being. This definition would indicate that stress is a very (subjective/objective) experience.

   1-2. What did Lazarus find with respect to minor hassles as compared to major stressful events?

   Answers: 1-1. subjective 1-2. Minor hassles are more strongly related to mental health.

2. **Describe the key processes and factors in our appraisals of stress.**

   2-1. When you appraise an event as either irrelevant, relevant but not threatening, or stressful, you are making a ___primary___ appraisal.

   2-2. When you appraise an event as stressful and then you evaluate your coping resources and options you are making a ___secondary___ appraisal.

   2-3. While a variety of factors influence stress evaluation, two are particularly important. Identify them in the situations described below.
   (a) A salesperson friend of mine is a frequent flyer, yet she still finds flying is stressful and can quickly tell you why this is so. What do you think she says?
   ___because she's not in control___

   (b) Why are natural disasters such as earthquakes and tornadoes particularly stressful?
   ___unpredictable___

   Answers: 2-1. primary 2-2. secondary 2-3. (a) She feels a lack of personal control when she flies. (b) because they are unpredictable.

3. **Describe the four principal types of stress discussed in the text.**

   3-1. The text lists four principal types of stress: frustration, conflict, change, and pressure. Identify these types of stress in the following situations.
   (a) You have three major exams coming up next week and you are also in charge of your sorority's fast-approaching homecoming celebration. _pressure_

   (b) Your family moves from a large city to a rather small rural community. _change_

   (c) You are late for an appointment and stuck in a traffic jam. _frustration_

   (d) Your are forced to choose between two good movies on television. _conflict_

   3-2. There are two kinds of pressure. One is the pressure to get things accomplished, or the pressure to ___perform___. The other is the pressure to abide by rules, or the pressure to ___conform___.

   Answers: 3-1. (a) pressure (b) change (c) frustration (d) conflict   3-2. perform, conform.

4. **Identify the three basic types of conflict and discuss which types are most troublesome.**

   4-1. Many persons do not want to pay their income taxes, but, on the other hand, they don't want to go to jail either. These persons are faced with an ___avoidance___ - ___avoidance___ conflict.

   4-2. Getting married has both positive and negative aspects that make it an excellent example of an ___approach___ - ___avoidance___ conflict.

   4-3. Consider the problem of the coed who has to choose between scholarships for two different universities. Since she can't accept both she is faced with an ___approach___ ___approach___ conflict.

   4-4. Now that you have correctly identified the three basic types of conflict, list them below in their order of troublesomeness, beginning with the least troublesome.
   (a) ___approach___ - ___approach___
   (b) ___approach___ - ___avoidance___
   (c) ___avoidance___ - ___avoidance___

   Answers: 4-1. avoidance-avoidance   4-2. approach-avoidance   4-3. approach-approach   4-4. (a) approach-approach (b) approach-avoidance (c) avoidance-avoidance.

CHAPTER THIRTEEN

5. **Summarize evidence on life change as a form of stress.**

5-1.   The Social Readjustment Rating Scale (SRRS) measures the stress induced by _changes_

in daily living routines. The developers of this scale theorized that all kinds of life changes, both

pleasant and unpleasant, would induce stress. Early research showed that high scores on the SRRS were

correlated with physical _illness_ .

5-2.   Later research began to indicate that high scores on the SRRS were primarily the result of (<u>pleasant/</u>

<u>unpleasant</u>) life changes. Other independent research has found that change by itself can induce stress,

but the greatest stress appears to be induced by _unpleasant_ life changes?

Answers: 5-1. changes, illness   5-2. unpleasant, unpleasant.

RESPONDING TO STRESS

6. **Identify some common emotional responses to stress and discuss the effects of emotional arousal.**

6-1.   The text describes three different dimensions of emotions that are particularly likely to be triggered by
stress. Identify which of these dimensions is most likely to be present in the following situations.
(a) This dimension is likely to be found when a person feels helpless and unable to cope.
dejection, sadness, & grief

(b) This dimension is likely to be found when a person feels put upon and treated unfairly.
annoyance, anger, & rage

(c) This dimension is likely to be found when a person faces conflict or uncertainty.
apprehension, anxiety, & fear

6-2.   What do optimal-arousal theories say about what happens to the optimal-arousal level as tasks become
more complex?
the optimal-arousal level decreases as tasks become more complex

Answers: 6-1. (a) dejection, sadness, and grief (b) annoyance, anger, and rage (c) apprehension, anxiety, and
fear   6-2. The optimal-arousal level decreases.

7. **Describe the fight-or-flight response and the three stages of the General Adaptation Syndrome.**

7-1.   What division of the autonomic nervous system mediates the fight-or-flight response?
sympathetic

7-2.   Although the body's fight-or-flight response appears to be an evolutionary carry-over from the past, why
is it perhaps of more harm than help to modern human beings?
because most stressful situations generally require a more complex response than simple fight or flight

7-3. Indicate which of the three stages of the General Adaptation Syndrome is being described in each of the following.
(a) This is the initial stage in which the body prepares for the fight-or-flight response.

alarm reaction

(b) This is the second stage in which the body stabilizes its physiological changes as it begins to effectively cope with the stress.   *stage of resistance*

(c) This is the third stage in which the body's coping resources are becoming depleted and the resistance to many diseases declines.   *stage of exhaustion*

7-4. Why did Hans Selye call this body-defense system the *General* Adaptation Syndrome?

because it is a general response to all kinds of stressful situations

Answers: 7-1. sympathetic nervous system   7-2. because most stressful situations generally require a more complex response than simple fight or flight   7-3. (a) stage of alarm (b) stage of resistance (c) stage of exhaustion
7-4. because it is a *general* response to all kinds of stressful situations.

8. **Discuss the two major pathways along which the brain sends signals to the endocrine system in response to stress.**

   8-1. Fill in the missing parts in the diagram below detailing the two major pathways along which the brain sends signals to the endocrine system.

   CEREBRAL CORTEX

   (a) *hypothalamus*

   SYMPATHETIC NS   PITUITARY GLAND
                                                                   ACTH

   (b) *adrenal medulla* GLAND   (c) *adrenal cortex* GLAND

   CATECHOLAMINES   CORTICOSTEROIDS

   Increases heart rate & respiration, etc.   Increases energy, inhibits tissue inflammation, etc.

   Answers: 8-1. (a) hypothalamus (b) adrenal medulla (c) adrenal cortex.

9. **Describe and evaluate aggression, giving up, and self-indulgence as behavioral responses to stress.**

   9-1. Answer the following questions regarding aggression, giving up, and self-indulgence as responses to stress.

   (a) Which of these responses is frequently, but not always, triggered by frustration?

   aggression

   (b) Which of these responses often results from a cognitive appraisal that one lacks control over problems? *giving up*

   (c) Which of these responses is illustrated by the saying, "When the going gets tough the tough go shopping"? *self-indulgence*

9-2. What is a common fault of all three of these behavioral responses to stress? _they divert effort away from solutions to problems._

Answers: 9-1. (a) aggression (b) giving up (c) self-indulgence   9-2. They divert effort away from solutions to problems.

10. Discuss defensive coping and constructive coping as mechanisms for dealing with stress.

10-1. Indicate whether each of the following situations illustrates defensive or constructive coping.

(a) This kind of coping is much more oriented to reality. _Constructive_

(b) This kind of coping is largely unconscious, although it can occur at conscious levels.
defensive

(c) This kind of coping uses self-deception to distort reality. _defensive_

(d) This kind of coping is much more task-relevant and action oriented. _constructive_

10-2. What two major problems arise from using defensive coping?
avoidance strategy - rarely provides a genuine solution
often leads to delaying facing up to a problem - lets problems fester/grow

10-3. What is perhaps the major emotion that triggers the onset of defensive coping? _anxiety_

Answers: 10-1. (a) constructive (b) defensive (c) defensive (d) constructive   10-2. They avoid the problem and they delay a possible solution   10-3. anxiety.

THE EFFECTS OF STRESS ON PSYCHOLOGICAL FUNCTIONING

11. Discuss the effects of stress on task performance, including the burnout syndrome.

11-1. Baumeister's theory as to why stress affects task performance is that pressure to perform makes us self-conscious and this elevated self-consciousness disrupts our _attention_. Attention may be distorted in two ways. One way is that the person fails to focus sufficient attention on the task, or to put it another way, becomes _distracted_. The second way is that the self-conscious person may focus too much attention on the task. The term we commonly use for this is _choking_ under pressure.

11-2. Indicate whether each of the following statements regarding the burnout syndrome is true or false.

_T_ Burnout is a potential problem in all occupations and may be caused by non-work-related stress as well.

_F_ The onset of of burnout is usually sudden.

11-3. What three general areas of functioning does the exhaustion produced by burnout affect?
physical, mental, emotion

Answers: 11-1. attention, distracted, choking   11-2. true, false   11-3. physical, mental, and emotional (in any order).

12. **Summarize the procedure, results, and implications of the Featured Study on choking under pressure.**

12-1.   What did Baumeister's theory predict about the relationship between home team advantage and the pressure to win? *As the pressure to win increases, the home team advantage becomes negative*

12-2.   How did the study distinguish between high pressure and low pressure games? *Final playoff games were assumed to be high pressure, games previous to the final games were assumed to be of less pressure*

12-3.   What did the study find regarding the home team winning percentage in the final playoff games? *the winning percentage dropped dramatically*

12-4.   What did the study find regarding the home team performance with respect to fielding errors and free-throw shooting percentages in the final games? *# of home team fielding errors increases, and the shooting percentage for free throws decreased*

12-5.   What advice can we offer persons who bet on athletic events? *don't bet on the home team on final playoff games.*

Answers: 12-1. As the pressure to win increases, the home team advantage becomes negative.   12-2. Final playoff games were assumed to be high-pressure games, while games previous to the final games were assumed to be of less pressure.   12-3. The winning percentage dropped dramatically.   12-4. The number of home team fielding errors increased and the shooting percentage for free throws decreased.   12-5. Don't bet on the home team on final playoff games.

13. **Discuss posttraumatic stress disorder and other psychological problems and disorders that may result from stress.**

13-1.   Answer the following questions regarding posttraumatic stress syndrome.
(a) What is unique about posttraumatic stress disorder? *the disturbed behavior occurs sometime after the stressful event*

(b) What are the two most common causes of this syndrome among men? *combat experiences or seeing someone die*

(c) What are the two most common causes of this syndrome among women? *physical attack/rape, seeing someone die*

(d) What were the three most common symptoms found in a diverse collection of persons suffering from this syndrome? *nightmares, sleeping difficulties, feelings of jumpiness.*

13-2.   The text lists five psychological disorders that research has shown to be related to chronic stress. List these disorders below. *poor academic performance, insomnia, sexual difficulties, drug abuse, and anxiety/dejection*

THE EFFECTS OF STRESS ON PHYSICAL HEALTH

14. **Describe the Type A behavior pattern and summarize the evidence linking it to coronary heart disease.**

   14-1. While the Type A behavior pattern is marked by competitive, aggressive, hostile behavior, two characteristics of Type A behavior appear to be most closely linked to coronary heart disorder. What are these two characteristics? *quick-tempered anger and hard-driving competitiveness.*

   14-2. Early research indicated that Type A persons were ___*6*___ times more likely to suffer from coronary heart disease than were Type B persons. Continuing research has since shown that the coronary risk is more (severe/moderate) than originally thought. It appears that Type A behavior increases coronary risk for (all/some) persons; perhaps those who are genetically predisposed to heart disorder.

   Answers: 14-1. quick-tempered anger and hard-driving competitiveness 14-2. six, moderate, some.

15. **Discuss and evaluate other evidence linking stress to immunosuppression and a variety of physical illnesses.**

   15-1. Research has found stress to be related to numerous diseases and disorders. What effect on the lymphocytes (the specialized white blood cells that are important in initiating the immune response) appears to be the link between stress and so many disorders? *Stress appears to suppress the proliferation of the lymphocytes (suppressing the immune system in general)*

   15-2. While many studies have shown a relationship between stress and numerous physical illness, we can still not state definitely that stress leads to physical illness. Why is this? *Because all of the relevant research that has been done is correlational —you cannot infer cause & effect*

   Answers: 15-1. Stress appears to suppress the proliferation of the lymphocytes (thus suppressing the immune system in general). 15-2. because almost all of the data are correlational (and you cannot infer cause and effect relationships with these kinds of data).

16. **Discuss how social support, hardiness, optimism, and autonomic reactivity moderate individual differences in stress tolerance.**

   16-1. What do persons who report good social support during times of stress really mean according to research? *their friends & family aren't contributing to the stress*

   16-2. What three personality characteristics were found to differentiate hardy executives from less-hardy executives? *more committed, felt more in control, had bigger appetites for challenge*

16-3. What difference was found between optimists and pessimists with respect to good physical health?

Optimists were most likely to enjoy good physical health

16-4. What condition related to rapid autonomic reactivity may also contribute to heart disease?

cardiovascular reactivity

16-5. What common element links social support, hardiness, optimism, and a placid autonomic nervous system? *they all are related to good health*

Answers: 16-1. Their friends and family aren't contributing to the stress. 16-2. high commitment, seeking challenge, a feeling of being in control 16-3. Optimists were more likely to enjoy good physical health. 16-4. cardiovascular reactivity 16-5. They are all related to good health.

HEALTH-IMPAIRING LIFESTYLES

17. **Discuss the negative impact of smoking, poor nutrition, lack of exercise, and alcohol and drug use on physical health.**

17-1. Answer the following questions regarding the negative impact of smoking, poor nutrition, lack of exercise, and substance abuse on physical health.
(a) How many fewer years can a 30-year-old smoker expect to live than a 30-year-old nonsmoker?
8 years
(b) List the three most frequent chronic diseases that are related to smoking.
lung cancer, bronchitis & emphysema, and cancer of the larynx

(c) What two pieces of advice can be gained from the text's review of poor nutritional habits?
don't overeat and watch what you eat

(d) Which class of diseases has been found among persons who get little exercise?
heart diseases

(e) How should one develop and follow an exercise program?
develop it gradually and follow it regularly

(f) Which of the recreational drugs causes the most physical damage in the United States?
alcohol

Answers: 17-1. (a) 8 years (b) lung cancer, bronchitis and emphysema, and cancer of the larynx (c) Don't overeat and watch what you eat. (d) heart diseases (e) Develop it gradually and follow it regularly. (f) alcohol.

18. **Discuss the relationship between lifestyle factors and AIDS.**

18-1. How is AIDS transmitted? *through bodily fluids (particularly blood & semen)*

18-2. What two general groups have the highest incidence of AIDS?
gay/bisexual males & intravenous drug users.

18-3. How can one virtually guarantee that he or she will not contact AIDS?

19. **Explain how health-impairing lifestyles develop.**

19-1. The text lists four complementary explanations as to why health-impairing lifestyles develop. Given the hints below, list these four reasons.

(a) slowly *- creep up on*

(b) immediate *- gratification/ pleasure*

(c) delayed *- risk associated*

(d) "not to me" *- will happen to someone else*

REACTIONS TO ILLNESS

20. **Discuss individual differences in willingness to seek medical treatment and to comply with medical advice.**

20-1. Indicate whether the following statements regarding individual differences in willingness to seek medical treatment are true or false.

___F___ Men are generally more willing than women to seek medical treatment.

___T___ The perception of pain and illness is highly subjective.

___T___ Some persons seek treatment because they actually like the "sick role."

20-2. The text lists three reasons for failure to comply with medical advice. One is that patients often fail to completely __understand__ treatment instructions. A second is that the treatment may prove to be quite __unpleasant__. The third reason is not directly related to either instructions or treatment but rather to the attitude towards the __physician__. A negative attitude makes compliance (more/(less)) likely.

PUTTING IT IN PERSPECTIVE

21. **Explain how this chapter highlighted our unifying themes about multifactoral causation and the subjectivity of experience.**

21-1. The fact that the amount of stress in any given situation primarily lies in the eyes of the beholder nicely illustrates the theme that experience is __subjective__.

21-2. The fact that stress interacts with numerous other factors that affect health illustrates the theme of
_____multifactoral_____ ___Causation_____.

Answers: 21-1. subjective   21-2. multifactoral causation.

APPLICATION: IMPROVING COPING AND STRESS MANAGEMENT

22. Summarize Albert Ellis's ideas about controlling one's emotions.

22-1. The main idea behind Albert Ellis's rational-emotive therapy is that stress is largely caused by
_____irrational_____ *thinking*. Therefore, by changing one's catastrophic thinking and taking a
more rational approach one can reduce ___stress_____.

22-2. Ellis illustrates this theory by postulating an A-B-C series of events. Describe below what is going on
during each of these events.
(A) activating event: that produces stress

(B) belief: about the event

emotional (C) consequence: that result from the belief

22-3. Since the emotional turmoil in the A-B-C sequence is caused by the ___B___ sequence, effort must be
directed toward changing irrational beliefs. Ellis proposes two techniques for doing this. One must first
learn to ___detect_____ instances of irrational beliefs. Then one must learn to actively
___dispute_____ those irrational beliefs.

Answers: 22-1. catastrophic, stress   22-2. (A) the activating event that produces the stress (B) the belief about the
event (C) the emotional consequences that result from the belief   22-3. B, detect, dispute.

23. Summarize other approaches to coping and stress management discussed in the Application.

23-1. The text describes three additional practices that can be used to reduce stress. Identify these practices
from their descriptions given below.
(a) Talking or writing about a problem with a sympathetic friend can lead to a releasing of:
pent-up emotions

(b) A quiet environment, a mental device, a passive attitude, and a comfortable position are conditions that
facilitate: learning to relax

(c) Eating a balanced diet, getting adequate sleep and exercise, and staying away from overeating and
harmful drugs can help to minimize: physical vulnerability

Answers: 23-1. (a) pent-up emotions (b) learning to relax (c) physical vulnerability.

REVIEW OF KEY TERMS

Aggression
Approach-approach conflict
Approach-avoidance conflict
Avoidance-avoidance conflict
Biopsychosocial model
Burnout
Catastrophic thinking
Catharsis
Conflict
Constructive coping
Coping

Defense mechanisms
Fight-or-flight response
Frustration
General adaptation syndrome
Hardiness
Health psychology
Immune response
Learned helplessness
Life changes
Optimism

Posttraumatic stress disorder
Pressure
Primary appraisal
Psychosomatic diseases
Rational-emotive therapy
Secondary appraisal
Social support
Stress
Type A pattern
Type B pattern

_____ 1. Holds that physical illness is caused by a complex interaction of biological, psychological, and sociocultural factors.

_____ 2. Concerned with how psychosocial forces relate to the promotion and maintenance of health, and the causation, prevention, and treatment of illness.

_____ 3. Any circumstances that threaten or are perceived to threaten our well-being and thereby tax our coping abilities.

_____ 4. An initial evaluation of whether an event is irrelevant, relevant but not threatening, or stressful.

_____ 5. An evaluation of one's coping resources and options for dealing with a particular stress.

_____ 6. Occurs in any situation in which the pursuit of some goal is thwarted.

_____ 7. Occurs when two or more incompatible motivations or behavioral impulses compete for expression.

_____ 8. Occurs when a choice must be made between two attractive goals.

_____ 9. Occurs when a choice must be made between two unattractive goals.

_____ 10. Occurs when a choice must be made whether to pursue a single goal that has both attractive and unattractive aspects.

_____ 11. Any noticeable alterations in one's living circumstances that require readjustment.

_____ 12. Expectations or demands that one behave in a certain way.

_____ 13. A physiological reaction to threat in which the autonomic nervous system mobilizes an organism for either attacking or fleeing an enemy.

_____ 14. A model of the body's stress response consisting of three stages: alarm, resistance and exhaustion.

_____ 15. An active effort to master, reduce or tolerate the demands created by stress.

_____ 16. Involves any behavior that is intended to hurt someone, either physically or verbally.

_____ 17. Passive behavior produced by exposure to unavoidable aversive events.

_____ 18. Largely unconscious reactions that protect a person from unpleasant emotions such as anxiety and guilt.

_____ 19. Relatively healthy efforts to deal with stressful events.

_____ 20. Involves physical, mental, and emotional exhaustion that is attributable to work-related stress.

_____ 21. Disturbed behavior that emerges after a major stressful event is over.

_____ 22. A behavior pattern marked by competitive, aggressive, impatient, hostile behavior.

_____ 23. A behavior pattern marked by relaxed, patient, easy-going, amicable behavior.

_____ 24. The body's defensive reaction to invasion by bacteria, viral agents, or other foreign substances.

_____ 25. Various types of aid and succor provided by members of one's social network.

_____ 26. A personality syndrome marked by commitment, challenge, and control that is purportedly associated with strong stress resistance.

_____ 27. A general tendency to expect good outcomes.

_____ 28. An approach to therapy that focuses on altering clients' patterns of irrational thinking to reduce maladaptive emotions and behavior.

_____ 29. The release of emotional tension.

_____ 30. Unrealistic and pessimistic appraisal of stress that exaggerates the magnitude of a problem.

_____ 31. Physical ailments caused in part by psychological factors, especially emotional distress.

Answers: 1. biopsychosocial model 2. health psychology 3. stress 4. primary appraisal 5. secondary appraisal 6. frustration 7. conflict 8. approach-approach conflict 9. avoidance-avoidance conflict 10. approach-avoidance conflict 11. life changes 12. pressure 13. fight-or-flight response 14. general adaptation syndrome 15. coping 16. aggression 17. learned helplessness 18. defense mechanisms 19. constructive coping 20. burnout 21. posttraumatic stress disorder 22. Type A pattern 23. Type B pattern 24. immune response 25. social support 26. hardiness 27. optimism 28. rational-emotive therapy 29. catharsis 30. catastrophic thinking 31. psychosomatic diseases.

REVIEW OF KEY PEOPLE

Walter Cannon   Thomas Holmes & Richard Rahe   Neal Miller
Albert Ellis   Suzanne Kobasa   Hans Selye
Meyer Friedman & Ray Rosenman   Richard Lazarus

_____ 1. Observed that minor hassles were more closely related to mental health than were major stressful events.

_____ 2. Noted for his extensive investigations of the three types of conflict.

_____ 3. These researchers developed the Social Readjustment Rating Scale.

_____ 4. One of the first theorists to describe the "fight-or-flight" response.

_____ 5. Coined the word "stress" and described the General Adaptation Syndrome.

_____ 6. These researchers found a connection between coronary risk and what they called Type A behavior.

_____ 7. Researched the notion that some persons may be hardier than others in resisting stress.

_____ 8. The developer of Rational-Emotive Therapy.

Answers: 1. Lazarus 2. Miller 3. Holmes & Rahe 4. Cannon 5. Selye 6. Friedman & Rosenman 7. Kobasa 8. Ellis.

SELF-QUIZ

1. Which of the following statements is not correct.
   a. Stress is a subjective experience.
   b. Stress involves both primary and secondary appraisals.
   c. Minor hassles are less stressful than major ones.
   d. One should not seek to avoid all stress.

2. You've been invited to dinner at a nice restaurant on the final night of a TV mini series you've been watching and thus find yourself confronted with:
   a. pressure
   b. frustration
   c. an approach-avoidance conflict
   d. an approach-approach conflict

3. The week of final exams subjects most students to what kind of stress?
   a. pressure
   b. change
   c. frustration
   d. conflict

4. High scores on the Social Readjustment Rating Scale were found to be correlated with:
   a. psychiatric disorders
   b. physical illness
   c. pessimistic attitudes
   d. all of the above

5. According to optimal-arousal theories, which of the following situations would be least affected by a high optimal-arousal level?
   a. taking a psychology exam
   b. looking up a word in a dictionary
   c. buttoning a shirt
   d. explaining to your parents why you need more money

6. The General Adaptation Syndrome shows that the body eventually successfully adapts to long-term stress. This statement is:
   a. true
   b. false

7. Which of the following organs is involved in both of the body's two major stress pathways?
   a. the adrenal gland
   b. the sympathetic nervous system
   c. the pituitary gland
   d. the pineal gland

8. Aggression is frequently triggered by:
   a. helplessness
   b. frustration
   c. loneliness
   d. change

9. Seeing someone die is one of the principal causes of:
   a. posttraumatic stress disorder
   b. burnout
   c. learned helplessness
   d. coronary heart disorder

10. Fred Fritz owns his own business, to which he is highly committed, and loves it because he likes the challenge and the feeling that he is in control. Fred Fritz has the characteristics found in:
   a. Type A executives
   b. Type B executives
   c. hardy executives

11. One of the key links between stress and physical illness may be that the body's response to stress:
   a. increases the optimal-arousal level
   b. suppresses the immune system
   c. decreases the optimal-arousal level
   d. suppresses the adrenal gland

12. Smoking is to lung cancer as Type A behavior is to:
   a. coronary disease
   b. AIDS
   c. defensive coping
   d. mental disorders

13. A major idea behind Rational-Emotive Therapy is that stress is caused by:
   a. conflict
   b. frustration
   c. catastrophic thinking
   d. pressure

14. Social support, hardiness, and optimism are all related to:
   a. the Type B personality pattern
   b. a low level of stress
   c. defensive-coping strategies
   d. good physical health

15. The best way to deal with stress is to:
   a. avoid it as much as possible
   b. learn defensive-coping strategies
   c. both of the above
   d. none of the above

   Answers: 1. c   2. d   3. a   4. b   5. c   6. b   7. a   8. b   9. a   10. c   11. b   12. a   13. c   14. d   15. d.

14 PSYCHOLOGICAL DISORDERS

ABNORMAL BEHAVIOR: MYTHS, REALITIES, AND CONTROVERSIES

1. **Describe and evaluate the medical model of abnormal behavior.**

   1-1. The medical model asserts that a psychological disorder is analogous to a disease. Thus, under the medical model, maladaptive behavior is referred to as mental _____illness_____.

   1-2. The term *mental illness* is so familiar to all of us that we rarely think about the meaning of the concept and whether or not the analogy with disease is a sensible one. The medical model has been strongly criticized, however. For example, Thomas Szasz asserts that the word *disease* is correctly used only in reference to the _____body_____ and that it is more appropriate to view abnormal behavior as a deviation from accepted social _____norms_____ than as an illness.

   1-3. Other critics object to the disease model because they believe that the labeling inherent in medical diagnosis tends to carry a strong social _____stigma_____. People tend to be _____prejudiced (biased)_____ against those who are labeled mentally ill.

   1-4. Still others argue that technical sounding diagnostic labels create an illusion that we understand more about the causes of a disorder than we do. Consider this pseudoexplanation: Ralph constantly washes his hands because he is obsessive-compulsive. The label *obsessive-compulsive* simply _____labels (describes)_____ the behavior; it does not _____explain_____ it.

   1-5. Some critics also suggest that the medical model encourages sufferers to adopt the _____passive_____ role of patient rather than the more active role generally required in psycho-therapy.

1-6.   The text concludes that a mental (or psychological or behavioral) disorder really isn't a

_____disease_____ and that the analogy with medicine may lead to some false conclusions.

Nonetheless, the disease analogy of the medical model can be useful as long as one understands that it

is just an _____analogy_____ and not a true explanation.

Answers: 1-1. illness (disease)   1-2. body, norms (behavior, standards)   1-3. stigma, prejudiced (biased)
1-4. describes (labels), explain   1-5. passive   1-6. disease, analogy.

2.   Explain the most commonly used criteria of abnormality and discuss two complexities that arise in their application.

2-1.   What does abnormal mean? Next to the descriptions below list the three criteria most frequently used in making judgments of abnormality.

(a) ___deviant___ : Does not conform to cultural norms or standards.

(b) ___maladaptive___ : Behavior which interferes with the individual's social or occupational functioning.

(c) ___personal distress___ : Intense discomfort produced by depression or anxiety.

2-2.   Following are three statements that describe a person with a particular type of disorder. Which criterion of abnormal behavior is illustrated by each statement? Place the letters from the list above in the appropriate blanks.

___b___   Ralph washes his hands several dozen times a day. His handwashing interferes with his work and prevents him from establishing normal friendships.

___a___   Even if Ralph's handwashing compulsion did not interfere with his work and social life, his behavior still would be considered strange. That is, most people do not do what he does.

___c___   It is also the case that Ralph's skin is very raw, and he becomes extremely anxious when he does not have immediate access to a sink.

2-3.   The first complexity in judging abnormality is that the difference between normal and abnormal

behavior is (very clear/not very clear). We all have some behaviors that interfere with our lives, that

cause us discomfort, and that others may consider strange. Thus, the difference between normal and

abnormal is not black and white but exists along a ___continuum___ .

2-4.   Second, we make value judgments that are influenced by our ___culture___ . In some

cultures, hearing voices or speaking with gods may be valued. In our culture, however, such behavior is

likely to be considered abnormal. Thus, there are no ___value/culture___ -free criteria for psycho-

logical disorders.

Answers: 2-1. (a) deviance (b) maladaptive behavior (c) personal distress   2-2. b, a, c   2-3. not very clear, continuum   2-4. culture (or society), value (or culture).

3. **List four stereotypes of people with psychological disorders.**

    3-1.   In the space below list four stereotypes of people with psychological disorders:

    (a) The disorders are a sign of ___personal___ ___weakness___ .

    (b) The disorders are ___Incurable___ .

    (c) People with the disorders are ___violent___ and ___dangerous___ .

    (d) People with the disorders behave in a ___bizarre___ manner and are very ___different___ from normal people.

    Answers: 3-1. (a) personal weakness (b) incurable (c) violent, dangerous (d) bizarre, different.

4. **Summarize the Featured Study by Rosenhan (1973) on the admission of pseudopatients to mental hospitals.**

    4-1.   What type of people did Rosenhan seek to have admitted to mental hospitals?

    normal

    4-2.   Once they were admitted, did the pseudopatients continue to complain of hearing voices, or did they behave normally? *normally*

    4-3.   What proportion of the pseudopatients were admitted to the hospital? *all of them*

    4-4.   For each of the following statements, indicate whether it is true of false.

    *F*___ Once the patients no longer claimed to hear voices, the professional staff rapidly recognized that they were not abnormal.

    *F*___ Most of the pseudopatients were dismissed within a couple of days.

    *F*___ The diagnosis for most of the pseudopatients was that they suffered from a relatively mild form of mental disorder.

    4-5.   What is the major implication to be drawn from Rosenhan's study?

    it is difficult, even for mental health professionals, to distinguish normal from abnormal behavior. there is a bias in the mental health community toward seeing abnormality where it may not exist

    Answers: 4-1. normal individuals   4-2. behaved normally   4-3. all of them   4-4. false, false (the shortest stay was 7 days; the longest was 52 days), false (most were diagnosed with schizophrenia, a severe form of mental illness) 4-5. The major implication is that it is difficult, even for mental health professionals, to distinguish normal from abnormal behavior. The study also suggests that there is a bias in the mental health community toward seeing abnormality where it may not exist.

5. **List the five diagnostic axes of DSM-III and discuss some of the controversial aspects of this classification system.**

5-1. Below are descriptions of the five axes of the DSM-III classification system. Label each with the correct axis number (I through V).

III Listing of physical disorders.

_II_ Diagnosis of personality or developmental disorders.

_I_ Diagnosis of the major disorders.

_V_ Estimates of the individual's current level of adaptive functioning.

_IV_ Notes concerning the severity of stress experienced by the individual in the past year.

5-2. Two changes introduced in the DSM-III produced a considerable amount of controversy. What were these changes? _did away with the categories of neurosis and psychosis, new system includes everyday problems not previously considered to be mental illnesses, such as underachievement and nicotine dependence_

5-3. While the terms *neurosis* and *psychosis* are no longer official diagnostic categories, they are still used informally as broadly descriptive terms. Which of the two terms refers to the more severe forms of mental illness characterized by impaired contact with reality? _psychosis_

5-4. Although it is quite a change to include some of the previously unlisted everyday problems in the DSM-III, what is the advantage of doing so? _insurance purposes_

Answers: 5-1. III, II, I, V, IV 5-2. First, DSM-III did away with the categories of neurosis and psychosis. Second, the new system included everyday problems not previously considered to be mental illnesses, such as underachievement and nicotine dependence. 5-3. psychosis 5-4. Many problems were added to DSM-III to permit people to bill their insurance companies for treatments related to these problems.

6. **Discuss estimates of the prevalence of psychological disorders.**

6-1. Epidemiological studies assess the prevalence of various disorders across a specific period of time. Prevalence refers to the _percentage_ of a population that exhibits a disorder during a specified period of time. For mental disorders, what is the time period usually considered? _the entire lifespan_

6-2. According to our best (if still approximate) estimates, what is the prevalence of mental illness in the United States? _approx. 1/3 of our population suffers from some form of mental illness @ some point in their lives._

6-3. List the three most prevalent forms of mental disorder. _anxiety disorders, substance use disorders, mood disorders._

Answers: 6-1. percentage (proportion), the entire lifespan 6-2. Approximately one-third of our population suffers from some form of mental illness at some point in their lives. 6-3. anxiety disorders, substance use disorders, mood disorders.

ANXIETY DISORDERS

7. **List four types of anxiety disorders and describe the symptoms associated with each.**

   7-1. List the names of the four anxiety syndromes in the space below. As hints, some initial letters of key words are listed at the left.

   GA: _generalized_ _anxiety_ _syndrome_

   Ph: _phobic disorder_

   O-C: _obsessive compulsive disorder_

   Pa: _panic disorder_ and _agoraphobia_

   7-2. Match the anxiety disorders with the symptoms that follow by placing the appropriate letters (from the previous question) in the blanks.

   _Pa_ Sudden, unexpected, and paralyzing attacks of anxiety.

   _GA_ Not tied to a specific object or event.

   _O-C_ Senseless, repetitive rituals.

   _GA_ Brooding over decisions.

   _Ph_ Fear of specific objects or situations.

   _O-C_ Persistent intrusion of distressing and unwanted thoughts.

   _GA_ Free-floating anxiety.

   _Pa_ Frequently includes fear of going out in public.

   Answers: 7-1. generalized anxiety disorder, phobic disorder, obsessive-compulsive disorder, panic disorder and agoraphobia   7-2. Pa, GA, O-C, GA, Ph, O-C, GA, Pa (in this case, agoraphobia).

8. **Discuss the contribution of biological factors, conditioning, observational learning, and stress to the etiology of anxiety disorders.**

   8-1. There is some evidence of a relatively weak genetic predisposition to anxiety disorders. These data support the theory that people with especially reactive _autonomic_ nervous systems are more likely to develop these disorders.

   8-2. Some research also links anxiety disorders with a heart defect known as a _mitral_ _valve_ _prolapse_, a problem associated with heart palpitations, faintness, and chest pains.

   8-3. Another source of biological evidence concerns the _neurotransmitters_, chemicals such as GABA and serotonin that carry nerve impulses across the synapse.

   8-4. Conditioning or learning clearly plays a role as well. For example, if an individual is bitten by a dog, he or she may develop a fear of dogs through the process of _classical_ conditioning and may then avoid contact with dogs in the future. Avoiding dogs is an operant response that is _negatively_ reinforced by a reduction in anxiety. Thus, phobias may be acquired through _classical_ conditioning and maintained by _operant_ conditioning.

8-5. People are more likely to be afraid of snakes than of baseballs. Using Seligman's notion of preparedness, explain why. *we are biologically prepared by our evolutionary history to acquire some fears much more easily than others.*

8-6. What two types of anecdotal evidence do not support the conditioning point of view? *people with phobias cannot remember the frightening experience, many people endure extremely traumatic experiences that should but don't create a phobia.*

8-7. As discussed in Chapter 6, the conditioning models are being extended to include a larger role for cognitive factors. For example, laboratory studies have demonstrated that conditioned fears can be produced in animals indirectly through ___observational___ learning. Children probably acquire fears in a similar manner by observing the behavior of anxious parents.

8-8. Finally, stress is related to the anxiety disorders. For example, one study found that men who experienced stress were 8.5 times as likely to develop ___generalized___ anxiety disorders as men under low stress. In another study patients with ___panic___ disorder were found to have experienced a dramatic increase in stress in the month prior to the onset of their disorder.

Answers: 8-1. autonomic **8-2.** mitral valve prolapse **8-3.** neurotransmitters **8-4.** classical, negatively, classical, operant **8-5.** Preparedness is Seligman's notion that human beings have evolved to be more prepared or ready to be conditioned to some stimuli than to others. It seems reasonable to suggest that we have evolved to be more afraid of snakes than of baseballs, the latter having appeared only relatively recently in our evolutionary history. **8-6.** First, people with phobias frequently cannot remember the frightening experience. Second, intensely frightening experiences do not produce phobias in all people. **8-7.** observational **8-8.** generalized, panic.

SOMATOFORM DISORDERS

9. Compare and contrast the three somatoform disorders and discuss their etiology.

9-1. For each of the following symptoms, indicate which disorder is described by placing the appropriate letters in the blanks: S for somatization, C for conversion, and H for hypochondriasis.

___C___ Serious disability that may include paralysis, loss of vision or hearing, loss of feeling, and so on.

___S___ Many different minor physical ailments accompanied by a long history of medical treatment.

___H___ Cannot believe the doctors report that one is not really ill.

___C___ Symptoms that appear to be organic in origin but don't match underlying anatomical organization.

___S___ Diverse complaints that implicate many different organ systems.

___H___ Usually does not involve disability so much as overreaction to slight possible signs of illness.

___C___ "Glove anesthesia"; seizures without loss of bladder control.

9-2. In the film *Hannah and Her Sisters* Woody Allen is convinced that certain minor physical changes are a sign of cancer. When tests eventually find no evidence of cancer, he is sure the tests have been done incorrectly. Which of the somatoform disorders does this seem to represent? ___hypochondriasis___

9-3. The somatoform disorders are associated with certain personality types and with learning. For example, the self-centered, excitable, and overly dramatic _histrionic_ personalities are particularly prone to somatoform disorders. With regard to learning, the sick role may be positively reinforced through _attention_ from others or negatively reinforced by _escaping_ certain problems, responsibilities, or unpleasant aspects of one's life.

Answers: 9-1. C, S, H, C, S, H, C   9-2. hypochondriasis   9-3. histrionic, attention, escaping (avoiding).

DISSOCIATIVE DISORDERS

10. Describe two dissociative disorders and discuss their etiology.

10-1. We've all seen media characterizations of individuals who can't remember who they are—what their names are, where they live, who their family is, and so on. This type of dissociative disorder, termed psychogenic _amnesia_, relates to loss of memory for one's _identity_.

10-2. Psychogenic amnesia may also involve loss of memory for a particular incident, such as a car accident, assault, or other _traumatic_ event.

10-3. The other dissociative disorder, characterized by more than one identity, is the _multiple_ _personality_ disorder.

10-4. What causes dissociative disorders? Psychogenic amnesia seems to be related to excessive _stress_, but little else is known about it. There is some evidence that multiple personalities are frequently _faked_ rather than real, but there is also evidence that what appear to be authentic cases are linked to a _disturbed_ home life that may include beatings and sexual abuse.

Answers: 10-1. amnesia, identity   10-2. traumatic   10-3. multiple-personality   10-4. stress, faked, disturbed (traumatic, abusive).

MOOD DISORDERS

11. Describe the two major affective disorders: depressive disorder and bipolar mood disorder.

11-1. One can view the manic and depressive states as polar opposites. Nothing is quite that simple, but this approach helps for purposes of remembering the symptoms. In the spaces below, in your own words, describe characteristics of the two states. (Before you make the lists, it may be a good idea to review Table 14.2 and the sections on depressive and bipolar mood disorders.)

	Manic	Depressive
mood:	elated/euphoric	depressed/negative
sleep:	little / goes without	insomnia
activity:	excessive/hyperactive	sluggish/inactive
speech:	talkative/very fast	very slow
self-esteem :	high	low
sex drive :	increased	decreased

11-2. Be sure to note that mania and depression are not the names of the two affective disorders. What is the name of the disorder accompanied only by depressive states? _depressive disorder_ By both manic and depressive states? _bipolar mood disorder_

Answers: 11-1. mood: euphoric vs. negative or depressed; sleep: goes without or doesn't want to vs. can't (insomnia); activity: hyperactive vs. sluggish and inactive; speech: very fast vs. very slow; self-esteem: very high vs. very low; sex drive: increased vs. decreased   11-2. depressive disorder, bipolar mood disorder.

12. Explain how genetic and neurochemical factors may be related to the development of mood disorders.

12-1. Twin studies implicate genetic factors in the development of mood disorders. In a sentence, summarize the results of these studies. _the concordance rate for mood disorders for identical twins is much higher than that for fraternal twins—67% in former, 15% in latter_

12-2. While the exact mechanism is not known, levels of norepinephrine and other _neurotransmitters_ are associated with mood disorders. In support of the role played by these body chemicals, it has been found that administering _drugs_ known to affect the availability of neurotransmitters in the brain tends to lessen the severity of mood disorders.

Answers: 12-1. The concordance rate for mood disorders for identical twins is much higher than that for fraternal twins—about 67% for the former compared to 15% for the latter.   12-2. neurotransmitters, drugs.

13. Explain how cognitive factors, interpersonal factors, and stress may be related to the development of mood disorders.

13-1. Below are possible thoughts that a person may have after performing poorly—on a test in school, in an athletic event, in a social encounter, in a public speech, or whatever. Following each thought are three dimensions of attributional style. Circle the one pole from each pair that best describes the sample cognition.

(a) "I've never been very good at this type of thing and I'm not doing well now."

internal ————————— external
stable ————————— unstable
global ————————— specific

(b) "I messed up the test this time because I was lazy, but next time I'll work harder."

internal ————————— external
stable ————————— unstable
global ————————— specific

(c) "I just can't seem to do anything well."

internal ————————— external
stable ————————— unstable
global ————————— specific

(d) "I messed up, but on the day of the event I had the flu and a high fever. I'm rarely sick."

internal ————————— external
stable ————————— unstable
global ————————— specific

13-2. Which of the above attributional styles (represented by a, b, c, or d) is most likely to characterize

depressed people? _____*c*_____ Least likely to characterize depressed people? _____*d*_____

13-3. I (R. S.) sometimes ask my social psychology class this question: If you had the choice between being depressed but keenly in touch with reality versus being happy but unable to accurately perceive reality, which would you choose? Answers from the class vary, depending on the semester and the way I ask the question. In any case, this issue relates to the finding by Alloy and Abramson that depressed people tend to be (more/less) realistic than nondepressed people.

13-4. For example, nondepressed people have been found to overestimate their control in a laboratory task, to recall positive but not negative feedback from others, and so on. Thus, nondepressed people tend to be (realistic/overly optimistic/overly pessimistic) while depressed people tend to be (realistic/overly optimistic/overly pessimistic). (This finding is surprising because theories of mental health usually stress realistic thinking. In some respects the Genesis story is a metaphor for this issue: After you've bitten the fruit of the Tree of Knowledge of Good and Evil you know more but are less happy outside the Garden.)

13-5. With regard to interpersonal factors, depressed people tend to lack _____*social*_____ skills.

How does this affect the ability to obtain reinforcers? *the deficit leads to difficulty in acquiring certain reinforcers, such as good friends and desirable jobs.*

13-6. Why do we tend to reject depressed people? *depressed people complain a lot, are irritable, and tend to infect others with their mood.*

13-7. What is the relationship among stress, the onset of depression, and genetic makeup? *stress is related to the onset of depression, some people are more vulnerable to stress and the resulting depression than are others. These differences in vulnerability seem to depend in large part on one's genetic makeup.*

Answers: 13-1. (a) internal, stable, specific (b) internal, unstable, specific (c) internal, stable, global (d) external, unstable, specific 13-2. c, d 13-3. more 13-4. overly optimistic, realistic 13-5. social. The deficit leads to difficulty in acquiring certain reinforcers, such as good friends and desirable jobs. 13-6. Depressed people complain a lot, are irritable, and tend to infect others with their mood. 13-7. Stress is related to the onset of depression, and some people are more vulnerable to stress and the resulting depression than are others. These individual differences in vulnerability seem to depend in large part on one's genetic makeup.

SCHIZOPHRENIC DISORDERS

14. Describe the general characteristics (symptoms) of schizophrenia.

14-1. Following are words relating to four of the five general characteristics of schizophrenia discussed in the text. What types of behaviors illustrate these categories? Next to each word give examples of some of the behaviors that describe them.

(a) thinking: *irrational, chaotic, various kinds of delusions are common.*

(b) behavior: *deteriorated behavior, neglects personal hygiene, doesn't function well @ work, little capacity for social relationships*

(c) perception: *distorted perceptions, hallucinations, esp. auditory*

(d) emotion: *disturbed emotions, flattened affect or inappropriate affect, erratic emotional outbursts*

14-2. The fifth category, other features, may include social __withdrawal__, a disturbed sense of __self__, very little __speech__, and abnormal __motor__ behavior (e.g., rocking back and forth).

Answers: 14-1. (a) irrational, chaotic thinking generally characterized by delusions (b) deteriorated behavior: neglects personal hygiene, doesn't function well at work, has little capacity for social relationships (c) distorted perceptions: hallucinations, especially auditory (d) disturbed emotion: flattened affect or inappropriate affect (crying when most people laugh); erratic, emotional outbursts   14-2. withdrawal, self, speech (verbal behavior), motor.

15. **Describe two classification systems for schizophrenic subtypes and discuss the course of schizophrenia (including factors related to prognosis).**

15-1. Write the names of the four recognized subcategories of schizophrenia next to the descriptions that follow.

(a) __Paranoid__ type: Particularly severe deterioration, incoherence, complete social withdrawal, aimless babbling and giggling, delusions centering on bodily functions.

(b) __Catatonic__ type: Muscular rigidity and stupor at one extreme, or random motor activity, hyperactivity, and incoherence at the other; now quite rare.

(c) __disorganized__ type: Delusions of persecution and grandeur.

(d) __undifferentiated__ type: Clearly schizophrenic but doesn't fit other three categories.

15-2. Some critics have asserted that there are no meaningful differences among the categories listed above and have proposed an alternative classification system. Nancy Andreasen and others have described a classification system consisting of only two categories, one that consists of __positive__ symptoms and the other of __negative__ symptoms.

15-3. In Andreasen's system "positive" and "negative" do not mean pleasant and unpleasant: Positive symptoms add something to "normal" behavior (like chaotic speech); negative symptoms subtract something (like social withdrawal). Indicate which of the following are positive and which negative by placing a P or an N in the appropriate blanks.

__N__ flattened emotions

__P__ hallucinations

__P__ delusions

__P__ bizarre behavior

__N__ socially withdrawn

__N__ apathetic

__N__ can't pay attention

__P__ nonstop babbling

__N__ doesn't speak

15-4. Across approximately what age range does schizophrenia tend to occur? generally during adolescence or early adulthood, rarely after age 45

15-5. Which characteristics tend to predict recovery from schizophrenia? Describe the favorable prognostic indicators with regard to rapidity of onset, age of onset, prior social and work history, and family situation. Sudden onset, at a later age, accompanied by good previous social & work adjustment, and a good family to return to.

Answers: 15-1. (a) disorganized (b) catatonic (c) paranoid (d) undifferentiated   15-2. positive, negative   15-3. N, P, P, P, N, N, N, P, N   15-4. generally during adolescence or early adulthood, rarely after age 45   15-5. The favorable prognostic indicators are sudden onset, at a later age, accompanied by good previous social and work adjustment, and a supportive family to return to.

16. **Explain how genetic vulnerability, neurochemical factors, and structural abnormalities in the brain may contribute to the etiology of schizophrenia.**

   16-1. As with mood disorders, twin studies implicate genetic factors in the development of schizophrenia. In a sentence, summarize the general results of these studies.

   48% identical twins, 17% fraternal

   16-2. As with mood disorders, neurotransmitter substances in the brain are implicated in the etiology of schizophrenia. Although the evidence is somewhat clouded, what is the name of the neurotransmitter thought to be involved? *dopamine* What evidence from drug treatments implicates this particular neurochemical? *most drugs useful in treatment of schizophrenia are known to decrease dopamine activity in the brain.*

   16-3. In addition to possible neurochemical factors, certain differences in brain structure may be associated with schizophrenia. What are these structural differences? Why is it difficult to conclude that these differences are definitely related to schizophrenia? *Enlarged brain ventricles are associated with chronic schizophrenia. They are associated with a # of pathologies besides schizophrenia, so it is difficult to determine whether or not this brain abnormality is causally related to schizophrenia*

   Answers: 16-1. For schizophrenia, the concordance rate for identical twins is about 48% compared to about 17% for fraternal twins. (For comparison, recall that the respective percentages for mood disorders are 67% and 15%.)   16-2. dopamine; most drugs useful in treatment of schizophrenia are known to decrease dopamine activity in the brain.   16-3. Enlarged brain ventricles are associated with chronic schizophrenia. Enlarged ventricles are associated with a number of pathologies besides schizophrenia, however, so it is difficult to determine whether or not this brain abnormality is causally related to schizophrenia.

17. **Summarize evidence on how family dynamics and stress may be related to the development of schizophrenia.**

   17-1. Families that communicate in an unintelligible manner (e.g., speech consisting of contradictions or vague, muddled, or fragmented sentences) have a communication style which may be described as *deviant*. Children brought up in these families are somewhat more likely to develop *schizophrenia* than those brought up with a more normal communication pattern.

17-2. Prognosis for recovery from schizophrenia has been found to be related to expressed

_____emotion_____ within the family. Patients returning to families high in expressed emotion

have a relapse rate that is about ___3-4___ (how many?) times as high as that of patients returning

to families low in expressed emotion. What is meant by expressed emotion in these studies? Give

several examples. _Critical comments, expressions of resentment, excessive emotional involvement idicated by overprotectiveness._

17-3. What role does stress play in the etiology of schizophrenia? _Stress seems to precipitate schizophrenia in those with a vulnerability to the disorder._

Answers: 17-1. deviant (defective), schizophrenia 17-2. emotion; 3 or 4; critical comments, expressions of resentment, excessive emotional involvement indicated by overprotectiveness 17-3. As with several other disorders, stress seems to precipitate schizophrenia in those with a vulnerability to the disorder.

PERSONALITY DISORDERS

18. **Discuss the nature of personality disorders and describe three broad clusters of such disorders.**

18-1. The personality disorders, which are recorded on Axis II, are (less/more) severe than most of the disorders on Axis I. They consist of relatively extreme and (flexible/inflexible) sets of personality traits that cause subjective distress or impaired functioning.

18-2. Complete the terms used to describe the three broad clusters of personality disorders.

(a) _____anxious_____-fearful cluster

(b) _____odd_____-eccentric cluster

(c) _____dramatic_____-impulsive cluster

18-3. Match the clusters listed in the previous question with the following descriptions by placing the appropriate letters in the blanks.

_b_ Inability to connect emotionally with others.

_a_ Fear concerning social rejection.

_c_ Theatrical or whimsical behavior.

18-4. It is beyond our purpose to list all of the subcategories of personality disorders, but to give the major clusters somewhat more meaning, the subcategories are briefly described in the following. Match the descriptions with the three clusters by placing the appropriate letters in the blanks.

_c_ Egocentric and excitable; or grandiose and hypersensitive; or unstable in emotions and full of self-doubt; or irresponsible, manipulative, and exploitive.

_b_ Not interested in intimate contact with others; or feels threatened by, and suspicious of, others; or shows poor social skills, strange behavior.

_a_ Is overly submissive to others; or is perfectionistic and rigid; or may be stubborn and procrastinating as a way of getting at others; or is timid, fears rejection.

Answers: 18-1. less, inflexible 18-2. anxious, odd, dramatic 18-3. b, a, c 18-4. c, b, a.

19. Describe the antisocial personality disorder and discuss its etiology.

19-1. The classification of personality disorders in the DSM-III has been criticized because of extensive overlap among the diagnoses. Of the 11 types of personality disorder listed, more is probably known about the antisocial personality disorder than the others, and it is described in more detail in your text. Check the concepts from the following list that correctly describe the antisocial personality.

✓ sociable	✓ aggressive
✓ friendly	✓ sexually promiscuous
___ bumbling	✓ manipulative
___ feels guilty	✓ irresponsible
___ genuinely affectionate	✓ impulsive
✓ lacks an adequate conscience	✓ charming

✓ much more likely to occur in males than females

✓ may be a con artist, thug, or unprincipled business executive

19-2. What findings support the idea that biological factors are involved in the etiology of the antisocial personality? Which environmental factors seem to be involved?

twin studies suggest that genetic factors are involved, and there has been some limited support for Eysenck's idea that antisocial personalities are chronically lower in autonomic arousal and are therefore less likely to develop classically conditioned inhibitions

Answers: 19-1. All the terms describe the antisocial personality except for bumbling, feels guilty, and genuinely affectionate. 19-2. Twin studies suggest that genetic factors are involved, and there has been some limited support for Eysenck's idea that antisocial personalities are chronically lower in autonomic arousal and are therefore less likely to develop classically conditioned inhibitions. With regard to environmental factors, studies suggest that inconsistent or ineffective discipline, along with modeling of antisocial behaviors, may be involved.

PSYCHOLOGICAL DISORDERS AND THE LAW

20. Distinguish between the legal concepts of insanity and incompetency and explain the grounds for involuntary commitment.

20-1. While the words *insane*, *psychotic*, and *incompetent* may in some cases apply to the same person, the terms do not mean the same thing. Two of the terms have a meaning in law and one is a descriptive term which may be used in psychological diagnosis. Distinguish between the use of these words by placing them in the appropriate blanks.

(a) An individual is troubled by hallucinations and delusions and in general seems out of touch with reality. The individual is __psychotic__.

(b) A court decides that an individual is in an extreme state of confusion, does not know where he is or what is going on around him, and is therefore not mentally fit to stand trial. The individual has been declared __incompetent__.

(c) A court declares that, because of a mental illness, an individual is not responsible for his criminal actions. The individual is __insane__.

20-2. What is the difference between the legal concepts of insanity and incompetence?

20-3. Answer the following questions concerning the procedures needed for involuntary commitment to a psychiatric facility.

(a) What three criteria are used to determine whether an individual should be committed?

mental health & legal authorities must judge the individual to be 1) dangerous to themself 2) dangerous to others or 3) in extreme need of treatment

(b) What is required to temporarily commit an individual for one to three days? *temporary commitment (24-72 hrs) may be done in emergencies by a psychologist or psychiatrist*

(c) What is required for longer-term commitment? *longer term commitments are issued by a court and require a formal hearing.*

Answers: 20-1. (a) psychotic (b) incompetent (c) insane   20-2. Insane means that a court has declared an individual not responsible for his or her actions because of a mental illness. Incompetent means that the court has decided that the individual does not have the capacity to understand the nature of the legal proceedings.   20-3. (a) In general, for a person to be involuntarily committed, mental health and legal authorities must judge the individual to be (1) dangerous to himself or herself, (2) dangerous to others, or (3) in extreme need of treatment. (b) Temporary commitment (usually 24 to 72 hours) may be done in emergencies by a psychologist or psychiatrist. (c) Longer-term commitments are issued by a court and require a formal hearing.

PUTTING IT IN PERSPECTIVE

21. Explain how this chapter highlighted three of our organizing themes: multifactorial causation, the interplay of heredity and environment, and the sociohistorical roots of psychology.

21-1. Below are examples of the highlighted themes. Indicate which theme fits each example by writing the appropriate abbreviations in the blanks: MC for multifactorial causation, HE for the interplay of heredity and environment, and SH for sociohistorical context.

 (a) Homosexuality is no longer considered to be a psychological disorder.

 (b) Psychological disorders are caused by neurochemical factors, brain abnormalities, styles of child rearing, life stress, and so on.

_HE_ (c) Mood and schizophrenic disorders will occur if one has a genetic vulnerability to the disorder *and* if one experiences a considerable amount of stress.

Answers: 21-1. (a) SH (b) MC (c) HE.

APPLICATION: UNDERSTANDING AND PREVENTING SUICIDE

22. **Summarize how age, sex, marital status, and occupational status are related to the prevalence of suicide.**

   22-1.   Summarize the effects of factors related to suicide by answering the following questions.
   (a) Across which age range does the largest number of suicide attempts occur?   *24-44*

   (b) Which sex attempts more suicides?   *females*

   (c) Which sex successfully completes more suicides?   *males*

   (d) Among men, are there more successful suicides before age 55 or after? Does the same relationship hold true for women?   *after, no*

   (e) Which marital status is associated with fewer suicides?   *married*

   (f) What types of occupational status are associated with suicide?   *Unemployed, and those among the more prestigious & pressured professions.*

   Answers: 22-1. (a) between ages 24 and 44 (b) females (c) males (d) Among men suicide is more more frequent after age 55 than before. Among women that is not the case; women's suicide rates decline slightly after age 55. (e) married (f) Suicide rates tend to be higher both among the unemployed and among those in the more prestigious and pressured professions.

23. **List four myths about suicidal behavior and summarize advice provided on preventing a suicide.**

   23-1.   For each of the following statements, indicate whether it is true of false.

   _T_   (a) Many suicidal individuals talk about committing suicide before they actually make the attempt.

   _T_   (b) The majority of suicides are preceded by some kind of warning.

   _T_   (c) A small minority of those who attempt suicide are fully intent on dying.

   _T_   (d) Many people are suicidal for a limited period of time, not for their entire lives.

23-2. While it is probably true that no one knows exactly what to do about suicide, your text makes some suggestions that may be useful if you ever find yourself face to face with someone contemplating suicide. Label each of the following statements with one of the six suggestions for dealing with a suicidal person.

(a) "Look, there's a number I want you to call, so that you can talk with someone about this and make an appointment for professional help."

Encourage professional consultation

(b) "You say that you're not sure whether your family would be better off without you. My guess is that they would be much worse off." *Capitalize on any doubts*

(c) "You think no one cares. I know that I care, and that's why I'm here. I think I can understand what you've been going through, and I want to help." *provide empathy & social support*

(d) "O.K., let's really try to put a finger on what's bothering you. You consider yourself a failure, both in terms of your job and your relationship with your family. Does that seem to be the main problem?"

identify & clarify the crucial problem

(e) "As an exercise, let's try to come up with some possibilities about what to do to solve this situation. Let's brainstorm, just listing possibilities for right now without considering how good they may be."

suggest alternative courses of action

(f) "You've been talking about things that sound like they're related to suicide. Are you contemplating suicide? Because if you are, I want to talk to you about it."

take suicidal talk seriously.

Answers: 23-1. All of these statements are true and are thus contrary to the four myths of suicide.
23-2. (a) Encourage professional consultation. (b) Capitalize on any doubts. (c) Provide empathy and social support. (d) Identify and clarify the crucial problem. (e) Suggest alternative courses of action. (f) Take suicidal talk seriously.

REVIEW OF KEY TERMS

Agoraphobia
Antisocial personality disorder
Anxiety disorders
Attributions
Bipolar mood disorder
Catatonic schizophrenia
Competency
Concordance rate
Conversion disorder
Delusions
Depressive disorders
Diagnosis
Disorganized schizophrenia
Dissociative disorders

Epidemiology
Etiology
Generalized anxiety disorder
Hallucinations
Hypochondriasis
Insanity
Involuntary commitment
Medical model
Mood disorders
Multiple personality disorder
Neurotic
Obsessive-compulsive disorder
Panic disorder
Paranoid schizophrenia

Personality disorders
Phobic disorder
Prevalence
Prognosis
Psychogenic amnesia
Psychosomatic diseases
Psychotic
Schizophrenic disorders
Seasonal affective disorder (SAD)
Somatization disorder
Somatoform disorders
Transvestism
Undifferentiated schizophrenia

_____ 1. Proposes that it is useful to think of abnormal behavior as a disease.

_____ 2. Involves distinguishing one illness from another.

_____ 3. Refers to the apparent causation and developmental history of an illness.

_____ 4. A forecast about the possible course of an illness.

_____ 5. A sexual disorder in which a man achieves sexual arousal by dressing in women's clothing.

_____ 6. An older category that includes the less severe forms of mental illness; refers to behavior marked by subjective distress (usually chronic anxiety) and reliance on avoidance coping.

_____ 7. Refers to behavior marked by impaired reality contact and profound deterioration of adaptive functioning.

_____ 8. The study of the distribution of mental or physical disorders in a population.

_____ 9. Refers to the percentage of a population that exhibits a disorder during a specified time period.

_____ 10. A class of disorders marked by feelings of excessive apprehension and anxiety.

_____ 11. Disorder marked by a chronic high level of anxiety that is not tied to any specific threat.

_____ 12. Disorder marked by a persistent and irrational fear of an object or situation that presents no realistic danger.

_____ 13. Disorder that involves recurrent attacks of overwhelming anxiety that usually occur suddenly and unexpectedly.

_____ 14. Disorder marked by persistent uncontrollable intrusions of unwanted thoughts and urges to engage in senseless rituals.

_____ 15. A fear of going out in public places.

_____ 16. Physical ailments with a genuine organic basis that are caused in part by psychological factors.

_____ 17. A class of disorders involving physical ailments that have no authentic organic basis and are due to psychological factors.

_____ 18. Disorder marked by a history of diverse physical complaints that appear to be psychological in origin.

_____ 19. Disorder that involves a significant loss of physical function (with no apparent organic basis), usually in a single organ system.

_____ 20. Disorder that involves excessive preoccupation with health concerns and incessant worrying about developing physical illnesses.

_____ 21. A class of disorders in which people lose contact with portions of their consciousness or memory, resulting in disruptions in their sense of identity.

_____ 22. A sudden loss of memory that is too extensive to be due to normal forgetting.

_____ 23. The coexistence in one person of two or more largely complete, and usually very different, personalities.

_____ 24. A class of disorders marked by depressed or elevated mood disturbances that may spill over to disrupt physical, perceptual, social, and thought processes.

_____ 25. Mood disorder that tends to repeatedly occur at about the same time of the year.

_____ 26. Disorders marked by persistent feelings of sadness and despair and a loss of interest in previous sources of pleasure.

_____ 27. Disorder marked by the experience of both depressive and manic periods.

_____ 28. Statistic indicating the percentage of twin pairs or other pairs of relatives who exhibit the same disorder.

_____ 29. Inferences that people draw about the causes of events, others' behavior, and their own behavior.

_____ 30. A class of disorders marked by disturbances in thought that spill over to affect perceptual, social, and emotional processes.

_____ 31. False beliefs that are maintained even though they clearly are out of touch with reality.

_____ 32. Sensory perceptions that occur in the absence of a real, external stimulus, or gross distortions of perceptual input.

_____ 33. Type of schizophrenia dominated by delusions of persecution, along with delusions of grandeur.

_____ 34. Type of schizophrenia marked by striking motor disturbances, ranging from muscular rigidity to random motor activity.

_____ 35. Type of schizophrenia marked by a particularly severe deterioration of adaptive behavior.

_____ 36. Type of schizophrenia marked by idiosyncratic mixtures of schizophrenic symptoms.

_____ 37. A class of disorders marked by extreme, inflexible personality traits that cause subjective distress or impaired social and occupational functioning.

_____ 38. Disorder marked by impulsive, callous, manipulative, aggressive, and irresponsible behavior; reflects a failure to accept social norms.

_____ 39. A legal status indicating that a person cannot be held responsible for his or her actions because of mental illness.

_____ 40. A defendant's capacity to stand trial.

_____ 41. Legal situation in which people are hospitalized in psychiatric facilities against their will.

Answers: 1. medical model 2. diagnosis 3. etiology 4. prognosis 5. transvestism 6. neurotic 7. psychotic 8. epidemiology 9. prevalence 10. anxiety disorders 11. generalized anxiety disorder 12. phobic disorder 13. panic disorder 14. obsessive-compulsive disorder 15. agoraphobia 16. psychosomatic diseases 17. somatoform disorders 18. somatization disorder 19. conversion disorder 20. hypochondriasis 21. dissociative disorders 22. psychogenic amnesia 23. multiple personality disorder 24. mood disorders 25. seasonal affective disorder (SAD) 26. depressive disorders 27. bipolar mood disorder 28. concordance rate 29. attributions 30. schizophrenic disorders 31. delusions 32. hallucinations 33. paranoid schizophrenia 34. catatonic schizophrenia 35. disorganized schizophrenia 36. undifferentiated schizophrenia 37. personality disorders 38. antisocial personality disorder 39. insanity 40. competency 41. involuntary commitment.

REVIEW OF KEY PEOPLE

Lauren Alloy & Lyn Abramson   David Rosenhan   Thomas Szasz
Nancy Andreasen   Martin Seligman

_____ **1.** Critic of the medical model; argues that abnormal behavior usually involves a deviation from social norms rather than an illness.

_____ **2.** Did a study on admission of pseudopatients to a mental hospital; concluded that our mental health system is biased toward seeing pathology where it doesn't exist.

_____ **3.** Developed the concept of "preparedness"; believes that classical conditioning creates most phobic responses.

_____ **4.** Found that depressed people's views may be more realistic than those of nondepressed people.

_____ **5.** Proposed an alternative approach to subtyping that divides schizophrenic disorders into just two categories based on the presence of negative versus positive symptoms.

Answers: 1. Szasz 2. Rosenhan 3. Seligman 4. Alloy & Abramson 5. Andreasen.

SELF-QUIZ

1. Which of the following concepts or people asserts that abnormal behavior is best thought of as a disease?
   a. the behavioral model
   b. the medical model
   c. Thomas Szasz
   d. Arthur Staats

2. Judgments of abnormality are usually based on assessments of:
   a. deviance from cultural standards
   b. degree of emotional distress
   c. the extent to which the behavior is maladaptive
   d. all of the above

3. In Rosenhan's study involving admission of pseudopatients to psychiatric facilities, most of the "patients" were:
   a. diagnosed as seriously disturbed.
   b. diagnosed as suffering from a mild neurosis.
   c. dismissed within two days.
   d. misdiagnosed by the ward attendants but correctly diagnosed by the professional staff.

4. Sue Ellen gets sudden, paralyzing attacks of anxiety and fears going out in public away from her house. Which anxiety disorder does this describe?
   a. generalized anxiety disorder
   b. phobic disorder
   c. obsessive-compulsive disorder
   d. agoraphobia

5. Ralph cleans and scrubs the cupboards in his house seven times each day. Which anxiety disorder does this describe?
   a. generalized anxiety disorder
   b. phobic disorder
   c. obsessive-compulsive disorder
   d. panic disorder

6. Human beings may have evolved to be more easily conditioned to fear some stimuli than others. This is Seligman's notion of:
   a. preparedness
   b. anxiety differentiation
   c. somatization
   d. learned helplessness

7. Which of the following is included under the somatoform disorders?
   a. bipolar mood disorders
   b. hypochondria
   c. phobias
   d. schizophrenia

8. Paralysis or loss of feeling that does not match underlying anatomical organization is a symptom of:
   a. somatization disorder
   b. conversion disorder
   c. hypochondriasis
   d. malingering

9. Multiple personality is:
   a. an anxiety disorder
   b. a dissociative disorder
   c. a mood disorder
   d. a somatoform disorder

10. The disorder marked by striking motor disturbances ranging from rigidity to random motor activity and incoherence is termed:
    a. catatonic schizophrenia
    b. multiple personality
    c. dissociative disorder
    d. paranoid schizophrenia

11. Which of the following tends to be associated with recovery from schizophrenia?
    a. rapid, as opposed to gradual, onset of the disorder
    b. onset at an early age
    c. an avoidant family situation
    d. all of the above

12. Genetic factors probably play a role in causing:
    a. anxiety disorders
    b. mood disorders
    c. schizophrenic disorders
    d. all of the above

13. An individual is described as impulsive, charming, lacking in conscience, manipulative, and incapable of forming close attachments. Which diagnostic category does this description fit?
    a. schizophrenic disorder
    b. multiple personality
    c. antisocial personality
    d. any of the Axis I categories

14. A court declares that, because of a mental illness, an individual is not responsible for his criminal actions. The individual is:
    a. insane
    b. incompetent to stand trial
    c. psychotic
    d. all of the above

15. Among males suicide occurs most frequently:
    a. between the ages of 15 to 19
    b. between the ages of 20 to 24
    c. between the ages of 24 to 44
    d. after age 55

Answers: 1. b 2. d 3. a 4. d 5. c 6. a 7. b 8. b 9. b 10. a 11. a 12. d 13. c 14. a 15. d.

15 PSYCHOTHERAPY

REVIEW OF KEY IDEAS

THE ELEMENTS OF PSYCHOTHERAPY: TREATMENT, CLIENTS, AND THERAPISTS

1. **Identify the three categories of therapy and discuss why people seek or do not seek therapy.**

   1-1. Imelda has suddenly developed an extreme fear of leaving her apartment (agoraphobia). She checks the Yellow Pages and calls three different psychotherapists regarding possible treatment.

   (a) One therapist tells her that treatment will require her to talk with the therapist so as to develop a better understanding of her inner feelings. This therapist probably belongs to the _____insight_____ school of psychotherapy.

   (b) Another therapist suggests that some form of medication may help alleviate her fear. This therapist probably pursues the ___biomedical___ approach to psychotherapy.

   (c) The third therapist is of the opinion that her fear results from learning and correcting it requires that she unlearn this fear. This therapist probably pursues the ___behavioral___ approach to psychotherapy.

   1-2. Indicate whether the following statements about people who seek and choose not to seek psychotherapy are true or false.

   __F__ Men are more likely than women to seek psychotherapy.

   __T__ The two most common presenting symptoms are excessive anxiety and depression.

   __F__ Persons seeking psychotherapy always have identifiable disorders.

   __T__ Only a minority of persons needing psychotherapy actually receive treatment.

   __T__ Many people feel that seeking psychotherapy is an admission of personal weakness.

   Answers: 1-1. (a) insight (b) biomedical (c) behavioral   1-2. false, true, false, true, true.

2. **Describe the various types of mental health professionals involved in the provision of psychotherapy.**

    2-1.   Identify the following kinds of mental health professionals:
(a) Medically trained persons (physicians) who generally use biomedical and insight approaches to psychotherapy. *Psychiatrists*

        (b) Persons with doctoral degrees who emphasize behavioral and insight approaches to psychotherapy in treating a full range of psychological problems (two types).
Psychologists – clinical & counseling

        (c) Nurses who usually work as part of the treatment team in a hospital setting.
Psychiatric nurses

        (d) These persons often work with both the patient and family to reintegrate the patient back into society.
psychiatric social workers

        (e) Persons who usually specialize in particular types of problems, such as vocational, drug, or marital counseling.
Counselors

Answers: 2-1. (a) psychiatrists (b) clinical and counseling psychologists (c) psychiatric nurses (d) psychiatric social workers (e) counselors.

INSIGHT THERAPIES

3. **Explain the logic of Freudian psychoanalysis and describe the techniques by which analysts probe the unconscious.**

    3-1.   Freud believed that psychological disturbances originate from unresolved conflicts deep in the unconscious levels of the mind. His theory of personality, which he called ___*psychoanalysis*___, would be classified as an ___*insight*___ approach to psychotherapy. The psychoanalyst plays the role of psychological detective to seek out problems largely in the (conscious/~~unconscious~~) thoughts of the patient.

    3-2.   The psychoanalyst employs two techniques to probe the unconscious. One technique requires the patient to tell whatever comes to mind no matter how trivial. This technique is called ___*free association*___. The other technique requires the patient to learn to remember his or her dreams, which are then probed for their hidden meaning by the psychoanalyst. This technique is called ___*dream analysis*___.

Answers: 3-1. psychoanalysis, insight, unconscious 3-2. free association, dream analysis.

4. Discuss resistance and transference in psychoanalysis.

4-1. Freud believed that people often (<u>do/do not</u>) want to know the true nature of their inner conflicts and will employ various strategies so as to offer ___*resistance*___ to the progress of therapy. As therapy progresses, the patient often begins to relate to the therapist as though he or she was actually one of the significant persons (mother, father, spouse, etc.) in the patient's life. This phenomenon is called ___*transference*___ .

Answers: 4-1. do not, resistance, transference.

5. Discuss trends in modern psychodynamic approaches to therapy.

5-1. Indicate whether the following statements about trends in modern psychodynamic approaches to therapy are true or false.

___T___ The new approaches have sought to decrease the length of psychotherapy.

___T___ The new approaches have emphasized conscious processes over unconscious processes.

___T___ The new approaches have deemphasized the couch and free association in favor of more direct communication with the patient.

___F___ The new approaches place a greater emphasis on probing into inner conflicts centering on sex and aggression.

___F___ The new approaches place a greater emphasis on delving into the patient's past.

Answers: 5-1. true, true, true, false, false.

6. Identify the elements of the therapeutic climate and discuss the therapeutic process in Rogers's client-centered therapy.

6-1. Client-centered therapy, as developed by Carl Rogers, holds that there are three important aspects necessary for a good therapeutic climate. These are genuineness, unconditional positive regard, and empathy. Match these terms with their correct definitions as given below.
(a) The ability to truly see the world from the client's point of view and communicate this understanding to the client. *empathy*

(b) The therapist's openness and honesty with the client.
genuineness

(c) The complete and nonjudgmental acceptance of the client as a person without necessarily agreeing with what the client has to say.
unconditional positive regard

6-2. For client-centered therapy, the major emphasis is to provide feedback and ___*clarification*___ as the client expresses his or her thoughts and feelings. The idea here is that the client (<u>does/does not</u>) need direct advice. What is needed is help in sorting through personal confusion in order to gain greater ___*insight*___ into true inner feelings.

Answers: 6-1. (a) empathy (b) genuineness (c) unconditional positive regard 6-2. clarification, does not, insight.

7. **Discuss the logic, goals, and techniques of cognitive therapy.**

   7-1.   Answer the following questions regarding the logic, goals and techniques of cognitive therapy.
   (a) What is the basic logic behind cognitive therapy? Or to put it another way, what is the origin of many psychological problems according to cognitive therapy?

   negative illogical thinking

   (b) What is the primary goal of cognitive therapy?

   the change way of thinking

   (c) How do cognitive therapists go about trying to change a client's negative illogical thinking?

   through argument & persuasion

   (d) Cognitive therapy is actually a blend of insight therapy and behavior therapy. What technique from behavior therapy do cognitive therapists frequently employ?

   homework assignments

   Answers: 7-1. (a) Many problems arise from negative illogical thinking. (b) to change the client's negative illogical thinking (c) through argument and persuasion (d) homework assignments.

8. **Describe how group therapy is generally conducted and identify some advantages of this approach.**

   8-1.   When conducting group therapy, the therapist generally plays a(an) (active/subtle) role, one that is primarily aimed at promoting ___*group*___ cohesiveness. Participants essentially function as ___*therapists*___ for each other, providing acceptance and emotional support.

   8-2.   Besides being less expensive, group therapy also has three other advantages: (1) the realization by the participants that their problems (are/are not) unique, (2) the opportunity to work in a safe environment to build ___*social*___ skills, and (3) the fact that group therapy is particularly appropriate for certain kinds of problems, as is illustrated by many peer ___*self help*___ groups that work with such diverse problems as alcoholism, overeating, child abuse, etc.

   Answers: 8-1. subtle, group, therapists   8-2. are not, social, self-help.

9. **Discuss Eysenck's critique of insight therapy and more recent evidence on the efficacy of insight therapies.**

   9-1.   In his review of therapeutic outcome studies with neurotic patients, Eysenck found that about ___*2/3*___ of all patients recovered within 2 years. The rate of recovery was (the same/ different) for patients treated with insight therapy and untreated patients. Eysenck concluded that ___*spontaneous*___ remission accounted for most of the cures ascribed to insight therapies.

   9-2.   More recent outcome studies have found that a better estimate of spontaneous remission is in the range of 30 to ___*40*___ %. Recent studies have also concluded that insight therapies appear to help about ___*80*___ % of the clients when compared to untreated controls.

9-3. Which of the following characteristics have been recently found to be related to successful outcomes with insight therapies?

young   attractive
verbal   intelligent
successful   motivated
positive attitude about therapy

Answers: 9-1. two-thirds, the same, spontaneous   9-2. 40, 70 to 80   9-3. intelligent, successful, motivated, positive attitude about therapy.

BEHAVIOR THERAPIES

10. **Summarize the general principles underlying behavioral approaches to therapy.**

10-1. In contrast to insight therapists who believe that pathological symptoms are signs of an underlying problem, behavior therapists believe that the _____Symptoms_____ are the problem. Thus behavior therapists focus on employing the principles of learning to directly change _____behavior_____. The two general principles underlying this approach are first, one's behavior is a product of _____learning_____, and second, what has been learned can be _____unlearned_____.

Answers: 10-1. symptoms, behavior, learning, unlearned.

11. **Describe the goals and procedures of systematic desensitization and aversion therapy.**

11-1. State if the following situations would be most applicable to systematic desensitization or to aversion therapy.

(a) The goal of this treatment is to lessen the attractiveness of particular stimuli and behaviors that are personally or socially harmful. _aversion therapy_

(b) The goal of this treatment is to reduce irrational fears such as found in phobias and other anxiety disorders. _systematic desensitization_

(c) This three-step treatment involves pairing an imagined anxiety hierarchy with deep muscle relaxation. _systematic desensitization_

(d) This treatment involves presenting an unpleasant stimulus, such as electric shock, while a person is engaged in performing a self-destructive, but personally appealing, act. _aversion therapy_

(e) This would be the treatment of choice for students who are unduly anxious about public speaking. _systematic desensitization_

Answers: 11-1. (a) aversion therapy (b) systematic desensitization (c) systematic desensitization (d) aversion therapy (e) systematic desensitization.

12. **Describe the goals and techniques of social skills training and biofeedback.**

12-1. As the name implies, social skills training is a behavior therapy designed to improve a client's social or ____*interpersonal*____ skills. Three different behavioral techniques are employed. First, one is required to closely watch the behavior of socially skilled persons, a technique called ____*modeling*____. Next the client is expected to imitate and practice the behavior he or she has just witnessed, a technique called behavior ____*rehearsal*____. Finally, the client is expected to perform in social situations requiring increasingly more difficult social skills, a technique called ____*shaping*____.

12-2. Biofeedback works by providing the client with immediate ____*feedback*____ about some bodily function, such as blood pressure or muscle tension, thus leading to better control of these functions. For example, it has been found that clients can lessen the intensity and frequency of tension headaches by learning to ____*lessen/reduce*____ the muscle tension in their neck and facial muscles.

Answers: 12-1. interpersonal, modeling, rehearsal, shaping 12-2. feedback, lessen (reduce).

13. **Discuss evidence on the effectiveness of behavior therapies.**

13-1. Compared to the evidence in support of insight therapies, the evidence in favor of behavior therapy is somewhat (weaker/stronger). It is important to remember, however, that behavior therapies are best suited for treating (specific/general) psychological disorders and that all of the various behavioral techniques (are/are not) equally effective.

Answers: 13-1. stronger, specific, are not.

BIOMEDICAL THERAPIES

14. **Describe the principal categories of drugs used in the treatment of psychological disorders.**

14-1. Valium and Librium, popularly called tranquilizers, are used to treat psychological disorders in which anxiety is a major feature. Thus they are collectively called ____*anti-anxiety*____ drugs.

14-2. Another class of drugs is used to treat severe psychotic symptoms, such as hallucinations and confusion. These drugs are collectively called ____*antipsychotic*____ drugs.

14-3. Two other classes of drugs, tricyclics and MAO inhibitors, have been found to be useful in alleviating depression. These drugs are collectively called ____*antidepressant*____ drugs.

14-4. A rather unique drug can function as both an antidepressant and antimanic agent. This drug is ____*lithium*____.

Answers: 14-1. antianxiety 14-2. antipsychotic 14-3. antidepressant 14-4. lithium.

15. **Discuss evidence on the effects and problems of drug treatments for psychological disorders.**

15-1. Drug therapies have proven useful in the treatment of many psychological disorders. However, they remain controversial for at least two reasons. List these two reasons below.

side effects, may only mask problem, over prescribed & medicated

Answers: 15-1. They alleviate rather than cure psychological distress and they are overprescribed and patients are overmedicated.

16. **Describe ECT and discuss its therapeutic effects and its risks.**

16-1. Answer the following questions about the nature and therapeutic effects and risks of ECT.
(a) What is the physical effect of the electric shock on the patient?

it produce convulsive seizures

(b) What general class of disorders warrant conservative use of ECT as a treatment technique.

severe mood disorders

(c) Why does ECT work?

unknown

(d) What is the major risk of ECT?

ECT can produce both short-term & long-term intellectual impairment.

Answers: 16-1. (a) It produces convulsive seizures. (b) severe mood disorders (c) It is unknown at this time. (d) It can produce both short-term and long-term intellectual impairment.

BLENDING APPROACHES TO PSYCHOTHERAPY

17. **Discuss the merits of blending or combining different approaches to therapy.**

17-1. A significant trend in modern psychotherapy is to blend or combine many different treatment approaches. Psychologists who advocate and use this approach are said to be _____*eclectic*_____.

One outcome study cited by the text suggests there may be merit to this approach. In this study, three different groups of depressed patients were treated by either insight therapy, drug therapy, or both. The greatest improvement was found in patients treated by _____*both*_____.

Answers: 17-1. eclectic, both.

INSTITUTIONAL TREATMENT IN TRANSITION

18. **Explain why people grew disenchanted with mental hospitals and describe the community mental health movement.**

18-1. After more than a century of reliance on state mental hospitals the evidence began to grow that these institutions were not helping the patients; in many instances these institutions were worsening the patients' condition. What two conditions, unrelated to funding, were said to be responsible for this state of affairs? *paternalistic care made the patients feel helpless, the removal of patients from their communities separated them from essential support groups*

18-2. In order to correct for these shortcomings, the community mental health movement arose as an alternative treatment option. The four key services they generally provide are (select the correct four from the following):
   a. long-term inpatient therapy
   b. short-term inpatient therapy
   c. outpatient therapy
   d. emergency services
   e. education and consultation
   f. vocational rehabilitation

Answers: 18-1. The paternalistic care made the patients feel helpless, and the removal of patients from their communities separated them from essential support groups. 18-2. b, c, d, e.

19. **Describe the deinstitutionalization trend and evaluate its effects.**

19-1. The transferring of mental health care from large state institutions to community-based facilities is what is meant by the term *deinstitutionalization*. As a result of deinstitutionalization, the number of mental patients in large institutional hospitals has *declined* remarkably. The length of stay by patients in mental hospitals has also *decreased*.

19-2. While deinstitutionalization has resulted in a decrease in the number of patients, as well as their length of stay, the number of admissions to psychiatric hospitals has actually *increased*. This is because of a large number of readmissions for short-term care, which the text calls "the *revolving door* problem". Another problem brought about by deinstitutionalization is that a large number of discharged patients who have meager job skills and no close support groups make up a large portion of the nation's *homeless* persons.

Answers: 19-1. deinstitutionalization, declined (or decreased), declined   19-2. increased, revolving door, homeless.

20. **Summarize the method, results, and implications of the Featured Study on homelessness among the mentally ill.**

　20-1.　Answer the following questions regarding the Featured Study.
　　　　(a) How did the study systematically estimate the number of persons suffering from mental illness among the nation's homeless.

　　　　they interviewed all guests at a selected homeless facility in Boston

　　　　(b) What was the median age of the guests?　*34*

　　　　(c) While 91% of the guests were found to have psychological disorders, only 28% had been previously hospitalized. What possible explanation did the authors give to account for the large percentage of untreated guests.　*they became adults after deinstitutionalization*

　　　　(d) What did the authors conclude about the current status of community shelters?

　　　　Community shelters often serve as open asylums

　　　　Answers:　20-1. (a) They interviewed all guests at a selected homeless facility in Boston. (b) 34 (c) They came into adulthood after deinstitutionalization. (c) Community shelters often serve as open asylums.

PUTTING IT IN PERSPECTIVE

21. **Explain how this chapter highlighted our unifying theme about the benefits of theoretical diversity.**

　21-1.　What point does the text make about psychotherapy that nicely illustrates the benefits of theoretical diversity?　*the many diverse approaches have resulted in better treatment approaches.*

　　　　Answers:　21-1. The many diverse approaches have resulted in better treatment techniques.

APPLICATION: LOOKING FOR A THERAPIST

22. **Discuss when and where to seek therapy, and the potential importance of a therapist's sex, theoretical approach, and professional background.**

　22-1.　While one might seek psychotherapy just to get more out of life, serious thinking about seeking psychotherapy should begin when you have talked to friends and family and still feel *uncomfortable (helpless)* about a problem that is severely disrupting your life. The text lists five places where you might seek psychotherapy. List them.

　　　　Community mental health centers
　　　　hospitals
　　　　human service agencies
　　　　School & work places
　　　　private practitioners

22-2. The text concludes that the kind of degree and theoretical approach held by the psychotherapist (is/is not) important, although a verifiable degree indicating some kind of professional training is important. The sex of the therapist should be chosen according to the feelings of the _client_ ; it is unwise to engage a therapist whose sex makes the client feel uncomfortable.

Answers: 22-1. uncomfortable (or helpless), private practice, community mental health centers, hospitals, human service centers, schools and work places   22-2. is not, client.

23. Summarize what one should look for in a prospective therapist and what one should expect out of therapy.

23-1. The text lists three areas to evaluate when looking for a therapist. Complete the following statements describing these areas.

(a) Can you talk to the therapist _in a candid, non defensive manner_ ?

(b) Does the therapist appear to have _empathy & understanding_ ?

(c) Does the therapist appear to be _self-assured & confident_ ?

23-2. What did the Ehrenbergs say about what to expect from psychotherapy? _psychotherapy takes time, effort, & courage_

23-3. What should one consider before terminating therapy because of lack of progress? _is it due to resistance?_

Answers: 23-1. (a) in a candid nondefensive manner (b) empathy and understanding (c) self-assured and confident   23-2. It takes time, effort, and courage.   23-3. The lack of progress may be due to resistance on your part.

REVIEW OF KEY TERMS

Antianxiety drugs
Antidepressant drugs
Antipsychotic drugs
Aversion therapy
Behavior therapies
Biofeedback
Biomedical therapies
Client-centered therapy
Clinical psychologists
Cognitive therapy
Community mental health centers

Counseling psychologists
Deinstitutionalization
Dream analysis
Electroconvulsive therapy (ECT)
Free association
Group therapy
Insight therapies
Interpretation
Lithium
Mental hospitals

Psychiatrists
Psychoanalysis
Psychopharmacotherapy
Resistance
Social skills training
Spontaneous remission
Systematic desensitization
Tardive dyskinesia
Theoretical eclecticism
Transference

_____ 1. Two groups of professionals that specialize in the diagnosis and treatment of psychological disorders and everyday behavioral problems.

_____ 2. Physicians who specialize in the treatment of psychological disorders.

_____ 3. Therapies that involve verbal interactions intended to enhance client's self-knowledge and thus produce healthful changes in personality and behavior.

_____ 4. An insight therapy that emphasizes the recovery of unconscious conflicts, motives, and defenses through techniques such as free association and transference.

_____ 5. A technique in which clients are urged to spontaneously express their thoughts and feelings with as little personal censorship as possible.

_____ 6. A technique for interpreting the symbolic meaning of dreams.

_____ 7. A therapist's attempts to explain the inner significance of a client's thoughts, feelings, memories, and behavior.

_____ 8. A client's largely unconscious defensive maneuvers intended to hinder the progress of therapy.

_____ 9. Process that occurs when clients start relating to their therapist in ways that mimic critical relationships in their lives.

_____ 10. An insight therapy that emphasizes providing a supportive emotional climate for clients who play a major role in determining the pace and direction of their therapy.

_____ 11. An insight therapy that emphasizes recognizing and changing negative thoughts and maladaptive beliefs.

_____ 12. The simultaneous treatment of several clients in a group.

_____ 13. Therapies that involve the application of learning principles to change a client's maladaptive behaviors.

_____ 14. A behavior therapy used to reduce clients' anxiety responses through counterconditioning.

_____ 15. A behavior therapy in which an aversive stimulus is paired with a stimulus that elicits an undesirable response.

_____ 16. Recovery from a disorder that occurs without formal treatment.

_____ 17. A behavior therapy designed to improve interpersonal skills, that emphasizes shaping, modeling, and behavioral rehearsal.

_____ 18. A behavioral technique in which a bodily function is monitored and information about it is fed back to a person to facilitate control of the physiological process.

_____ 19. Therapies that use physiological interventions intended to reduce symptoms associated with psychological disorders.

_____ 20. The treatment of mental disorders with drug therapy.

_____ 21. Drugs that relieve tension, apprehension, and nervousness.

_____ 22. Drugs that gradually reduce psychotic symptoms.

_____ 23. A neurological disorder marked by chronic tremors and involuntary spastic movements.

_____ 24. Drugs that gradually elevate mood and help bring people out of a depression.

_____ 25. A chemical used to control mood swings in patients with bipolar mood disorder.

_____ 26. A treatment in which electric shock is used to produce cortical seizure accompanied by convulsions.

_____ 27. Selecting what appears to be the best from a variety of theories or systems of therapy rather than committing to one theoretical orientation.

_____ 28. A medical institution specializing in the provision of inpatient care for psychological disorders.

_____ 29. Centers that provide mental health care for their local communities.

30. Transfering the treatment of mental illness from inpatient institutions to community-based facilities that emphasize outpatient care.

Answers: 1. clinical and counseling psychologists 2. psychiatrists 3. insight therapies 4. psychoanalysis 5. free association 6. dream analysis 7. interpretation 8. resistance 9. transference 10. client-centered therapy 11. cognitive therapy 12. group therapy 13. behavior therapies 14. systematic desensitization 15. aversion therapy 16. spontaneous remission 17. social skills training 18. biofeedback 19. biomedical therapies 20. psychopharmacotherapy 21. antianxiety drugs 22. antipsychotic drugs 23. tardive dyskinesia 24. antidepressant drugs 25. lithium 26. electroconvulsive therapy (ECT) 27. theoretical eclecticism 28. mental hospitals 29. community mental health centers 30. deinstitutionalization.

REVIEW OF KEY PEOPLE

Aaron Beck   Sigmund Freud   Joseph Wolpe
Hans Eysenck   Carl Rogers

_____ 1. Developed a systematic treatment procedure that he called psycho-analysis.

_____ 2. The developer of client-centered therapy.

_____ 3. Noted for his work in the development of cognitive therapy.

_____ 4. His early research showed that insight therapies were ineffective.

_____ 5. The developer of systematic desensitization.

Answers: 1. Freud 2. Rogers 3. Beck 4. Eysenck 5. Wolpe.

SELF-QUIZ

1. Which of the three approaches to psychotherapy is most likely to use medication as part of the treatment package?
   a. insight
   b. biomedical
   c. behavioral
   d. all of the above

2. Which of the following is not a true statement?
   a. Women seek psychotherapy more than men.
   b. The two most common problems that lead to psychotherapy are sexual problems and depression.
   c. Persons seeking psychotherapy don't always have identifiable problems.
   d. Many people feel that seeking psychotherapy is an admission of personal weakness.

3. Which of the following mental health professionals is most likely to work with both the patient and family to reintegrate the patient back into society?
   a. psychiatric social workers
   b. clinical psychologists
   c. psychiatric nurses
   d. counselors

4. Psychoanalysis is an example of what kind of approach to psychotherapy?
   a. insight
   b. learning
   c. biomedical
   d. a combination of learning and biomedical

5. The release of emotional tensions by the client during the course of psychoanalysis is called:
   a. transference
   b. free association
   c. catharsis
   d. restructuring

6. Which of the following is correct concerning trends in modern psychodynamic approaches to therapy?
   a. The therapeutic process has been lengthened.
   b. A greater emphasis has been placed on unconscious forces.
   c. A greater emphasis has been placed on the here and now.
   d. All of the above are correct.

7. The major emphasis in client-centered therapy is to provide the client with:
   a. interpretation of unconscious thinking
   b. cognitive restructuring
   c. feedback and clarification
   d. good advice

8. Which of the following is likely to be commonly found in behavior therapy?
   a. free association
   b. emphasis on nonverbal cues
   c. transference
   d. none of the above

9. Which of the following is likely to be found in cognitive therapy?
   a. a search for automatic negative thoughts
   b. reality testing
   c. an emphasis on rational thinking
   d. all of the above

10. Which kind of therapist is likely to play the least active (most subtle) role in conducting therapy?
    a. behavior therapist
    b. cognitive therapist
    c. group therapist
    d. psychoanalytic therapist

11. Eysenck's study of outcome studies with neurotic patients found that the recovery rate:
    a. was best for treated patients
    b. was best for untreated patients
    c. was the same for treated and untreated patients

12. Which of the following therapies is most likely to see the symptom as the problem?
    a. psychoanalysis
    b. gestalt
    c. behavior
    d. cognitive

13. Which of the following behavior therapy techniques would most likely be used to treat a fear of flying?
    a. systematic desensitization
    b. aversive conditioning
    c. modeling
    d. biofeedback

14. In comparison to other forms of therapy, behavior therapy is most applicable to all kinds of psychological disorders. This statement is:
    a. true
    b. false

15. Electroconvulsive therapy (ECT) is now primarily used to treat patients suffering from:
    a. anxiety
    b. phobia
    c. severe mood disorders
    d. psychosis

16. Psychotherapists who combine several different approaches in their approach to therapy are said to be:
    a. enigmatic
    b. eclectic
    c. unspecific
    d. imaginative

17. The trend toward deinstitutionalization largely came about because large mental institutions:
    a. were becoming too expensive
    b. were actually worsening the condition of many patients
    c. could not be properly staffed
    d. both a and c

Answers: 1. b 2. b 3. a 4. a 5. c 6. c 7. c 8. d 9. d 10. c 11. c 12. c 13. a 14. b 15. c 16. b 17. b.

16 SOCIAL BEHAVIOR

REVIEW OF KEY IDEAS

PERSON PERCEPTION: FORMING IMPRESSIONS OF OTHERS

1. **Describe how various aspects of physical appearance may influence our impressions of others.**

   1-1. What *general* types of characteristics do we tend to attribute to physically attractive people?

   1-2. We also tend to associate specific personality characteristics with specific aspects of appearance. For example, suppose you see several people who happen to have the following physical characteristics. What are you likely to assume about their personalities? Name one (or more) of the traits that people are likely to associate with each of the following:
   (a) tall men:

   (b) baby-faced people:

   (c) people with a youthful gait:

   Answers: 1-1. generally desirable characteristics (e.g., more sensitive, kind, sociable, pleasant, likable, intelligent, competent, and interesting)   1-2. (a) leadership ability, competence (b) warmth, submissiveness, kindness, naiveté (c) happiness, power.

2. **Explain how schemas, stereotypes, and other factors contribute to selectivity in person perception.**

   2-1. Briefly define the following:
   (a) schemas:

   (b) stereotypes:

   2-2. As mentioned earlier, people tend to associate large eyes and rounded features (a baby-faced appearance) with submissiveness and warmth. Forgetting baby-faced Nelson, the notorious killer, they may justify this association by saying that everyone they've heard of with those features also has those characteristics. As this example illustrates, our memory for events is _____: we tend to recall events that fit our schemas and not to recall events that do not fit our schemas.

   2-3. The type of exaggeration illustrated above, in which we tend to remember more confirmations of an association between traits than have actually occurred, is an example of selective perception referred to as _____ _____.

   2-4. In one study presented in the text, subjects watched a videotape of a woman engaged in various activities. For one set of subjects she was described as a librarian and for another group as a waitress. What effect did the occupational labels have on subjects' recall of the woman's activities? What does this study demonstrate?

   Answers: 2-1. (a) Social schemas are cognitive structures or *clusters of ideas* that guide our perceptions of people and events. (b) Stereotypes are a type of schema about groups or categories of people, acquired from our culture, that affect our perceptions of people who are members of those groups. 2-2. selective 2-3. illusory correlation 2-4. Subjects tended to recall activities consistent with stereotypes of librarians and waitresses. The study demonstrates that schemas, in this case stereotypes, affect what we remember; we selectively perceive; we exhibit illusory correlation, the tendency to exaggerate the correlation between traits (in this case occupational status and personality).

ATTRIBUTION PROCESSES: EXPLAINING BEHAVIOR

3. **Explain what attributions are, and why and when we make them.**

   3-1. What are attributions?

3-2. Why do we make attributions?

3-3. We make attributions when:

(a) _____ events grab our attention, when . . .

(b) events have _____ consequences for us, and when . . .

(c) people behave in _____ ways.

Answers: 3-1. Attributions are inferences that we make about the causes of events, especially about the causes of our own and other people's behavior.   3-2. We seem to have a strong need to understand, to explain, our experiences; explanations may guide behavior to enhance chances of success or hide evidence that there is a problem. 3-3. (a) unusual (unexpected) (b) personal (c) unexpected (unusual).

4. Describe the distinction between internal and external attributions and summarize Kelley's and Weiner's theories of attribution.

4-1. Which of the following involve internal and which external attributions? Label each sentence with an I or an E.

_____ He flunked because he's lazy.

_____ Our team lost because the officials were biased against us.

_____ The accident was caused by poor road conditions.

_____ He achieved by the sweat of his brow.

_____ Criminal behavior is caused by poverty.

_____ His success is directly derived from his parents' wealth and influence.

4-2. Ralph cried when he watched the Santa Claus parade. No one else seemed to be crying, so according to Kelley's model, Ralph's behavior would be (low/high) in (consistency/distinctiveness/consensus). Further, Ralph always cries when he watches parades, so Ralph's crying is (low/high) in (consistency/distinctiveness/consensus). Ralph also cries when he watches a movie, attends the ballet, watches a sporting event, or on almost any other occasion; thus, Ralph's crying is _____ in _____.

4-3. When people behave in a manner that is *high* in consistency, distinctiveness, and consensus, we are likely to attribute their behavior to *external* factors. On the other hand, when people behave in a manner that is high in consistency but *low* in both distinctiveness and consensus, we are likely to attribute their behavior to *internal* causes. Thus, according to Kelley's model, Ralph's crying behavior in the previous question would be attributable to _____ factors.

4-4. Weiner proposed that attributions are made not only in terms of an internal-external dimension but also in terms of a stable-unstable dimension. Suppose that Sally makes a high score on an exam. Her score could be attributed to the fact that she worked hard, an (internal/external) factor. If she *always* works hard, the factor is also (stable/unstable), while if she *does not* always work hard the factor is (stable/unstable).

4-5. Alternatively, Sally's high score might be attributed to an easy test, an (internal/external) factor. If the tests are always easy, then this factor is also (stable/unstable); if the tests are sometimes easy and sometimes difficult, then the factor is (stable/unstable).

4-6. As discussed in Chapter 14, theorists working with Weiner's model have developed an additional dimension along a *global-specific* continuum. These three dimensions allow one to make certain predictions about personality. For example, which of the following attributional styles are most likely to characterize depressed people?
a. internal, stable, and global
b. external, unstable, and specific
c. internal, unstable, and specific

Answers: **4-1.** I, E, E, I, E, E   **4-2.** low, consensus, low, distinctiveness, high, consistency   **4-3.** internal **4-4.** internal, stable, unstable   **4-5.** external, stable, unstable   **4-6.** c. (For more practice with these concepts see item 13 in Chapter 14 of this study guide.)

5. Describe several types of attributional bias and their relation to marital stress.

5-1. Define or describe the following:
(a) fundamental attribution error:

(b) actor-observer bias:

(c) defensive attribution:

(d) self-serving bias:

5-2. In what situation is the self-serving bias the same as the actor-observer bias, and when is it not the same?

5-3. While in marital therapy Ed described his wife as very selfish. He indicated that she had always been selfish in her treatment of him, and he took this as evidence that she was unable to have normal, caring relationships with people. Once in a while she would treat him nicely, Ed reported, when they were in public and she was under social pressure. How do Ed's attributions reflect the typical attributions of distressed couples?

Answers: **5-1.** (a) the tendency for observers to attribute an individual's behavior to internal rather than external factors (b) the tendency for observers to attribute an actor's behavior to internal rather than external factors *and the tendency for actors to attribute their own behavior to external causes* (Yes, there is overlap between definitions.) (c) the tendency to attribute other people's misfortunes to internal causes; in other words, the tendency to blame the victim (d) the tendency to attribute our successes to internal factors and our failures to situational factors   **5-2.** We tend to explain others' failures in terms of internal factors and our own in terms of external factors, as the actor-observer bias indicates. However, we tend to attribute our successes to internal factors, while others will tend to attribute them to external factors, an exception to the actor-observer rule.   **5-3.** As Ed has done in this example, distressed spouses tend to explain their mate's negative behavior in terms of internal, stable, and global factors and to explain his or her positive behavior in terms of external, unstable, and specific factors. The opposite tends to be the case with happily married couples.

INTERPERSONAL ATTRACTION: LIKING AND LOVING

6. Summarize evidence on four key factors in attraction discussed in the text.

6-1.   In the blanks below list the four key factors associated with attraction, then briefly explain what each concept means and how it is related to attraction.

(a) _____:

(b) _____:

(c) _____:

(d) _____:

6-2.   What is the matching hypothesis?

Answers: 6-1. (a) proximity: We are more likely to form friendships with others who are spatially closer than those further away. (Closeness or proximity in this case refers to where people live, shop, sit, work, etc.) (b) physical attractiveness: Our preferences for whom to date, marry, or form friendships with are strongly influenced by their physical attractiveness. (c) similarity: We tend to like others who are like us (in attitudes, personality, social background, etc.). (d) reciprocity: We tend to reciprocate liking; in other words, we tend to like others who like us.
6-2. This is the notion, backed up by a considerable amount of research, that people tend to date and marry others who are similar to themselves in physical attractiveness.

7. List several myths about love and describe theories that analyze love into components.

7-1.   In the space below list the three myths about love described in your text.

7-2.   Hatfield and Berscheid divide love into two types: _____ and

_____ love. Sternberg further divides companionate love into two subtypes, thus

producing three factors: _____, _____, and

_____. Of the three factors, which tends to drop off rapidly and which tend to

increase gradually over time?

Answers: 7-1. When you fall in love you'll know it. Love is a purely positive experience. True love lasts forever.
7-2. passionate, companionate, passion, intimacy, commitment. Passion drops off rapidly; intimacy and commitment (the subcategories of companionate love) increase gradually over time.

8. **Discuss evidence on the hypothesized relationship between love and attachment.**

   8-1. What *general* conclusion did Hazen and Shaver reach concerning the association between types of infant attachment and the love relationships of adults?

   8-2. Write the names of the three attachment styles next to the appropriate letters below.

   S: _____

   A-A: _____

   A: _____

   8-3. Using the letters from the previous question, match the three types of relationship with the descriptions.

   _____ Experiences difficulty in having a close relationship.

   _____ Preoccupied with love, expectant of rejection, volatile.

   _____ Characterized by close relationships.

   _____ Trusting.

   _____ Jealous.

   _____ Lacking intimacy.

   Answers: 8-1. The three types of infant-caretaker attachments (also described in Chapter 11) tend to predict the love relationships that these children have as adults. 8-2. secure, anxious-ambivalent, avoidant 8-3. A, A-A, S, S, A-A, A.

ATTITUDES: MAKING SOCIAL JUDGMENTS

9. **Describe the components of attitudes and the relations between attitudes and behavior.**

   9-1. Attitudes are said to be made up of three components: cognition, affect, and behavior. What do the words *cognition* and *affect* refer to? List synonyms (one or two words for each) in the blanks below.

   (a) cognition: _____

   (b) affect: _____

   9-2. The behavioral component refers, of course, to behavior. When expressed, it is the component we can readily observe, but it is not always expressed. Thus, this component is described in terms of behavioral _____ or tendencies.

   9-3. As LaPiere found in his travels with the Chinese couple, attitudes are relatively (poor/excellent) predictors of behavior. In part, this seems to be true because attitudes and cognitions are highly general, while _____ tend to be quite specific.

   9-4. In addition, attitudes may be poor predictors because the behavioral component is merely a *predisposition* that may be changed by norms and other aspects of the situation. People may want or plan or intend a certain course of action but may be deterred by characteristics of the immediate situation. For example, why might the restaurateurs have served the Chinese couple even though they said that they would not?

Answers: 9-1. (a) beliefs (or thoughts, thinking) (b) emotion (or feelings) 9-2. predispositions 9-3. poor, behaviors 9-4. The situational factors present at the time the couple asked to be served may have included: the embarrassment of confrontation, pressure from others, loss of income, the unanticipated pleasant characteristics of the couple, and so on.

10. Summarize evidence on source factors, message factors, and receiver factors that influence the process of persuasion.

10-1. Suppose you are the *source* of a communication, the message giver.
(a) What factors mentioned in your text could you use to make yourself more believable?

(b) Other than credibility, what else about yourself would you hope to emphasize?

10-2. Answer the following questions about *message* factors.
(a) In general, which is more effective, a one-sided argument or a two-sided argument? When is a one-sided message more effective?

(b) When do fear appeals work?

10-3. Answer the following questions about the role of the *receiver* in persuasive communications.
(a) What is the effect of forewarning on persuasive appeals?

(b) What does "latitude of acceptance" refer to?

Answers: 10-1. (a) To enhance credibility you would demonstrate your expertise and especially your trustworthiness. (b) Emphasize your likability by enhancing your physical attractiveness and the other factors that affect attraction. 10-2. (a) In general, two-sided appeals are more effective: That's the kind of speech Mark Antony gave over the body of Caesar. One-sided appeals are better when the audience is uneducated about the issue or when they are already very favorably disposed to your point of view. (b) They work only if the audience is persuaded that the described negative consequences are exceedingly unpleasant, likely to occur if they don't take your advice, and avoidable if they do take your advice. 10-3. (a) If you know that someone is going to attempt to persuade you on a particular topic, you will be less easy to persuade. Forewarning reduces the impact of persuasive arguments. (b) that people will be persuaded only if their view is not too different from that of the message.

11. **Explain how cognitive dissonance can account for the effects of counterattitudinal behavior and effort justification.**

11-1. Ralph bought a used car. However, the car uses a lot of gas, which he doesn't like because he strongly supports conserving energy. He rapidly concludes that conserving fuel isn't so important after all.
(a) Ralph has engaged in counterattitudinal behavior. What were the two contradictory cognitions? (One is a thought about his *behavior*. The other is a thought about an important *attitude*.)

(b) Suppose the car was a real beauty, a rare antique worth much more than the price paid. Alternatively, suppose that the car was only marginally worth what was paid for it. In which case would dissonance be stronger? In which case would the attitude about gas guzzling be more likely to change?

11-2. Suppose Bruce decides to join a particular club. (l) One possible scenario is that he must travel a great distance to attend, the club is very expensive, and he must give up much of his free time to become a member. (2) Alternatively, suppose that the traveling time is short, the club in inexpensive, and he need not give up any free time. In which case (1 or 2) will he tend to value his membership more, according to dissonance theory? Briefly, why?

Answers: 11-1. (a) cognition about behavior: I know I bought the car. cognition about attitude: I'm against the purchase of cars that waste gas. (b) The additional reward in the first situation produces less dissonance and will tend to leave Ralph's original attitude about gas consumption intact. Ralph's attitude about gas consumption will change more when there is less justification (in terms of the value of the car) for his action. As described in your text, we tend to have greater dissonance, and greater attitude change, when *less reward* accompanies our counterattitudinal behavior. 11-2. According to dissonance theory, he will value the membership more under alternative 1, even if the benefits of membership are slight, because people attempt to justify the effort expended in terms of the benefits received. (Note: Both questions in this section are contrary to a common sense idea of reward and punishment. Item 11-1 indicates that we like behaviors accompanied by less, not more, reward; item 11-2 indicates that we like behaviors accompanied by more, not less, discomfort.)

12. **Relate learning theory, balance theory, self-perception theory, and the elaboration likelihood model to attitude change.**

12-1. Following are examples that relate learning theory to attitude change. Indicate which type of learning—classical conditioning (CC), operant conditioning (OC), or observational learning (OL)—is being illustrated.

_____ Ralph hears a speaker express a particular political attitude, which is followed by thunderous applause. Thereafter, Ralph tends to express the same attitude.

_____ Advertisers pair soft drinks (and just about any other product) with attractive models. The audience likes the models and develops a stronger liking for the product.

_____ If you express an attitude that I like, I will agree with you, nod, say "mm-hmm," and so on. This will tend to strengthen your expression of that attitude.

12-2. Following are situations intended to illustrate three of the theories of attitude change described in the text. Label each example with the name of one of the theories: cognitive dissonance (CD), self-perception (SP), or balance (B).

_____ Workers in Group A are paid $100 per job. Workers in group B are paid $1000 per job (for the same work). The Group A workers enjoy their work more than the Group B workers.

_____ At a cocktail party Bruce eats caviar. When asked whether he likes caviar he responds, "I'm eating it, so I guess I must like it."

_____ Ed likes Sheila. Ed strongly favored gun control until he learned that Sheila strongly opposes it. Ed reversed his attitude on gun control.

12-3. In the situation with Ed and Sheila, was the original situation balanced or imbalanced, according to Heider's model? _____ How else could balance have been restored? List two possibilities.

12-4. To illustrate the elaboration likelihood model: Suppose that you are to travel in Europe and must decide between two options, whether to rent a car or go by train (e.g., on a Eurailpass, to be specific). In the blanks below indicate which persuasive route, central or peripheral, is referred to in these examples..

_____: On the basis of train brochures showing apparently wealthy and dignified travelers dining in luxury on the train while surveying the Alps, you opt for the train.

_____: Your travel agent, whose expertise you value and who usually knows what she is talking about, strongly recommends that you take the train. You decide on the train.

_____: You examine the costs of each mode of transportation, taking into account that four people will travel together. You interview several people who have used both methods. You factor in time, convenience, standing in line, the difficulty of reserving seats, and the cost of cab rides for the train option. You decide to rent a car.

12-5. In the elaboration likelihood model, the route that is easier, that involves the least amount of thinking, is the _____ route. The route in which relevant information is sought out and carefully pondered is the _____ route. Elaboration, which involves thinking about the various complexities of the situation, is more likely to occur when the _____ route is used. Elaboration leads to (more enduring/transient) changes in attitudes. In addition, attitudes formed by elaboration (i.e., the more central route) are (better/worse) predictors of behavior.

Answers: 12-1. OL, CC, OC   12-2. CD (assuming that other factors needed for cognitive dissonance are present), SP, B   12-3. imbalanced. Balance would also occur if Sheila changes her attitude regarding gun control or if Ed began to dislike Sheila.   12-4. peripheral, peripheral, central   12-5. peripheral, central, central, more enduring, better.

CONFORMITY AND OBEDIENCE: YIELDING TO OTHERS

13. **Describe Asch's work on conformity.**

13-1. Briefly summarize the general procedure and results of the Asch line-judging studies.

13-2. Conformity increased as number of accomplices increased, up to a point. At what number did conformity seem to peak? _____

13-3. Suppose there are five accomplices, one real subject, and another accomplice who dissents from the majority. What effect will this "dissenter" have on conformity by the real subject?

Answers: 13-1. Subjects were asked to judge which of three lines matched a standard line, a judgment that was actually quite easy to make. Only one of the subjects was a real subject, however; the others were accomplices of the experimenter who gave wrong answers on key trials. The result was that a majority of the real subjects tended to conform to the wrong judgments of the majority on at least some trials. 13-2. 7 13-3. Conformity will be dramatically reduced, to about one-fourth of its peak.

14. **Describe the procedure, results, and implications of the Featured Study (Milgram, 1963) on obedience to authority.**

14-1. Two individuals at a time participated in Milgram's initial study, but only one was a real subject. The other "subject" was an accomplice of the experimenter, an actor. By a rigged drawing of slips of paper the real subject became the _____ and the accomplice became the _____ . There were a total of _____ subjects, or "teachers," in the initial study.

14-2. The experimenter strapped the learner into a chair and stationed the teacher at an apparatus from which he could, supposedly, deliver electric shocks to the learner. The teacher was to start at 15 volts, and each time the learner made a mistake the teacher was supposed to _____ the level of shock by 15 volts—up to a level of 450 volts.

14-3. At 300 volts, the learner pounded on the wall and demanded to be released. Of the 40 subjects, how many quit the experiment at that point? _____ How many subjects had quit prior to that point? _____ What percentage of the subjects continued to obey instructions, thereby increasing the shock all the way up to 450 volts? _____

14-4. What is the major conclusion to be drawn from this study? Why are the results of interest?

Answers: 14-1. teacher, learner, 40 14-2. increase 14-3. 5, none, 65% 14-4. The major conclusion is that ordinary people will tend to obey an authority even when their obedience could result in considerable harm (and perhaps even death) to others. The result is of interest because it suggests that war crimes, such as occurred with the Nazis and the soldiers at Mai Lai, may occur not because of the evil nature of the participants but simply from situational pressures and the tendency to obey. The result is also of interest because most people would not expect this degree of obedience: psychiatrists, for example, predicted that fewer than 1% of the subjects would go all the way to 450 volts.

15. Describe the ensuing controversy generated by Milgram's obedience research.

15-1. Following are three objections raised against Milgram's studies on obedience. Beneath each indicate the counterargument raised either by Milgram or his supporters.
(a) "Subjects knew it was an experiment, so they went along only because they assumed everything must be okay."

(b) "Subjects in an experiment expect to obey an experimenter, so the results don't generalize to the real world."

(c) "Milgram's procedure, by which subjects were allowed to think that they had caved in to commands to harm an innocent victim, was potentially emotionally damaging to the subjects."

Answers: 15-1. (a) If subjects had thought everything was okay, they would not have shown the enormous distress that they did. (b) Obedience is also considered appropriate in the military and business worlds; that is, subjects expect to obey in the real world as well as in the laboratory. (c) The brief distress experienced by the subjects was a small price to pay for the insights that emerged. Furthermore, the subjects were thoroughly debriefed.

BEHAVIOR IN GROUPS: JOINING WITH OTHERS

16. Discuss the nature of groups and the bystander effect.

16-1. The word *group* doesn't have the same meaning for social psychologists that it does for everyone else. As I (R. S.) look out across my social psychology class on a Tuesday morning, I might say to myself, "Hm, quite a large group we have here today." Actually, my class (is/is not) a group in social psychological terms because it lacks one, and perhaps two, of the essential characteristics of a group. A group consists of two or more individuals who (a) _____ and (b) are _____.

16-2. Which of the following are groups, as defined by social psychologists?

_____ A husband and wife.

_____ The board of directors of a corporation.

_____ A sports team.

_____ Spectators at an athletic event.

_____ Shoppers at a mall.

16-3. What is the bystander effect?

16-4. Why does the bystander effect occur? Discuss the causes in terms of:
(a) ambiguity of the situation:

(b) diffusion of responsibility:

Answers: **16-1.** is not (a) interact (b) interdependent **16-2.** The first three are groups and the last two are not. **16-3.** When people are in groups (or at least in the presence of others), they are less likely to help than when they are alone. Or, the greater the number of onlookers in an emergency, the less likely any one of them is to assist the person in need. **16-4.** (a) The bystander effect is more likely to occur in ambiguous situations, when the need for help is not perfectly clear. The need for help is not clear when members of a group are looking around (to see how others are responding) rather than acting. (b) It occurs when others are present because responsibility can be spread out among the rest of the onlookers (e.g., "Someone else will do it" or, "We're all equally responsible.").

17. Summarize evidence on group productivity and group decision making.

17-1. Individuals tend to be less productive when working in groups than when working alone. Explain why the decreases in *efficiency* and decreases in *effort* tend to occur.
(a) less efficiency:

(b) less effort:

17-2. What is social loafing?

17-3. This and the following problem should help you understand the concept of group polarization. Suppose that a group of five corporate executives meet to decide whether to raise or lower the cost of their product, and by how much. Before they meet as a group, here are the decisions of the five executives (expressed as a percentage): +32%, +17%, +13%, +11%, and +2%. After they meet as a group, which of the following is most likely to be the result? Assume that group polarization occurs.
a. +30%, +10%, +3%, +3%, and +2%
b. +32%, +29%, +22%, +15%, and +20%
c. +3%, +13%, +11%, +9%, and +2%
d. −10%, −7%, −3%, 0%, and +7%

17-4. What is group polarization?

17-5. Have you ever been in a group when you thought to yourself, "This is a stupid idea, but my best friends seem to be going along with it, so I won't say anything." If so, you may have been in a group afflicted with groupthink. Groupthink is characterized by, among other things, an intense pressure to _____ accompanied by very low tolerance for _____.

17-6. The major cause of groupthink is _____ _____, which may be described or defined as:

Answers: 17-1. (a) Individuals in a group may be less efficient because they lack coordination, as when the efforts of one person interfere with those of another. (b) According to Latane, individuals in a group expend less effort due to diffusion of responsibility. 17-2. Social loafing is the reduction in effort expended by individuals working in groups as compared to when they work by themselves. 17-3. b 17-4. Group polarization is the tendency for a group's decision to shift toward a more extreme position in the direction that individual members are already leaning. 17-5. conform, dissent (disagreement, nonconformity) 17-6. group cohesion; the degree of liking that members have for each other and for the group, a "we" feeling, group spirit.

PUTTING IT IN PERSPECTIVE

18. **Explain how this chapter highlighted two of our unifying themes: the value of empiricism and the subjectivity of our experience.**

> **18-1.** As pointed out in the text, many individuals might conclude that the social psychological research simply confirms what we already know through common sense. Dispute this view by listing and describing two or three studies with results that are not predictable from commonsense assumptions.

> **18-2.** Most people believe that they view things objectively. Dispute this notion by explaining how the following factors affect our perception and understanding of the world, so that our judgments tend to be subjective rather than objective.
> (a) physical attractiveness:
>
> (b) social schemas:
>
> (c) pressure to conform:
>
> (d) groupthink:

Answers: 18-1. Milgram's studies: Psychiatrists incorrectly predicted that fewer than 1% of the subjects would go to 450 volts. Cognitive dissonance: Common sense would suggest that people would like tasks less when they are paid less; dissonance researchers found that under certain circumstances people like tasks *more* when they are paid less. The bystander effect: It might seem reasonable to suppose that the larger the number of people who observe someone in need of help, the more likely any one is to offer help. Bystander research consistently finds the opposite to be the case. 18-2. (a) Our judgments of people's ability and personality are biased by their physical attractiveness. Thus, we do not judge abilities objectively. (b) Social schemas, the frameworks or clusters of ideas about people and events, affect what we see. We do not see things objectively but only as filtered through our social schemas. (c) In Asch's studies, pressure to conform caused subjects to make incorrect judgments about line lengths. Thus, perception (or at least our report of our perception) may be distorted by our desire to conform. (d) Group cohesion, the feeling of belonging, may cause us to suspend logical evaluation in favor of compliance with the group decision.

APPLICATION: UNDERSTANDING PREJUDICE

19. Relate person perception and attributional bias to prejudice.

19-1.   Explain how *selective perception* maintains attitudes of prejudice.

19-2.   People's *attributional biases* also tend to maintain or augment prejudice. Give several examples to illustrate how this occurs.

Answers: 19-1. People with a stereotype about a particular group will tend to selectively perceive, or selectively remember, those behaviors congruent with that stereotype. For example, if someone views women as incapable of leading, he (or she) will tend to see and remember female behaviors that are congruent with lack of leadership. 19-2. For example, people tend to attribute success in men to ability but success in women to luck (or sheer effort, or the ease of the task), thereby enhancing prejudice against women. People also tend to attribute others' behavior to internal traits (the fundamental attribution error) and to blame people for their misfortunes (defensive attribution or victim blaming).

20. Relate principles of attraction, attitude formation, and group processes to prejudice.

20-1.   The text discusses two factors important in producing interpersonal attraction; lack of these factors would tend to maintain prejudice. List and describe these factors.

20-2.   Principles of attitude formation also contribute to our understanding of prejudice. For example, if

someone makes a prejudiced remark that is followed by approval, the approval is likely to function as a

_____ that increases that person's tendency to make similar remarks in the future.

This is the learning process known as _____ _____. Or, if

someone observes another person receiving approval for making such a remark, the observer may

acquire the tendency to make similar remarks through the process known as _____

_____.

20-3. In addition, the theory of _____ _____, which emphasizes inconsistencies between behavior and belief, may help explain the enhancement of prejudice in some situations. According to this point of view, questioning the fair-mindedness of people making prejudiced remarks is likely to increase dissonance and thereby (increase/decrease) the prejudiced attitude.

20-4. We tend to perceive outgroups differently from ingroups. Our perceptions are based not on characteristics of the groups but simply on the fact that the outgroup is different from our ingroup. Following are key words or hints relating to two cognitive biases that influence people in their perception of outgroups. Explain each.
(a) evaluation:

(b) homogeneity:

Answers: 20-1. *Proximity* effects dictate that people tend to become friends with those who live near them; thus, segregated housing patterns reduce the chances for friendship formation between races. *Similarity* with regard to attitudes, personality traits, and other factors is also a major factor in friendship formation. The extent to which groups are dissimilar will tend to be a force in creating and maintaining prejudice. 20-2. reinforcer, operant conditioning, observational learning 20-3. cognitive dissonance, increase 20-4. (a) We tend to evaluate outgroup members less favorably than members of our own group. (b) We overestimate the homogeneity of outgroups. We tend to view outgroup members as alike, not only in personality but in appearance.

REVIEW OF KEY TERMS

Attitudes
Attributions
Balance
Bystander effect
Channel
Cognitive dissonance
Commitment
Companionate love
Compliance
Conformity
Defensive attribution
Discrimination
Ethnocentrism
External attribution

Fundamental attribution error
Group
Group cohesiveness
Group polarization
Groupthink
Illusory correlation
Ingratiation
Ingroup
Internal attribution
Interpersonal attraction
Intimacy
Latitude of acceptance
Matching hypothesis
Message

Obedience
Outgroup
Passionate love
Person perception
Prejudice
Proximity
Receiver
Reciprocity
Self-serving bias
Social loafing
Social psychology
Social schemas
Source
Stereotypes

_____ 1. The branch of psychology concerned with the way individuals' thoughts, feelings, and behaviors are influenced by others.

_____ 2. The process of forming impressions of others.

_____ 3. Clusters of ideas about categories of social events and people that we use to organize the world around us.

_____ 4. Widely held beliefs that people have certain characteristics because of their membership in a particular group.

_____ 5. Error that occurs when we estimate that we have encountered more confirmations of an association between social traits than we have actually seen.

_____ 6. Inferences that people draw about the causes of events, others' behavior, and their own behavior.

_____ 7. Attributing the causes of behavior to personal dispositions, traits, abilities, and feelings.

_____ 8. Attributing the causes of behavior to situational demands and environmental constraints.

_____ 9. The tendency of an observer to favor internal attributions in explaining the behavior of an actor.

_____ 10. The tendency to blame victims for their misfortune so that we feel less likely to be victimized in a similar way.

_____ 11. The tendency to attribute our positive outcomes to personal factors and our negative outcomes to situational factors.

_____ 12. Liking or positive feelings toward another.

_____ 13. Geographic, residential, and other forms of spatial closeness.

_____ 14. The observation that males and females of approximately equal physical attractiveness are likely to select each other as partners.

_____ 15. Liking those who show that they like us.

_____ 16. A conscious effort to cultivate others' liking by complimenting them, agreeing with them, doing favors for them, etc.

_____ 17. A complete absorption in another person that includes tender sexual feelings and the agony and ecstasy of intense emotion.

_____ 18. A warm, trusting, tolerant affection for another whose life is deeply intertwined with one's own.

_____ 19. Warmth, closeness, and sharing in a relationship.

_____ 20. The intent to maintain a relationship in spite of the difficulties and costs that may arise.

_____ 21. Responses that locate the objects of thought on dimensions of judgment; have cognitive, behavioral, and emotional components.

_____ 22. The person who sends a communication.

_____ 23. The person to whom the message is sent.

_____ 24. The information transmitted by the source.

_____ 25. The medium through which the message is sent.

_____ 26. A range of potentially acceptable positions on an issue centered around one's initial attitude position.

_____ 27. Using positive and negative signs to analyze the attraction between two people and the similarity of their attitudes toward an object.

_____ 28. Situation that exists when cognitions about behavior and attitudes are inconsistent.

_____ 29. Yielding to real or imagined social pressure.

_____ 30. Yielding to social pressure in one's public behavior even though one's private beliefs have not changed.

_____ 31. A form of compliance that occurs when people follow direct commands, usually from someone in a position of authority.

_____ 32. Two or more individuals who interact and are interdependent.

_____ 33. The apparent paradox that people are less likely to provide help when they are in groups than when they are alone.

_____ 34. A reduction in effort by individuals when they work together as compared to when they work by themselves.

CHAPTER SIXTEEN

_____ 35. Situation that occurs when group discussion strengthens a group's dominant point of view and produces a shift toward a more extreme decision in that direction.

_____ 36. Phenomenon that occurs when members of a cohesive group emphasize concurrence at the expense of critical thinking in arriving at a decision.

_____ 37. The group one belongs to and identifies with.

_____ 38. People who are not a part of the ingroup.

_____ 39. The strength of the liking relationships linking group members to each other and to the group itself.

_____ 40. A negative attitude held toward members of a group.

_____ 41. Behaving differently, usually unfairly, toward the members of a group.

_____ 42. A tendency to evaluate people in outgroups less favorably than those in one's ingroup.

Answers: 1. social psychology 2. person perception 3. social schemas 4. stereotypes 5. illusory correlation 6. attributions 7. internal attribution 8. external attribution 9. fundamental attribution error 10. defensive attribution 11. self-serving bias 12. interpersonal attraction 13. proximity 14. matching hypothesis 15. reciprocity 16. ingratiation 17. passionate love 18. companionate love 19. intimacy 20. commitment 21. attitudes 22. source 23. receiver 24. message 25. channel 26. latitude of acceptance 27. balance 28. cognitive dissonance 29. conformity 30. compliance 31. obedience 32. group 33. bystander effect 34. social loafing 35. group polarization 36. groupthink 37. ingroup 38. outgroup 39. group cohesiveness 40. prejudice 41. discrimination 42. ethnocentrism.

REVIEW OF KEY PEOPLE

Solomon Asch   Elaine Hatfield   Harold Kelley
Ellen Berscheid   Fritz Heider   Stanley Milgram
Leon Festinger   Irving Janis

_____ 1. Was the first to describe the crucial dimension along which we make attributions; developed balance theory.

_____ 2. Devised a theory that identifies important factors relating to internal and external attributions.

_____ 3. With Hatfield did research describing two types of romantic love: passionate and companionate.

_____ 4. Originator of the theory of cognitive dissonance.

_____ 5. Devised the "line-judging" procedure in pioneering investigations of conformity.

_____ 6. In a series of "fake shock" experiments, studied the tendency to obey authority figures.

_____ 7. First described groupthink.

_____ 8. Under the name of Walster did early study on dating and physical attractiveness; with Berscheid, described types of romantic love.

Answers: 1. Heider 2. Kelley 3. Berscheid 4. Festinger 5. Asch 6. Milgram 7. Janis 8. Hatfield.

SELF-QUIZ

1. Which of the following characteristics do we tend to attribute to physically attractive people?
   a. coldness
   b. competence
   c. unpleasantness
   d. all of the above

2. Cognitive structures that guide our perceptions of people and events are termed:
   a. attributions
   b. stigmata
   c. schemas
   d. denkmals

3. Inferences that we make about the causes of our own and others' behavior are termed:
   a. attributions
   b. stigmata
   c. schemas
   d. denkmals

4. Bruce performed very well on the examination, which he attributed to native ability and hard work. Which bias does this illustrate?
   a. the fundamental attribution error
   b. the actor-observer bias
   c. the self-serving bias
   d. all of the above

5. Which of the following are related to interpersonal attraction?
   a. proximity
   b. similarity
   c. physical attractiveness
   d. all of the above

6. Which of the following could be an example of the fundamental attribution error?
   a. Ralph described himself as a failure.
   b. Ralph thought that the reason he failed was that he was sick that day.
   c. Jayne said Ralph failed because the test was unfair.
   d. Sue explained Ralph's failure in terms of his incompetence and laziness.

7. Bruce had what could be described as a secure attachment to his parents during his infancy. What kind of relationship is he likely to develop as an adult?
   a. trusting and close
   b. jealous
   c. volatile and preoccupied with love
   d. difficult

8. Which of the following is, in general, likely to *reduce* the persuasiveness of a message?
   a. The receiver's viewpoint is already fairly close to that of the message.
   b. The receiver has been forewarned about the message.
   c. A two-sided appeal is used.
   d. The source is physically attractive.

9. Osmo is frequently seen in the company of Cosmo. When asked if he likes Cosmo, Osmo replies, "I guess I must, since I hang out with him." Which theory does this example best illustrate?
   a. balance
   b. cognitive dissonance
   c. self-perception
   d. observational learning

10. In making a decision you rely on the opinion of experts and the behavior of your best friends. According to the elaboration likelihood model, which route to persuasion have you used?
    a. central
    b. peripheral
    c. attributional
    d. 66

11. Which of the following is the best statement of conclusion concerning Milgram's classic study involving the learner, teacher, and ostensible shock?
    a. Under certain circumstances, people seem to enjoy the opportunity to be cruel to others.
    b. People have a strong tendency to obey an authority even if their actions may harm others.
    c. The more people there are who observe someone in need of help, the less likely any one is to help.
    d. Aggression seems to be a more potent force in human nature than had previously been suspected.

12. Which of the following is most likely to function as a group?
    a. shoppers at a mall
    b. the audience in a theater
    c. the board of trustees of a college
    d. passengers in an airplane

13. Vanessa witnesses a car accident. In which of the following cases is she most likely to stop and render assistance?
    a. Only she saw the accident.
    b. She and one other individual saw the accident.
    c. She and 18 others saw the accident.
    d. The other observers are pedestrians.

14. Suppose the original decisions of members of a group are represented by the following numbers in a group polarization study: 9, 7, 5, 5, 4. The range of numbers possible in the study is from 0 to 9. Which of the following possible shifts in decisions would demonstrate polarization?
    a. 2, 3, 3, 4, 5
    b. 7, 7, 6, 5, 5
    c. 5, 4, 0, 2, 3
    d. 9, 9, 7, 7, 5

15. What is the major cause of groupthink?
    a. strong group cohesion
    b. weak group cohesion
    c. the tendency of group members to grandstand
    d. group conflict

Answers: 1. b 2. c 3. a 4. c 5. d 6. d 7. a 8. b 9. c 10. b 11. b 12. c 13. a 14. d 15. a.

APPENDIX B:
STATISTICAL METHODS

REVIEW OF KEY IDEAS

1. **Describe several ways of using frequency distributions and graphs to organize numerical data.**

   1-1. Identify the following methods that are commonly used to present numerical data.

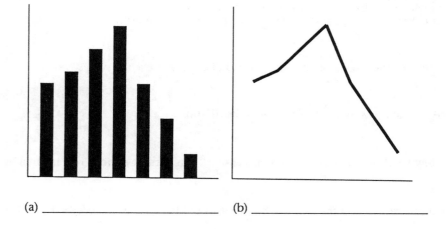

   (a) _____   (b) _____

   1-2. What data are usually plotted along the:
   (a) horizontal axis?

   (b) vertical axis?

   Answers: 1-1. (a) histogram (b) frequency polygram 1-2. (a) the possible scores (b) the frequency of each score.

2. Describe the measures of central tendency and variability discussed in the text.

2-1. Tell which measure of central tendency, the mean, median, or mode, would be most useful in the following situations.

(a) Which measure would be best for analyzing the salaries of all workers in a small, low-paying printshop that includes two high-salaried managers. Explain your answer.

(b) Which measure would be best for selecting a single ice cream flavor for an upcoming party?

(c) Which measure would be best for pairing players at a bowling match, using their individual past scores, so that equals play against equals?

(d) Where do most of the scores pile up in a positively skewed distribution?

Answers: 2-1. (a) the median, because the high salaries of the two management persons would distort the mean (b) the mode (c) the mean (d) at the bottom end of the distribution.

3. Describe the normal distribution and its use in psychological testing.

3-1. Answer the following questions regarding the normal distribution.

(a) Where do the mean, median, and mode fall in a normal distribution?

(b) Where are most of the scores located in a normal distribution?

(c) What is the unit of measurement in a normal distribution?

(d) Approximately what percentage of scores falls above 2 standard deviations in a normal distribution?

(e) If your percentile ranking on the SAT was 84, what would your SAT score be (see Fig. B.7 in the text)?

Answers: 3-1. (a) at the center (b) around the mean (plus or minus 1 standard deviation) (c) the standard deviation (d) 2.3% (e) 600 (approximately).

4. **Explain how the magnitude and direction of a correlation are reflected in scatter diagrams and how correlation is related to predictive power.**

4-1.   Answer the following questions about the magnitude and direction of a correlation as reflected in scattergrams.
(a) Where do the data points fall in a scattergram that shows a perfect correlation?

(b) What happens to the data points in a scattergram when the magnitude of correlation decreases?

(c) What does a high negative correlation indicate?

4-2.   Answer the following questions regarding the predictive power of correlations.
(a) How does one compute the coefficient of determination?

(b) What does the coefficient of determination tell us?

(c) What could we say if the sample study used in the text showed a correlation of –.50 between SAT scores and time watching television?

Answers: 4-1. (a) in a straight line (b) They scatter away from a straight line. (c) High scores on one variable (X) are accompanied by low scores on the other variable (Y).   4-2. (a) by squaring the correlation coefficient (b) It indicates the percentage of variation in one variable that can be predicted based on the other variable. (c) We could say that knowledge of TV viewing habits allows one to predict 25% of the variation on SAT scores (.50 × .50 = .25).

5. **Explain how the null hypothesis is used in hypothesis testing and relate it to statistical significance.**

5-1.   Answer the following questions regarding the null hypothesis and statistical significance.
(a) In the sample study correlating SAT scores and television viewing, the findings supported the null hypothesis. What does this mean?

(b) What level of significance do most researchers demand as a minimum before rejecting the null hypothesis?

(c) What is the probability of making an error when a researcher rejects the null hypothesis at the .01 level of significance?

Answers: 5-1. (a) We cannot conclude that there is a significant negative correlation between SAT scores and television viewing. (b) the .05 level (c) 1 in 100.

REVIEW OF KEY TERMS

Coefficient of determination
Correlation coefficient
Descriptive statistics
Frequency distribution
Frequency polygon
Histogram
Inferential statistics

Mean
Median
Mode
Negatively skewed distribution
Normal distribution
Null hypothesis
Percentile score

Positively skewed distribution
Scatter diagram
Standard deviation
Statistics
Statistical significance
Variability

_____ 1. The use of mathematics to organize, summarize, and interpret numerical data.

_____ 2. An orderly arrangement of scores indicating the frequency of each score or group of scores.

_____ 3. A bar graph that presents data from a frequency distribution.

_____ 4. A line figure used to present data from a frequency distribution.

_____ 5. Type of statistics used to organize and summarize data.

_____ 6. The arithmetic average of a group of scores.

_____ 7. The score that falls in the center of a group of scores.

_____ 8. The score that occurs most frequently in a group of scores.

_____ 9. A distribution in which most scores pile up at the high end of the scale.

_____ 10. A distribution in which most scores pile up at the low end of the scale.

_____ 11. The extent to which the scores in a distribution tend to vary or depart from the mean.

_____ 12. An index of the amount of variability in a set of data.

_____ 13. A bell-shaped curve that represents the pattern in which many human characteristics are dispersed in the population.

_____ 14. Figure representing the percentage of persons who score below (or above) any particular score.

_____ 15. A numerical index of the degree of relationship between two variables.

_____ 16. A graph in which paired X and Y scores for each subject are plotted as single points.

_____ 17. The percentage of variation in one variable that can be predicted based on another variable.

_____ 18. Statistics employed to interpret data and draw conclusions.

_____ 19. The hypothesis that there is no relationship between two variables.

_____ 20. Said to exist when the probability is very low that observed findings can be attributed to chance.

Answers: 1. statistics 2. frequency distribution 3. histogram 4. frequency polygon 5. descriptive statistics 6. mean 7. median 8. mode 9. negatively skewed distribution 10. positively skewed distribution 11. variability 12. standard deviation 13. normal distribution 14. percentile score 15. correlation coefficient 16. scatter diagram 17. coefficient of determination 18. inferential statistics 19. null hypothesis 20. statistical significance.

APPENDIX C: INDUSTRIAL/ORGANIZATIONAL PSYCHOLOGY

REVIEW OF KEY IDEAS

1. Discuss the settings, procedures, and content areas of I/O psychology.

1-1.   In a humorous commentary a few years ago psychologist Jerry Burger said he longed to hear, just once, someone in a theater asking, "Is there a social psychologist in the house?" (Burger, 1986). The writer's comments reflected not only his wish that psychology be recognized somewhere outside the halls of academia but his desire for application. Of course, the settings for the four applied fields of psychology (Chapter 1) frequently are outside university settings—clinical psychology and counseling psychology take place in mental health settings, school psychology occurs in educational settings, and I/O psychology is conducted in _____ settings.

1-2.   While research and application of I/O psychology may occur in the workplace, many of its principles derive from research in social psychology and other fields of psychology. In addition, I/O psychologists use (very different/much the same) research methods and statistics as the other fields of psychology.

1-3.   There are three primary areas of interest for the industrial psychologists. Write the names of these subareas in the blanks below next to the correct initial letters.

P: _____ psychology

O: _____ psychology

HF: _____ _____ psychology

1-4.   Below are descriptions of the three subareas of I/O psychology. Match the subareas with the descriptions by placing the appropriate letters in the blanks.

_____   Examines the way human beings fit the characteristics of the workplace; concerned with the interface between human beings and machines.

_____   Tests and selects employees, tries to match the abilities of the person to the job requirements.

_____   Concerned with job satisfaction, relationships among employees, social adaptation of the worker to the workplace.

1-5.   Below are possible problems encountered in a workplace. Match the subareas with the problems.

_____   The employees intentionally work at a slow place.

_____   Several employees unintentionally push the wrong buttons on their widget makers.

_____   Ralph tests out poorly in accounting but has potential for working with the widget machine.

Answers: 1-1. work (employment, industrial)   1-2. much the same   1-3. personnel, organizational, human factors   1-4. HF, P, O   1-5. O, HF, P.

2. Discuss how the systems approach relates to the subfields of I/O psychology.

2-1.   Your text makes the point that the three subareas of I/O psychology (operate independently/are interdependent). Thus, making a human factors decision to change the design of equipment, for example, (is likely to/will not) affect personnel and organizational functions.

2-2.   As described in your text, replacing a secretary's typewriter with a personal computer may affect not only the way the employee interfaces with the machine (the _____

_____ subarea) but interactions among employees in the workplace (the

_____ subarea) and the characteristics of the person who performs the job

(the _____ subarea). Recognizing that changes made in one part of the system

usually affect the other parts, the approach of I/O psychology is termed a _____

approach.

Answers: 2-1. are interdependent, is likely to   2-2. human factors, organizational, personnel, systems.

3. Describe how the three subfields of I/O psychology emerged historically.

3-1.   The first of the three subareas of I/O psychology to appear historically was _____

psychology. One could mark the origin of this field at the turn of the century, at about the time Binet

developed the _____ test.

3-2.   Two major events of the twentieth century spurred the use of ability testing on a massive scale and enhanced the importance of personnel psychology. What were these two events?

3-3.   Prior to 1930, the cost-benefit theories of Frederick _____ dominated industry's

thinking about behavior in the workplace. Productivity was thought to be determined solely by efficient

movements, the physical conditions of the plant, and rate of _____ to workers.

3-4.   In 1930, a now-famous study at a Western Electric plant near Chicago found that factors other than

pay and working conditions affected productivity, factors such as workers' _____

toward their supervisors. This experiment involving human relations in the workplace marks the

beginning of the field of _____ psychology.

3-5.   The subarea directed toward developing technical systems that can be used effectively by human beings

is known as _____ _____ psychology.

3-6.   Human factors developed in large part in response to the need to understand the best and safest ways for human beings to interact with airplanes and other weapons of war. What historical event may be used to mark the beginning of human factors psychology? _____.

Answers: 3-1. personnel, intelligence   3-2. World War I and World War II   3-3. Taylor, payment   3-4. attitudes, organizational   3-5. human factors   3-6. World War II.

4. Discuss the role of psychological testing in personnel psychology, job analysis, and performance evaluation.

4-1.   The function of personnel psychology is to match people's abilities with characteristics of the job.
(a) If there are more applicants than jobs, what is the role of psychological testing?

(b) If there are no applicants who have the skills needed for the job, what is likely to be the task of the personnel psychologist? What is the function of testing in this case?

4-2.   While the task of personnel psychology is to match the person to the job, characteristics of the job (are/ are not) always obvious. We know that accountants do accounting and managers do managing and so on, but these rough descriptions are not specific enough to permit prediction from tests. A more precise description is provided by the process known as job _____, a method for breaking a job into its constituent parts.

4-3.   Job analysis determines not only what tasks a person performs for a particular job but which of the tasks are _____ to the job and which are _____. Once the analysis has determined the components of the job and the skills needed, the personnel psychologist administers psychological _____ intended to assess those skills.

4-4.   After selection and hiring have taken place, the next step is to assess the quality of employees' work. The _____ evaluation should be guided by the job analysis; thus, it should emphasize tasks that are _____ rather than peripheral to the position.

4-5.   While in some instances it is possible to evaluate performance on the basis of objective products, in most cases it is not possible to attribute the product to just one person. Thus, the most common form of performance evaluation is _____ _____.

4-6. With regard to supervisor ratings:

(a) What are the major advantages of using this method?

(b) The major disadvantage of using rating scales is that the ratings can be influenced by irrelevant factors. Give one or two examples of these irrelevant factors.

(c) What steps can be taken to help prevent such rating errors?

Answers: 4-1. (a) to select the applicant with the best skills for the job (b) to develop training programs designed to provide candidates with the needed skills. In this case, the testing objective is to find individuals who have the capacity to develop the needed skills. 4-2. are not, analysis 4-3. central, peripheral, tests 4-4. performance, central 4-5. supervisor rating 4-6. (a) The supervisor may know the employee's work best, and evaluations are based on observations made over a long period of time. (b) Some supervisors are more lenient than others; supervisors may be influenced by how much they like the person. (c) Rating errors may be lessened by providing supervisors with special training and by designing less subjective (more behaviorally based) scales.

5. Describe and compare the equity and expectancy theories of work motivation.

5-1. Equity theory assumes that workers attempt to match inputs with outcomes. The workers' efforts (and skills, experience, loyalty, and so on) are considered _____; their wages (and other rewards) are the _____. To the extent that inputs match outcomes, a state of _____ is said to exist.

5-2. If employees perceive that the rewards do not match their efforts, and therefore that balance does not exist, equity theory indicates that they will make changes directed at producing equity. For example, what adjustments might they make if they perceive that they are *underpaid*?

5-3. If employees are *overpaid*, equity theory suggests that they will (increase/decrease) output or ask for (lower/higher) wages. The evidence indicates, however, that this type of adjustment (is/is not) likely to occur.

5-4. Expectancy theory has a different approach to understanding work motivation. It assumes that effort is in large part a function of an employee's evaluation of two main questions relating to the reward. What are these questions?

5-5.   Following are possible thoughts running through the minds of imaginary employees. Indicate which theory of work motivation is reflected in these examples.

_____: The boss has promised me a big raise if I increase sales by 10% . I could sure use the money. I don't think he will give it to me, though, so I'm not going to expend the extra effort.

_____: It's unfair that I'm the one with the skill but he's the one who gets the raise! I'm not going to work so hard in the future.

_____: My supervisor says that I'd become employee of the month if I could average two widgets per hour. Big deal! I can't eat employee of the month—what I need is cash.

_____: Next year's salary is just 5% higher than this year's. Considering my loyalty and the money I've made for the company, that just isn't enough. Next year I'm going to slow down and be sure to take all of my sick leave.

Answers: 5-1. inputs, outcomes, equity (or balance or homeostasis)   5-2. They could reduce effort, or they could ask for higher wages.   5-3. increase, lower, is not   5-4. Is the reward of value to me? Is it likely that I will receive the reward? (In other words: Do I want it, and will I get it?)   5-5. expectancy, equity, expectancy, equity.

6.   Summarize research on job satisfaction.

6-1.   What do people want in a job? Place check marks to indicate which of the following are primary factors associated with job satisfaction.

_____   adequate salary

_____   interesting work

_____   challenging work

_____   opportunities for advancement

_____   effective supervisors

_____   supportive supervisors

_____   acceptable company policies

6-2.   To assess job satisfaction most organizations distribute questionnaires that ask employees to rate their satisfaction on the factors listed above. Results indicate that job satisfaction is associated with which of the following? Check those that apply.

_____   low absenteeism

_____   low turnover

_____   high productivity

6-3.   While it might seem reasonable to expect that job satisfaction leads to greater productivity, a great deal of research has failed to find this to be the case. There is, however, some evidence that the reverse is true, that _____ leads to more _____.

Answers: 6-1. Thousands of studies have found that all of these are primary sources of job satisfaction!
6-2. low absenteeism, low turnover   6-3. productivity, job satisfaction.

7. Discuss how human engineering can enhance work environments.

7-1. There are two major points of interaction, or interface, between humans and machines: the first involves the devices that _____ information; the second is the action taken by the person, the _____ part of the system.

7-2. For example, dashboards in cars provide the _____ interface. Based on that information, the human being operates the pedals and knobs that provide the _____ interface.

7-3. The major problems encountered in using machines are the result of either confusing _____ or confusing _____. To alleviate these problems human factors specialists design displays more readily understood at a glance or control components that resemble the functions they control. For example, after World War II the knobs that operated the flaps on airplanes were redesigned to be shaped like _____.

7-4. Most people have certain expectations about the way things work. For example, people generally expect to unscrew things in a counterclockwise direction. Thus, another design principle is to build in accordance with *response stereotype*, people's natural _____ when using controls.

7-5. As I sit here at my computer completing the last part of this study guide, I (R. S.) am aware that the field of human factors is not irrelevant to my life. Yesterday (8/22/91) the coup in the USSR failed, in part due to the availability of communications devices designed by human factors specialists. Today I interact with my display screen and keyboard and mouse, all designed to make my life easier. To the question of how human engineering can enhance work environments: Well designed machines permit more work in less time, more efficiency; are less confusing, less frustrating, and so cause fewer _____-related health problems; and, with less stress and careful attention to the areas of interface, cause fewer _____ in the workplace.

Answers: 7-1. display, control   7-2. display, control   7-3. displays, controls, flaps   7-4. tendencies (expectations, responses, preferences, etc.)   7-5. stress, accidents (mistakes).

Reference: Burger, J. M. (1986). Is there a Ph.D. in the house? *APA Monitor, 17,* 4.